Safety Symbols

These symbols appear in laboratory activities. They warn of possible dangers in the laboratory and remind you to work carefully.

 Safety Goggles Wear safety goggles to protect your eyes in any activity involving chemicals, flames or heating, or glassware.

 Lab Apron Wear a laboratory apron to protect your skin and clothing from damage.

 Breakage Handle breakable materials, such as glassware, with care. Do not touch broken glassware.

 Heat-Resistant Gloves Use an oven mitt or other hand protection when handling hot materials such as hot plates or hot glassware.

 Plastic Gloves Wear disposable plastic gloves when working with harmful chemicals and organisms. Keep your hands away from your face, and dispose of the gloves according to your teacher's instructions.

 Heating Use a clamp or tongs to pick up hot glassware. Do not touch hot objects with your bare hands.

 Flames Before you work with flames, tie back loose hair and clothing. Follow instructions from your teacher about lighting and extinguishing flames.

 No Flames When using flammable materials, make sure there are no flames, sparks, or other exposed heat sources present.

 Corrosive Chemical Avoid getting acid or other corrosive chemicals on your skin or clothing or in your eyes. Do not inhale the vapors. Wash your hands after the activity.

 Poison Do not let any poisonous chemical come into contact with your skin, and do not inhale its vapors. Wash your hands when you are finished with the activity.

 Fumes Work in a ventilated area when harmful vapors may be involved. Avoid inhaling vapors directly. Only test an odor when directed to do so by your teacher, and use a wafting motion to direct the vapor toward your nose.

 Sharp Object Scissors, scalpels, knives, needles, pins, and tacks can cut your skin. Always direct a sharp edge or point away from yourself and others.

 Animal Safety Treat live or preserved animals or animal parts with care to avoid harming the animals or yourself. Wash your hands when you are finished with the activity.

 Plant Safety Handle plants only as directed by your teacher. If you are allergic to certain plants, tell your teacher; do not do an activity involving those plants. Avoid touching harmful plants such as poison ivy. Wash your hands when you are finished with the activity.

 Electric Shock To avoid electric shock, never use electrical equipment around water, or when the equipment is wet or your hands are wet. Be sure cords are untangled and cannot trip anyone. Unplug equipment not in use.

 Physical Safety When an experiment involves physical activity, avoid injuring yourself or others. Alert your teacher if there is any reason you should not participate.

 Disposal Dispose of chemicals and other laboratory materials safely. Follow the instructions from your teacher.

 Hand Washing Wash your hands thoroughly when finished with the activity. Use antibacterial soap and warm water. Rinse well.

⚠ **General Safety Awareness** When this symbol appears, follow the instructions provided. When you are asked to develop your own procedure in a lab, have your teacher approve your plan before you go further.

Earth's Changing Surface

PRENTICE HALL Science Explorer

PEARSON

Prentice Hall

Needham, Massachusetts
Upper Saddle River, New Jersey

Earth's Changing Surface

Book-Specific Resources

Student Edition
Interactive Textbook
Teacher's Edition
All-in-One Teaching Resources
Guided Reading and Study Workbook
Student Edition on Audio CD
Discovery Channel Video
Lab Activity Video
Consumable and Nonconsumable Materials Kits

Program Print Resources

Integrated Science Laboratory Manual
Computer Microscope Lab Manual
Inquiry Skills Activity Books
Test Preparation Blackline Masters
Test Preparation Workbook
Test-Taking Tips With Transparencies
Teacher's ELL Handbook
Reading in the Content Area

Program Technology Resources

Teacher Express™ CD-ROM
Interactive Textbook
Presentation Pro CD-ROM
Exam*View*®, Computer Test Bank CD-ROM
Lab zone™ Easy Planner CD-ROM
Student Edition Worksheet Library CD-ROM
Probeware Lab Manual With CD-ROM
Computer Microscope and Lab Manual
Materials Ordering CD-ROM
Discovery Channel DVD Library
Lab Activity DVD Library
Web Site at PHSchool.com

Spanish Print Resources

Spanish Student Edition
Spanish Guided Reading and Study Workbook
Spanish Teaching Guide With Tests

Acknowledgments appear on page 198, which constitutes an extension of this copyright page.

Cover
Sunrise illuminates the Pinnacles in Nambung National Park, Western Australia (top). A thorny devil leaves footprints in the sand (bottom).

ISBN 0-13-115092-8
1 2 3 4 5 6 7 8 9 10   08 07 06 05 04

Program Authors

Michael J. Padilla, Ph.D.
Professor of Science Education
University of Georgia
Athens, Georgia

Michael Padilla is a leader in middle school science education. He has served as an author and elected officer for the National Science Teachers Association and as a writer of the National Science Education Standards. As lead author of *Science Explorer,* Mike has inspired the team in developing a program that meets the needs of middle grades students, promotes science inquiry, and is aligned with the National Science Education Standards.

Ioannis Miaoulis, Ph.D.
President
Museum of Science
Boston, Massachusetts

Originally trained as a mechanical engineer, Ioannis Miaoulis is in the forefront of the national movement to increase technological literacy. As dean of the Tufts University School of Engineering, Dr. Miaoulis spearheaded the introduction of engineering into the Massachusetts curriculum. Currently he is working with school systems across the country to engage students in engineering activities and to foster discussions on the impact of science and technology on society.

Martha Cyr, Ph.D.
Director of K–12 Outreach
Worcester Polytechnic Institute
Worcester, Massachusetts

Martha Cyr is a noted expert in engineering outreach. She has over nine years of experience with programs and activities that emphasize the use of engineering principles, through hands-on projects, to excite and motivate students and teachers of mathematics and science in grades K–12. Her goal is to stimulate a continued interest in science and mathematics through engineering.

Book Author

Michael Wysession, Ph.D.
Associate Professor of Earth and
    Planetary Sciences
Washington University
St. Louis, Missouri

Contributing Writers

Rose-Marie Botting
Science Teacher
Broward County
    School District
Fort Lauderdale,
    Florida

Colleen Campos
Science Teacher
Laredo Middle School
Aurora, Colorado

Holly Estes
Science Teacher
Hale Middle School
Stow, Massachusetts

Edward Evans
Former Science
    Teacher
Hilton Central School
Hilton, New York

Sharon Stroud
Science Teacher
Widefield High School
Colorado Springs,
    Colorado

Consultants

Reading Consultant

Nancy Romance, Ph.D.
Professor of Science
    Education
Florida Atlantic University
Fort Lauderdale, Florida

Mathematics Consultant

William Tate, Ph.D.
Professor of Education and
    American Culture Studies
Washington University
St. Louis, Missouri

Reviewers

Tufts University Content Reviewers

Faculty from Tufts University in Medford, Massachusetts, participated in the development of *Science Explorer* chapter projects, reviewed the student books for content accuracy, and helped coordinate field testing.

Astier M. Almedom, Ph.D.
Department of Biology

Wayne Chudyk, Ph.D.
Department of Civil and Environmental Engineering

John Durant, Ph.D.
Department of Civil and Environmental Engineering

George S. Ellmore, Ph.D.
Department of Biology

David L. Kaplan, Ph.D.
Department of Chemical Engineering

Samuel Kounaves, Ph.D.
Department of Chemistry

David H. Lee, Ph.D.
Department of Chemistry

Doug Matson, Ph.D.
Department of Mechanical Engineering

Karen Panetta, Ph.D.
Department of Electrical Engineering and Computer Science

Jan Pechenik, Ph.D.
Department of Biology

John C. Ridge, Ph.D.
Department of Geology

William Waller, Ph.D.
Department of Astronomy

Content Reviewers

Jeff Bodart, Ph.D.
Chipola Junior College
Marianna, Florida

Michael Castellani, Ph.D.
Department of Chemistry
Marshall University
Huntington, West Virginia

Eugene Chiang, Ph.D.
Department of Astronomy
University of California–Berkeley
Berkeley, California

Charles C. Curtis, Ph.D.
Department of Physics
University of Arizona
Tucson, Arizona

Diane Doser, Ph.D.
Department of Geological Sciences
University of Texas at El Paso
El Paso, Texas

Richard Duhrkopf, Ph.D.
Department of Biology
Baylor University
Waco, Texas

Michael Hacker
Co-director, Center for Technological Literacy
Hofstra University
Hempstead, New York

Michael W. Hamburger, Ph.D.
Department of Geological Sciences
Indiana University
Bloomington, Indiana

Alice Hankla, Ph.D.
The Galloway School
Atlanta, Georgia

Donald Jackson, Ph.D.
Department of Molecular Pharmacology, Physiology, & Biotechnology
Brown University
Providence, Rhode Island

Jeremiah Jarrett, Ph.D.
Department of Biological Sciences
Central Connecticut State University
New Britain, Connecticut

Becky Mansfield, Ph.D.
Department of Geography
Columbus, Ohio

Joe McCullough, Ph.D.
Department of Natural and Applied Sciences
Cabrillo College
Aptos, California

Robert J. Mellors, Ph.D.
Department of Geological Sciences
San Diego State University
San Diego, California

Joseph M. Moran, Ph.D.
American Meteorological Society
Washington, D.C.

David J. Morrissey, Ph.D.
Department of Chemistry
Michigan State University
East Lansing, Michigan

Philip A. Reed, Ph.D.
Department of Occupational & Technical Studies
Old Dominion University
Norfolk, Virginia

Scott M. Rochette, Ph.D.
Department of Earth Sciences
State University of New York, College at Brockport
Brockport, New York

Laurence D. Rosenheim, Ph.D.
Department of Chemistry
Indiana State University
Terre Haute, Indiana

Ronald Sass, Ph.D.
Department of Ecology & Evolutionary Biology
Rice University
Houston, Texas

George Schatz, Ph.D.
Department of Chemistry
Northwestern University
Evanston, Illinois

Sara Seager, Ph.D.
Carnegie Institution of Washington
Washington, D.C.

John R. Villarreal, Ph.D.
College of Science and Engineering
The University of Texas–Pan American
Edinburg, Texas

Kenneth Welty, Ph.D.
School of Education
University of Wisconsin–Stout
Stout, Wisconsin

Edward J. Zalisko, Ph.D.
Department of Biology
Blackburn College
Carlinville, Illinois

Teacher Reviewers

Steve Barbato
Lower Merion School
Ardmore, Pennsylvania

David R. Blakely
Arlington High School
Arlington, Massachusetts

Jane Callery
Two Rivers Magnet Middle
School
East Hartford, Connecticut

Melissa Lynn Cook
Oakland Mills High School
Columbia, Maryland

James Fattic
Southside Middle School
Anderson, Indiana

Wayne Goates
Goddard Middle School
Goddard, Kansas

Katherine Bobay Graser
Mint Hill Middle School
Charlotte, North Carolina

Darcy Hampton
Deal Junior High School
Washington, D.C.

Karen Kelly
Pierce Middle School
Waterford, Michigan

David Kelso
Manchester High School Central
Manchester, New Hampshire

John G. Little
St. Mary's High School
Stockton, California

Benigno Lopez, Jr.
Sleepy Hill Middle School
Lakeland, Florida

Angie L. Matamoros, Ph.D.
ALM Consulting
Weston, Florida

Tim McCollum
Charleston Middle School
Charleston, Illinois

Bruce A. Mellin
Brooks School
North Andover, Massachusetts

Ella Jay Parfitt
Southeast Middle School
Baltimore, Maryland

Kathleen Poe
Duncan Fletcher Middle School
Jacksonville, Florida

Shirley Rose
Lewis and Clark Middle School
Tulsa, Oklahoma

Linda Sandersen
Greenfield Middle School
Milwaukee, Wisconsin

Mary E. Solan
Southwest Middle School
Charlotte, North Carolina

Mary Stewart
University of Tulsa
Tulsa, Oklahoma

Paul Swenson
Billings West High School
Billings, Montana

Thomas Vaughn
Arlington High School
Arlington, Massachusetts

Steve Wright
Butler Middle School
Waukesha, Wisconsin

Safety Reviewers

W. H. Breazeale, Ph.D.
Department of Chemistry
College of Charleston
Charleston, South Carolina

Ruth Hathaway, Ph.D.
Hathaway Consulting
Cape Girardeau, Missouri

Douglas Mandt
Science Education Consultant
Edgewood, Washington

Activity Field Testers

Nicki Bibbo
Russell Street School
Littleton, Massachusetts

Connie Boone
Fletcher Middle School
Jacksonville Beach, Florida

Rose-Marie Botting
Broward County School District
Fort Lauderdale, Florida

Colleen Campos
Laredo Middle School
Aurora, Colorado

Elizabeth Chait
W. L. Chenery Middle School
Belmont, Massachusetts

Holly Estes
Hale Middle School
Stow, Massachusetts

Laura Hapgood
Plymouth Community
Intermediate School
Plymouth, Massachusetts

Sandra M. Harris
Winman Junior High School
Warwick, Rhode Island

Jason Ho
Walter Reed Middle School
Los Angeles, California

Joanne Jackson
Winman Junior High School
Warwick, Rhode Island

Mary F. Lavin
Plymouth Community
Intermediate School
Plymouth, Massachusetts

James MacNeil, Ph.D.
Concord Public Schools
Concord, Massachusetts

Lauren Magruder
St. Michael's Country
Day School
Newport, Rhode Island

Jeanne Maurand
Austin Preparatory School
South Hamilton, Massachusetts

Warren Phillips
Plymouth Community
Intermediate School
Plymouth, Massachusetts

Carol Pirtle
Hale Middle School
Stow, Massachusetts

Kathleen M. Poe
Kirby-Smith Middle School
Jacksonville, Florida

Cynthia B. Pope
Ruffner Middle School
Norfolk, Virginia

Anne Scammell
Geneva Middle School
Geneva, New York

Karen Riley Sievers
Callanan Middle School
Des Moines, Iowa

David M. Smith
Eyer Middle School
Allentown, Pennsylvania

Gene Vitale
Parkland School
McHenry, Illinois

Zenovia Young
Meyer Levi Jr. HS/IS-285
Brooklyn, New York

Contents

Earth's Changing Surface

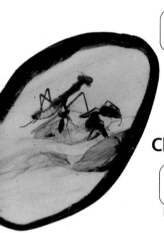

Reference Section

Enhance understanding through dynamic video.

Preview Get motivated with this introduction to the chapter content.

Field Trip Explore a real-world story related to the chapter content.

Assessment Review content and take an assessment.

Get connected to exciting Web resources in every lesson.

$SC\hspace{-2pt}{\overset{\displaystyle i}{L}}INKS_{_{TM}}$ **NSTA** Find Web links on topics relating to every section.

Active Art Selected visuals from every chapter become interactive online.

Planet Diary® Explore news and natural phenomena through weekly reports.

Science News® Keep up to date with the latest science discoveries.

Experience the complete text-book online and on CD-ROM.

Activities Practice skills and learn content.

Videos Explore content and learn important lab skills.

Audio Support Key terms are spoken and defined.

Self-Assessment Instant feed-back helps you track your progress.

Activities

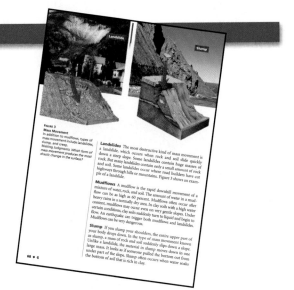

FIGURE 3
Mass Movement
In addition to mudflows, types of mass movement include landslides, slump, and creep. *Making Judgments* Which form of mass movement produces the most drastic change in the surface?

Landslides The most destructive kind of mass movement is a landslide, which occurs when rock and soil slide quickly down a steep slope. Some landslides contain huge masses of rock. But many landslides contain only a small amount of rock and soil. Some landslides occur where road builders have cut highways through hills or mountains. Figure 3 shows an example of a landslide.

Mudflows A mudflow is the rapid downhill movement of a mixture of water, rock, and soil. The amount of water in a mudflow can be as high as 60 percent. Mudflows often occur after heavy rains in a normally dry area. In clay soils with a high water content, mudflows may occur even on very gentle slopes. Under certain conditions, clay soils suddenly turn to liquid and begin to flow. An earthquake can trigger both mudflows and landslides. Mudflows can be very dangerous.

Slump If you slump your shoulders, the entire upper part of your body drops down. In the type of mass movement known as slump, a mass of rock and soil suddenly slips down a slope. Unlike a landslide, the material in slump moves down in one large mass. It looks as if someone pulled the bottom out from under part of the slope. Slump often occurs when water soaks the bottom of soil that is rich in clay.

68 ◆ G

Tyrannosaurus rex

Fossils Reveal Dinosaur Diet

Have you ever wondered what a *Tyrannosaurus rex* might have eaten for lunch? Paleontologist Karen Chin is looking for the answers to this question. She explores the world of ancient animals, including dinosaurs. But she doesn't do her research by digging up fossil bones. Instead, she relies on another kind of clue left behind by these fascinating animals.

Karen is a world-famous expert on coprolites—fossilized animal droppings. Because coprolites contain the undigested remains of food that has passed through an animal's digestive tract, they may provide clues about an animal's diet.

Studying coprolites may sound odd. But research can reveal important information about an animal and its environment. In fact, Karen has made some exciting discoveries about dinosaurs as a result of her research. And she's earned a nickname—The Queen of Coprolites.

Career Path

Dr. Karen Chin has a master's degree in biology from Montana State University. She earned a Ph.D. in geology from the University of California at Santa Barbara. Currently, Karen is an Assistant Professor of Geology at the University of Colorado at Boulder. She is also a curator of paleontology at the University of Colorado Museum of Natural History, where she helps oversee the museum's fossil collection.

Using a slicing machine, Karen cuts thin sections of fossils to examine.

Talking With
Dr. Karen Chin

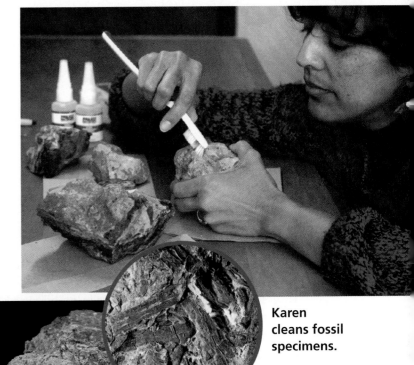

Karen cleans fossil specimens.

A complete *Maiasaura* coprolite is shown (left). A microscopic image of the fossil shows plant material (above).

? How did you become interested in fossils?

As a child, I was interested in animals and plants. But I wasn't interested in studying extinct animals, so I never thought about becoming a paleontologist. As a young adult, I worked for many summers as a National Park naturalist. I enjoyed talking with the public about nature and science.

When I entered graduate school at Montana State University, I wanted to learn about museums, so I took a part-time job at the Museum of the Rockies. I did all sorts of things there, including helping to glue together fossil dinosaur bones and writing text for fossil exhibits. I became fascinated by the mystery of how we can learn about the prehistoric world by using clues from fossils. It was during this time that I got interested in coprolites.

? How do you identify coprolites?

When a team of paleontologists finds the fossilized bones of dinosaurs or other animals, they sometimes come across coprolites in the same area. Not all coprolites look alike. But they do have some characteristics in common. Coprolites from smaller animals often have a shape that reminds you of dog droppings. But the shapes of coprolites from giant animals like *Tyrannosaurus rex* are not always easy to recognize. In some cases, the coprolites contain clues in the form of chopped-up remains of things an animal ate. I often have to do a lot of investigating to figure out whether a fossil is a coprolite or not.

? What do these fossils tell you?

They can give us a good idea of a dinosaur's diet and digestion. I've seen many different types of food remains, including fish scales, broken bits of dinosaur bone, shells, and fragments of wood and other plant material. Those food remains also tell us what kinds of organisms lived together in the same environment in the ancient past. The coprolites found in Montana are an example of what specimens can reveal.

Two Medicine Formation (above), located in northwestern Montana, is an important dinosaur site. The artwork (left) shows duck-billed dinosaurs in prehistoric Montana.

 ## What did you find in the fossils?

Many dinosaur fossils have been found at the Two Medicine Formation site in Montana. Dr. Jack Horner, one of the paleontologists who discovered these fossils, also found some specimens he thought might be coprolites. I decided to take a closer look at them.

The specimens looked like nothing more than broken, jagged black rocks. But when I looked closely, I could see they contained plant material. I prepared a very thin section, thin enough for light to shine through, so I could examine it under the microscope. It showed that the rock was filled with chopped-up wood. That material was wood from coniferous trees.

These coprolites were probably produced by duck-billed dinosaurs that lived about 75 million years ago. This particular dinosaur, called *Maiasaura*, was very large, about 7 meters long and about one or two metric tons.

What else did you learn?

I also noticed burrows in these coprolites. The burrows reminded me of dung beetles. Dung beetles are insects that feed on droppings. Some species of dung beetles create distinctive burrows as they feed. I asked a beetle expert to take a look. He confirmed that the burrows were the type made by dung beetles.

Now we had some new pieces of information. First of all, the presence of the dung beetles confirmed that these fossils were coprolites. Also, the coprolites showed that dung beetles and dinosaurs lived together in prehistoric Montana—something we didn't know before. Other coprolites at the site indicate the presence of snails. So we can infer that duck-billed dinosaurs, coniferous trees, dung beetles, and snails lived in close association.

This large coprolite is thought to be from *Tyrannosaurus rex*. It is being weighed.

What fossils did you examine in Canada?

Another paleontologist sent me a possible coprolite collected near where a *T. rex* skeleton was dug up in Saskatchewan, Canada. These giant dinosaur species lived about 65 million years ago. They grew to 14 meters long and weighed as much as 5 metric tons.

I did some chemical tests on the specimen. My results showed that it was a coprolite and that it was produced by a meat-eating animal. The specimen contained many bone fragments. By looking at the cell structure of the bone fragments, I was able to tell that they probably belonged to a young plant-eating dinosaur.

This coprolite specimen was found in the same rock layers as several species of meat-eating dinosaurs. All the dinosaurs were fairly small. The only large one was *T. rex*. Because of the large size of the Saskatchewan coprolite, we inferred that it was probably produced by *T. rex*.

What did you conclude?

This coprolite showed us that it is possible to find coprolites from large meat-eating dinosaurs. It gives us an idea of what to look for when we are searching for fossils. This coprolite provides physical evidence that *T. rex* ate other dinosaurs.

What is your most surprising finding?

I identified a very large tyrannosaur coprolite, though not from *T. rex*. It contains not only bone fragments, but also impressions of muscle tissue. It was surprising to find the fossilized remains of undigested meat in a coprolite. This discovery shows that it is possible for droppings to become fossilized much more quickly than we thought.

Why are these findings important?

It's exciting to use a different kind of fossil evidence to find out how these ancient animals lived and what their environments were like.

Karen looks at a very thin slice of coprolite under her microscope.

Writing in Science

Career Link Karen Chin uses the clues she finds in coprolites to figure out what ancient animals ate and what their environment was like. Make a list of what you'd like to know about animals and plants that lived in prehistoric times. In a paragraph describe ways that studying fossils could help you learn the answers to your questions.

Go Online
PHSchool.com

For: More on this career
Visit: PHSchool.com
Web Code: cfb-2000

Mapping Earth's Surface

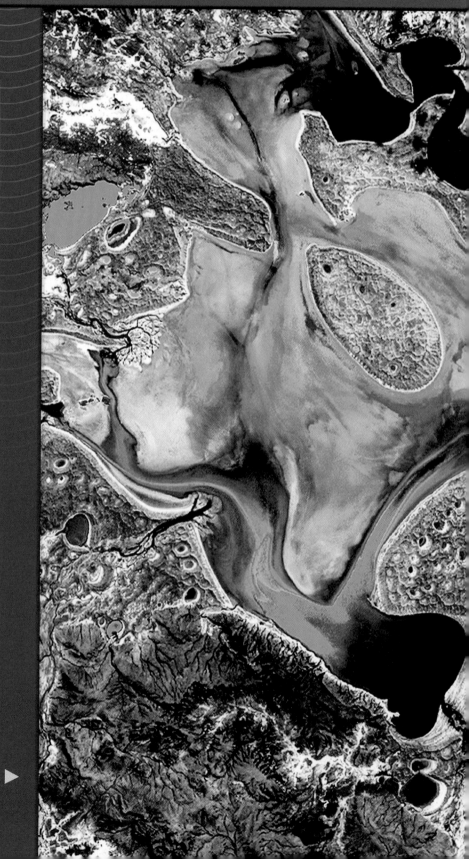

interactive
Textbook

This satellite image shows Lake Carnegie in Western Australia. ▶

Lab zone Chapter **Project**

Getting on the Map

For this chapter project, you will select a small piece of land and draw a map of its physical features.

Your Goal To create a scale map of a small area of your neighborhood

To complete this project, you must
● work with your teacher or an adult family member
● choose and measure a small square or rectangular piece of land
● use a compass to locate north
● draw a map to scale
● use symbols and a key to represent natural and human-made features of the land
● follow the safety guidelines in Appendix A

Plan It! Start by looking for a suitable site. Your site should be about 300 to 1,000 square meters in area. It could be part of a park, playground, or backyard. Look for an area that includes interesting natural features such as trees, a stream, and changes in elevation or slope. There may be some human-made structures on your site, such as a park bench or sidewalk. Once you have chosen a site, measure its boundaries and sketch its physical features. Then brainstorm ideas for symbols to include on your map. When you have completed your map, including a key and map scale, present it to your class.

Exploring Earth's Surface

Reading Preview

Key Concepts
- What does the topography of an area include?
- What are the main types of landforms?

Key Terms
- topography • elevation
- relief • landform • plain
- mountain • mountain range
- plateau • landform region

Target Reading Skill
Comparing and Contrasting
As you read, compare and contrast the characteristics of landforms by completing a table like the one below.

Characteristics of Landforms

Landform	Elevation	Relief
Plain	a. ___?___	Low
Mountain	b. ___?___	c. ___?___
d. ___?___	High	e. ___?___

Discover Activity

What Is the Land Like Around Your School?

1. On a piece of paper, draw a small square to represent your school.
2. Choose a word that describes the type of land near your school, such as flat, hilly, or rolling. Write the word next to the square.
3. Use a magnetic compass to determine the direction of north. Assume that north is at the top of your piece of paper.
4. If you travel due north 1 kilometer from your school, what type of land do you find? Choose a word to describe the land in this area. Write that word to the north of the square.
5. Repeat Step 4 for areas located 1 kilometer east, south, and west of your school.

Think It Over
Forming Operational Definitions What phrase could you use to describe the land in your area?

In 1804, an expedition set out from St. Louis to explore the land between the Mississippi River and the Pacific Ocean. The United States had just purchased a part of this vast territory, called Louisiana, from France. Before the Louisiana Purchase, the United States stretched from the Atlantic coast westward to the Mississippi River. Few United States citizens had traveled west of the Mississippi. None had ever traveled over land all the way to the Pacific.

Led by Meriwether Lewis and William Clark, the expedition first traveled up the Missouri River. Then the group crossed the Rocky Mountains and followed the Columbia River to the Pacific Ocean. They returned by a similar route. The purpose of the expedition was to map America's interior.

On the journey to the Pacific, the Lewis and Clark expedition traveled more than 5,000 kilometers. As they traveled, Lewis and Clark observed many changes in topography. **Topography** (tuh PAWG ruh fee) is the shape of the land. An area's topography may be flat, sloping, hilly, or mountainous.

◀ **The compass used by Meriwether Lewis**

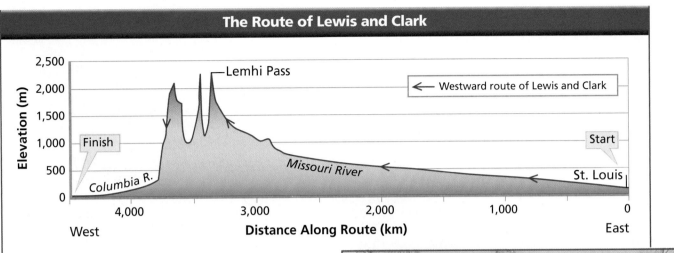

The Route of Lewis and Clark

Elevation (m) — vertical axis: 0, 500, 1,000, 1,500, 2,000, 2,500

Lemhi Pass

← Westward route of Lewis and Clark

Finish

Start

Columbia R.

Missouri River

St. Louis

Distance Along Route (km): 4,000 3,000 2,000 1,000 0

West   East

Topography

The topography of an area includes the area's elevation, relief, and landforms. The desktop where you do homework probably has piles of books, papers, and other objects of different sizes and shapes. Your desktop has both elevation and relief!

Elevation The height above sea level of a point on Earth's surface is its **elevation.** When Lewis and Clark started in St. Louis, they were about 140 meters above sea level. By the time they reached Lemhi Pass in the Rocky Mountains, they were more than 2,200 meters above sea level. Look at Figure 1 to see the changes in elevation along Lewis and Clark's route.

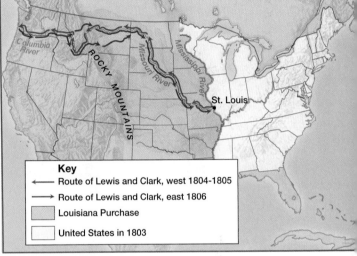

FIGURE 1
The route of the Lewis and Clark expedition crossed regions that differed greatly in elevation and relief. **Interpreting Graphs** *How much elevation did Lewis and Clark gain between St. Louis and Lemhi Pass?*

Relief The difference in elevation between the highest and lowest parts of an area is its **relief.** Early in their journey, Lewis and Clark encountered flat or rolling land with low relief, or small differences in elevation. In the Rocky Mountains, they crossed huge mountains separated by deep valleys. These areas had high relief, or great differences in elevation.

Landforms If you followed the route of the Lewis and Clark expedition, you would see many different landforms. A **landform** is a feature of topography, such as a hill or valley, formed by the processes that shape Earth's surface. Different landforms have different combinations of elevation and relief.

 Reading Checkpoint What is the difference between elevation and relief?

FIGURE 2

Landforms

Mountains, plains, and plateaus are just a few of the many landforms that make up the topography of Earth's surface.
Predicting *What do you think would be the main difference between interior plains and coastal plains?*

Plains
Plains may occur along a continent's edges or in the interior.

Go Online

SCi **NSTA** LINKS™

For: Links on landforms
Visit: www.SciLinks.org
Web Code: scn-0711

Types of Landforms

Landforms vary greatly in size and shape—from level plains extending as far as the eye can see, to low, rounded hills that you could climb on foot, to jagged mountains that would take you many days to walk around. **There are three main types of landforms: plains, mountains, and plateaus.**

Plains A **plain** is a landform made up of nearly flat or gently rolling land with low relief. A plain that lies along a seacoast is called a coastal plain. In North America, a coastal plain extends around the continent's eastern and southeastern shores. Coastal plains have both low elevation and low relief.

A plain that lies away from the coast is called an interior plain. Although interior plains have low relief, their elevation can vary. The broad interior plains of North America are called the Great Plains.

The Great Plains extend north from Texas into Canada. The Great Plains extend west to the Rocky Mountains from the states of North and South Dakota, Nebraska, Kansas, Oklahoma, and Texas. At the time of the Lewis and Clark expedition, the Great Plains were a vast grassland.

Mountains
A mountain's base usually covers an area of at least several square kilometers, but its peak may rise to a point. Mountains often have steeply sloping sides.

Plateaus
The top of a plateau forms a level surface.

Mountains A **mountain** is a landform with high elevation and high relief. Mountains usually occur as part of a mountain range. A **mountain range** is a group of mountains that are closely related in shape, structure, and age. After crossing the Great Plains, the Lewis and Clark expedition crossed a rugged mountain range in Idaho called the Bitterroot Mountains.

The different mountain ranges in a region make up a mountain system. The Bitterroot Mountains are one mountain range in the mountain system known as the Rocky Mountains.

Mountain ranges and mountain systems in a long, connected chain form a larger unit called a mountain belt. The Rocky Mountains are part of a great mountain belt that stretches down the western sides of North America and South America.

Plateaus A landform that has high elevation and a more or less level surface is called a **plateau.** A plateau is rarely perfectly smooth on top. Streams and rivers may cut into the plateau's surface. The Columbia Plateau in Washington State is an example. The Columbia River, which the Lewis and Clark expedition followed, slices through this plateau. The many layers of rock that make up the Columbia Plateau are stacked about 1,500 meters thick.

Lab zone Skills **Activity**

Classifying
You take a direct flight across the United States from Walla Walla in Washington State to Washington, D.C. You have a window seat. Write a postcard to friends describing the major landforms that you see on your trip. Use Figure 3 to determine what the land is like along your route.

Landform Regions of the United States

Key
- Coastal plains
- Interior plains or lowlands
- Mountains
- Plateaus or uplands
- Basins and mountains

FIGURE 3
The United States has many different landform regions.
Interpreting Maps *In what regions are Charleston, Santa Fe, and Topeka?*

Landform Regions A large area of land where the topography is made up mainly of one type of landform is called a **landform region.** The Great Plains and Rocky Mountains are major landform regions. Other terms can be used to describe landform regions. For example, an upland is a region of hilly topography. A lowland is a region of plains with low elevation. A basin is lower than the mountains around it.

Reading Checkpoint What terms can be used to describe landform regions?

Section 1 Assessment

Target Reading Skill Comparing and Contrasting Use the information in your table to help answer Question 2 below.

Reviewing Key Concepts

1. **a. Defining** What is elevation?
   b. Comparing and Contrasting What is relief? How does it differ from elevation?
   c. Calculating What is the relief in an area where the highest point is 1,200 meters above sea level and the lowest point is 200 meters above sea level?

2. **a. Listing** What are the three main types of landforms?
   b. Describing What are the characteristics of a mountain?
   c. Sequencing Place these features in order from smallest to largest: mountain system, mountain range, mountain belt, mountain.

Writing in Science

Description Look at Figure 3. Choose one of the landform regions on the map. Research the characteristics of your landform region using an encyclopedia or other reference. Write a description of the region, including characteristics such as elevation, relief, and the types of landforms found there.

Models of Earth

Reading Preview

Key Concepts

- How do maps and globes represent Earth's surface?
- What reference lines are used to locate points on Earth?
- What are three common map projections?

Key Terms

- map • globe • scale
- symbol • key • degree
- equator • hemisphere
- prime meridian • latitude
- longitude • map projection

Target Reading Skill

Asking Questions Before you read, preview the red headings. In a graphic organizer like the one below, ask a question for each heading. As you read, write the answers to your questions.

Models of Earth

Question	Answer
What are maps and globes?	

Lab zone Discover Activity

How Can You Flatten the Curved Earth?

1. Using a felt-tip pen, make a rough sketch of the outlines of the continents on the surface of an orange or grapefruit.
2. Using a plastic knife, carefully peel the orange. If possible, keep the peel in one large piece so that the continents remain intact.
3. Try to lay the pieces of orange peel flat on a table.

Think It Over

Observing What happens to the continents when you try to flatten the pieces? Is there any way to keep the shapes of the continents from being distorted?

Today, people know that Earth is a sphere located in space and moving around the sun. But it took hundreds of years to develop this scientific model of Earth. Around 600 B.C., one early Greek scientist, Thales of Miletus, hypothesized that Earth is a disk floating in a pool of water. Another Greek scientist, Anaximander, suggested that Earth is a cylinder floating in space. (He thought that people lived on the flat top of the cylinder!)

Around 350 B.C., the Greek scientist Aristotle used evidence from everyday observations to support the idea that Earth is a sphere. For example, Aristotle pointed out that a ship sailing away from shore appears to sink beneath the horizon because Earth's surface is curved. If Earth were flat, the ship would simply appear smaller as it moved away.

After Aristotle, other Greek scientists used the knowledge that Earth is a sphere to help them measure the size of Earth. Eratosthenes, a Greek scientist who lived in Egypt more than 2,200 years ago, calculated Earth's size. Using measurements and principles of geometry and astronomy, he arrived at a figure that was accurate to within 14 percent.

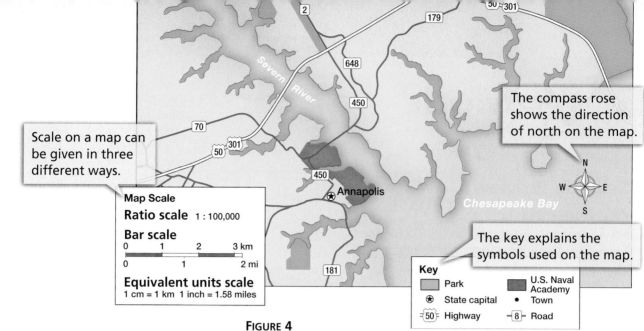

Scale on a map can be given in three different ways.

The compass rose shows the direction of north on the map.

Map Scale
Ratio scale 1 : 100,000

Bar scale
0   1   2   3 km
0   1   2 mi

Equivalent units scale
1 cm = 1 km   1 inch = 1.58 miles

The key explains the symbols used on the map.

Key
▢	Park	▢	U.S. Naval Academy
✪	State capital	•	Town
⁅50⁆	Highway	⊣8⊢	Road

FIGURE 4
What's in a Map?
A map is drawn to scale, uses symbols explained in a map key, and usually has a compass rose to show direction. This map shows the area around Annapolis, Maryland.
Interpreting Maps *What is the scale of this map?*

Maps and Globes

Maps and globes show the shape, size, and position of Earth's surface features. A **map** is a flat model of all or part of Earth's surface as seen from above. A **globe** is a sphere that represents Earth's entire surface. A globe correctly shows the relative size, shape, and position of landmasses and bodies of water, much as if you were viewing Earth from space.

Maps and globes are drawn to scale and use symbols to represent topography and other features on Earth's surface. A map's **scale** relates distance on a map to a distance on Earth's surface. Scale is often given as a ratio. For example, one unit on a map could equal 25,000 units on the ground. So one centimeter on the map would represent 0.25 kilometer. This scale, "one to twenty-five thousand," would be written "1 : 25,000." Figure 4 shows three ways of giving a map's scale.

Mapmakers use shapes and pictures called **symbols** to stand for features on Earth's surface. A symbol can represent a physical feature, such as a river, lake, mountain, or plain. A symbol also can stand for a human-made feature, such as a highway, city, or airport. A map's **key**, or legend, is a list of all the symbols used on the map with an explanation of their meaning.

Maps also include a compass rose or north arrow. The compass rose helps relate directions on the map to directions on Earth's surface. North usually is located at the top of the map.

Reading Checkpoint Where can you find the meaning of the symbols on a map?

Figure 5
A Grid System
The checkerboard pattern made by
this farmland is based on the grid
lines used on maps and globes.

An Earth Reference System

When you play checkers, the grid of squares helps you to keep track of where each piece should be. To find a point on Earth's surface, you need a reference system like the grid of squares on a checkerboard. Of course, Earth itself does not have grid lines, but most maps and globes show a grid. Because Earth is a sphere, the grid curves to cover the entire planet. **Two of the lines that make up the grid, the equator and prime meridian, are the baselines for measuring distances on Earth's surface.**

Measuring in Degrees To locate positions on Earth's surface, scientists use units called degrees. You probably know that degrees are used to measure the distance around a circle. As you can see in Figure 6, a **degree** (°) is $\frac{1}{360}$ of the distance around a circle. Degrees can also be used to measure distances on the surface of a sphere. On Earth's surface, each degree is a measure of an angle formed by lines drawn from the center of Earth to points on the surface. To help locate points precisely, degrees are further divided into smaller units called minutes and seconds.

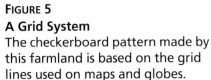

Figure 6
Degrees Around
Distances around a circle
are measured in degrees.
Interpreting Diagrams *How many
degrees are there in one quarter
of the distance around the circle?*

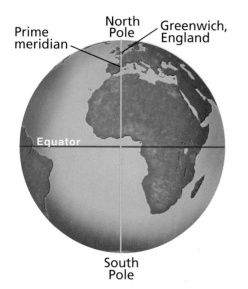

FIGURE 7
Equator and Prime Meridian
The equator and prime meridian divide Earth's surface into hemispheres.

The Equator Halfway between the North and South poles, the **equator** forms an imaginary line that circles Earth. The equator divides Earth into the Northern and Southern hemispheres. A **hemisphere** (HEM ih sfeer) is one half of the sphere that makes up Earth's surface. If you started at the equator and traveled to one of the poles, you would travel 90 degrees—one quarter of the distance in a full circle.

Science and History

Maps and Technology
Centuries ago, people invented instruments for determining compass direction, latitude, and longitude. Mapmakers developed techniques to show Earth's surface accurately.

1154
Scientific Mapmaking
The Arab mapmaker Al-Idrisi made several world maps for King Roger of Sicily. Idrisi's maps marked a great advance over other maps of that time. They showed the Arabs' grasp of scientific mapmaking and geography. But unlike modern maps, these maps placed south at the top!

Around 1300
Charts for Navigation
Lines representing wind directions criss-crossed a type of map called a portolan chart. These charts also showed coastlines and harbors. A sea captain would use a portolan chart and a compass when sailing from one harbor to another.

Around 1100
Magnetic Compass
Because the needle of a magnetic compass points north, ships at sea could tell direction even when the sun and stars were not visible. Arabs and Europeans adopted this Chinese invention by the 1200s.

| 1100 | 1200 | 1300 | 1400 |

The Prime Meridian Another imaginary line, called the **prime meridian,** makes a half circle from the North Pole to the South Pole. The prime meridian passes through Greenwich, England. Places east of the prime meridian are in the Eastern Hemisphere. Places west of the prime meridian are in the Western Hemisphere.

If you started at the prime meridian and traveled west along the equator, you would travel through 360 degrees before returning to your starting point. At 180 degrees east or west of the prime meridian is another half circle that lies directly opposite the prime meridian.

✔ **Reading Checkpoint** What two hemispheres are separated by the equator?

Writing in Science

Writing in Science Choose one period on the timeline to learn more about. Use the library to find information about maps in that time. Who used maps? Why were they important? Share what you learn in the form of a letter written by a traveler or explorer who is using a map of that period.

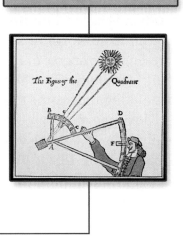

1595
Determining Latitude
To find latitude, sailors used a variety of instruments, including the backstaff. The navigator sighted along the backstaff's straight edge to measure the angle of the sun or North Star above the horizon. Later improvements led to modern instruments for navigation.

1569
Map Projections
Flemish mapmaker Gerardus Mercator invented the first modern map projection, which bears his name. Mercator and his son, Rumold, also made an atlas and maps of the world such as the one shown above.

1763
Determining Longitude
John Harrison, a carpenter and mechanic, won a prize from the British navy for building a highly accurate clock called a chronometer. Harrison's invention made finding longitudes quicker and easier. With exact longitudes, mapmakers could greatly improve the accuracy of their maps.

| 1500 | 1600 | 1700 | 1800 |

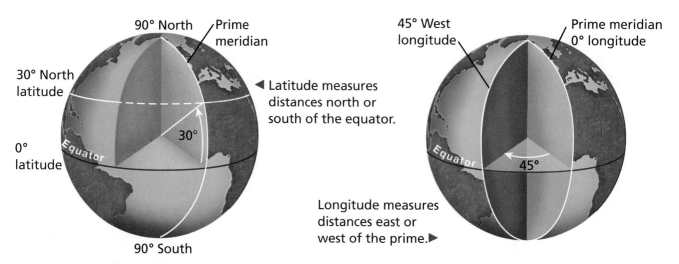

FIGURE 8
Latitude and Longitude
Points on Earth's surface can be located using the grid of latitude and longitude lines.

Locating Points on Earth's Surface

Using the equator and prime meridian, mapmakers have constructed a grid made up of lines of latitude and longitude. **The lines of latitude and longitude form a grid that can be used to find locations anywhere on Earth.**

Latitude The equator is the starting line for measuring **latitude,** or distance in degrees north or south of the equator. The latitude of the equator is 0°. Between the equator and each pole are 90 evenly spaced, parallel lines called lines of latitude. Each degree of latitude is equal to about 111 kilometers.

A line of latitude is defined by the angle it makes with the equator and the center of Earth. Figure 8 shows how lines drawn from the center of Earth to the equator and from the center of Earth to 30° North form an angle of 30 degrees.

Longitude The distance in degrees east or west of the prime meridian is called **longitude.** There are 360 lines of longitude that run from north to south, meeting at the poles. Each line represents one degree of longitude. A degree of longitude equals about 111 kilometers at the equator. But at the poles, where the lines of longitude come together, the distance decreases to zero.

The prime meridian, which is the starting line for measuring longitude, is at 0°. The longitude lines in each hemisphere are numbered up to 180 degrees. Half of the lines of longitude are in the Eastern Hemisphere, and half are in the Western Hemisphere.

Each line of longitude is defined by the angle it makes with the prime meridian and the center of Earth. As you can see in Figure 8, a line drawn from the center of Earth to the prime meridian and a line drawn from the center of Earth to 45° West form an angle of 45 degrees at the equator.

Lab zone Try This **Activity**

Where in the World?
Using a globe, determine what city is found at each of the following points:

2° S 79° W

38° N 9° W

34° N 135° E

34° S 58° W

55° N 3° W

1° N 103° E

What word is spelled by the first letters of these cities?

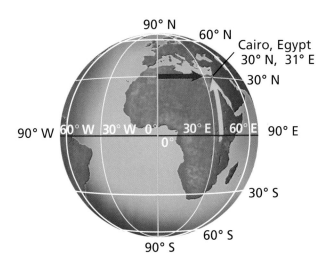

Cairo, Egypt
30° N, 31° E

◄ Cairo, Egypt, is located where the latitude line 30° N crosses the longitude line 31° E.

Using Latitude and Longitude The location of any point on Earth's surface can be expressed in terms of the latitude and longitude lines that cross at that point. For example, you can see on the map in Figure 9 that New Orleans is located where the line for 30° North latitude crosses the line for 90° West longitude. Notice that each longitude line crosses the latitude lines, including the equator, at a right angle.

FIGURE 9
Every point on Earth's surface has a particular latitude and longitude.
Interpreting Maps *What are the latitude and longitude of Mexico City? Of Sydney?*

✓ Reading Checkpoint **How are longitude lines numbered?**

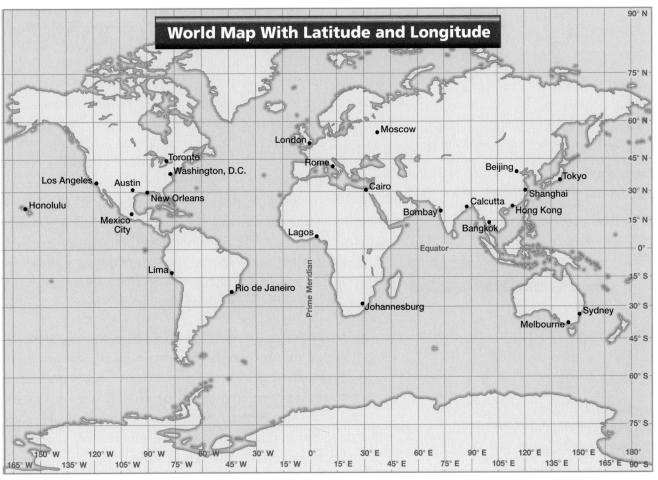

FIGURE 10
A Mercator projection is based on a cylinder with grid lines that has been flattened. On a Mercator projection, lines of longitude are parallel, so shapes near the poles are distorted.

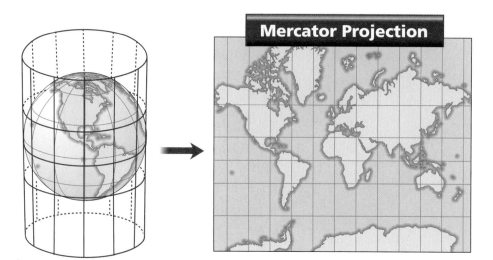

Mercator Projection

Map Projections

To show Earth's curved surface on a flat map, mapmakers use map projections. A **map projection** is a framework of lines that helps in transferring points on Earth's three-dimensional surface onto a flat map. Depending on which map projection a mapmaker chooses, features such as continents, oceans, islands, rivers, and lakes might appear to have somewhat different sizes and shapes on the map. **Three common map projections are the Mercator projection, the equal-area projection, and the conic projection.** Each map projection has advantages and disadvantages.

Mercator Projection On a Mercator projection, all the lines of latitude and longitude appear as straight, parallel lines that form a rectangle. On a Mercator projection, the size and shape of landmasses near the equator are distorted only a little. But as you can see in Figure 10, size and shape become more and more distorted as you go toward the poles. The reason for this distortion is that the lines of longitude on the map do not come together at the poles as they do on a globe. In fact, the North and South poles do not appear as points on a map drawn using a Mercator projection.

Equal-Area Projection To solve the problem of distortion on Mercator projections, mapmakers developed equal-area projections. An equal-area projection correctly shows the relative sizes of Earth's landmasses. But an equal-area projection also has distortion. The shapes of landmasses near the edges of the map appear stretched and curved.

FIGURE 11
An equal-area projection shows areas correctly, but distorts some shapes around its edges.
Comparing and Contrasting *Why does Greenland appear larger on the Mercator projection than on the equal-area projection?*

Equal-Area Projection

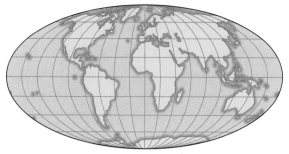

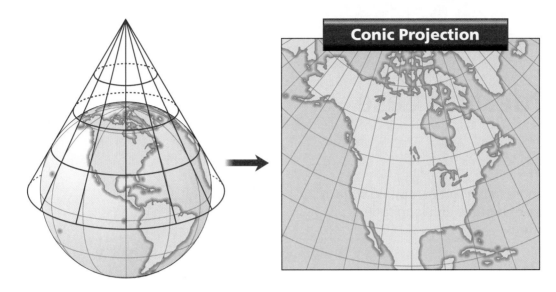

Conic Projection

Conic Projection Suppose you placed a clear plastic cone over a globe, as shown in Figure 12. Then you could trace the lines of latitude and longitude onto the cone, unwrap the cone, and place it flat. The result would be a conic projection. In a conic projection, lines of longitude appear as straight lines while lines of latitude are curved. There is little distortion on maps that use this projection to show limited parts of Earth's surface. A conic projection is frequently used for maps of the continental United States.

FIGURE 12
A conic projection is based on a cone that covers part of Earth and is then rolled out flat. A conic projection's grid is formed from straight lines of longitude and curved lines of latitude.

✓ **Reading Checkpoint** Why is a conic projection best suited to showing only part of Earth's surface?

Section 2 Assessment

🔁 **Target Reading Skill** Asking Questions
Work with a partner to check the answers in your graphic organizer.

Reviewing Key Concepts

1. **a. Defining** What is a map?
   b. Explaining What information does a globe present?
   c. Comparing and Contrasting How are maps and globes similar? How are they different?
2. **a. Identifying** What two lines are baselines for measurements on Earth's surface?
   b. Explaining How are these baselines used to locate points on Earth's surface?
   c. Interpreting Maps Look at the map in Figure 9. If you fly due north from Lima, through how many degrees of latitude must you travel to reach Washington, D.C.?

3. **a. Listing** What are three common map projections?
   b. Comparing and Contrasting What are the advantages and disadvantages of each of the three projections?

Math Practice

4. **Scales and Ratios** A globe has a scale of 1 : 40,000,000. Using a piece of string, you determine that the shortest distance between two cities on the globe is 7 cm. What is the actual distance between the two cities?

A Borderline Case

Problem

Which was more important in locating state borders: lines of latitude and longitude or physical features?

Skills Focus

classifying, observing, inferring

Materials

- United States map with latitude, longitude, and state borders
- tracing paper
- paper clips
- colored pencils

Procedure

1. Lay a sheet of tracing paper on top of a map of the United States.
2. Trace over the Pacific and Atlantic coasts of the United States with a blue pencil.
3. Using the blue pencil, trace all Great Lakes shorelines that reach nearby states.
4. Trace all state borders that go exactly north-south with a red pencil. (*Hint:* Some straight-line borders that appear to run north-south, such as the western border of Maine, do not follow lines of longitude.)
5. Use a green pencil to trace all state borders or sections of state borders that go exactly east-west. (*Hint:* Straight-line borders that are slanted, such as the southern border of Nevada, do not follow lines of latitude.)
6. Now use a blue pencil to trace the borders that follow rivers.
7. Use a brown pencil to trace any borders that are not straight lines or rivers.

Analyze and Conclude

1. **Classifying** How many state boundaries are completely defined by longitude and latitude? How many are partially defined by longitude and latitude? How many states do not use either one to define their borders?
2. **Observing** What feature is most often used to define a state border when longitude and latitude are not used? Give specific examples.
3. **Observing** Study the physical map of the United States in Appendix A. What other physical features are used to define borders? Which state borders are defined by these features?
4. **Inferring** In which region of the country were lines of latitude and longitude most important in determining state borders? What do you think is the reason for this?
5. **Communicating** Pick any state and describe its borders as accurately as you can in terms of latitude, longitude, and physical features.

More to Explore

Research the history of your state to find out when and how its borders were established. Are your state's borders based on longitude and latitude, landforms and topography, or both?

Review a map of your county or state. Are any features other than borders related to longitude and latitude? Which features seem to follow landforms and topography?

Maps and Computers

Reading Preview

Key Concepts
- How does computer mapping differ from earlier ways of making maps?
- What sources of data are used in making computer maps?

Key Terms
- surveying • digitizing
- satellite image • pixel
- Global Positioning System

Target Reading Skill

Identifying Main Ideas As you read the Maps and Computers section, write the main idea in a graphic organizer like the one below. Then write three supporting details that further explain the main idea.

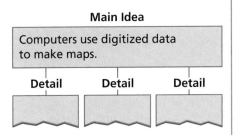

Main Idea

Computers use digitized data to make maps.

Detail	Detail	Detail

Lab zone Discover **Activity**

Can You Make a Pixel Picture?

1. With a pencil, draw a square grid of lines spaced 1 centimeter apart. The grid should have 6 squares on each side.
2. On the grid, draw the outline of a simple object, such as an apple.
3. Using a different color pencil, fill in all squares that are completely inside the object. If a square is mostly inside the object, fill it in completely. If it is mostly outside, leave it blank.
4. Each square on your grid represents one pixel, or bit of information, about your picture. Looking at your pixel picture, can you recognize the shape you started with?

Think It Over
Predicting How would the pixel picture change if you drew the object smaller? How would the pixel picture look if you used graph paper with squares that are smaller than your grid?

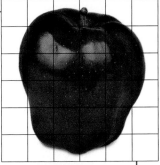

For centuries, mapmakers drew maps by hand. Explorers made maps by sketching coastlines as seen from their ships. More accurate maps were made by locating points on Earth's surface in a process called surveying. In **surveying,** mapmakers determine distances and elevations using instruments and the principles of geometry. In the twentieth century, people learned to make maps using photographs taken from airplanes.

Computer Mapping

Since the 1970s, computers have revolutionized mapmaking. **With computers, mapmakers can store, process, and display map data electronically.**

All of the data used in computer mapping must be written in numbers. The process by which mapmakers convert the location of map points to numbers is called **digitizing.** These numbers are stored on a computer as a series of 0's and 1's. The digitized data can easily be displayed on a computer screen, modified, and printed in map form.

▲ A computer produced this digital model of part of Earth's surface.

Sources of Map Data

Computer mapmakers use these up-to-the-minute data to produce maps quickly and easily. Computers can automatically make maps that might take a person hundreds of hours to draw by hand. **Computers produce maps using data from many sources, including satellites and the Global Positioning System.**

Data From Satellites Much of the data used in computer mapping is gathered by satellites in space. Mapping satellites use electronic devices to collect computer data about the land surface. Pictures of the surface based on these data are called **satellite images.**

A satellite image is made up of thousands of tiny dots called **pixels.** A painting made of pixels would have many separate dots of color. Each pixel in a satellite image contains information on the color and brightness of a small part of Earth's surface. For example, the pixels that represent a forest differ in color and brightness from the pixels that represent farmland. The data in each pixel are stored on a computer. When the satellite image is printed, the computer translates these digitized data into colors.

FIGURE 13

Views of Yellowstone

These views of Yellowstone National Park show how computers have changed the technology of map making.

◄ This early map of the Yellowstone region was produced through surveys on the ground. Yellowstone Lake is near the center of both images.

This satellite image made by the Landsat ► Thematic Mapper enables scientists to compare areas affected by forest fires (orange) with ambient forest (green).

Beginning in 1972, the United States launched a series of Landsat satellites designed to observe Earth's surface. Today, Landsat is just one of many different satellites used for this purpose. As a Landsat satellite orbits Earth, it collects and stores data about a strip of the surface that is 185 kilometers wide. The satellite relays the data back to a station on Earth, where computers use the data to create images. Landsat images show what covers the land surface—plants, soil, sand, rock, water, or snow and ice. Large, human-made features such as cities are also visible.

Scientists learn to identify specific features by the "signature," or combination of colors and shapes, that the feature makes on a satellite image. In a satellite image, areas covered by grass, trees, or crops are often shown as red, water as black or blue, and cities as bluish gray. Landsat images may show features such as grasslands, forests, and agricultural crops, as well as deserts, mountains, or cities.

Data From the Global Positioning System Today map-makers can collect data for maps using the Global Positioning System, or GPS. The **Global Positioning System** is a method of finding latitude, longitude, and elevation of points on Earth's surface using a network of satellites. To learn more about GPS, look at the Technology and Society feature on pages 24 and 25.

Mapping Earth's Surface

Video Preview
▶ Video Field Trip
Video Assessment

✔ **Reading Checkpoint**   **What is a satellite image?**

Section 3 Assessment

🎯 **Target Reading Skill** Identifying Main Ideas Use your graphic organizer to help you answer Question 1 below.

Reviewing Key Concepts

1. a. **Explaining** In what form is the information for a map stored on a computer?
   b. **Defining** What is digitizing?
   c. **Applying Concepts** What are the advantages of computer mapping?
2. a. **Reviewing** How do satellites gather data for a satellite image?
   b. **Explaining** In what form are data for a satellite image stored?
   c. **Summarizing** Summarize the process by which Landsat produces a satellite image of part of Earth's surface.

Lab zone **At-Home Activity**

Maps in the News Most of the maps that you see today in newspapers and magazines are made using computers. With family members, look through newspapers and news magazines. How many different types of maps can you find? Explain to your family the map's scale, symbols, and key. After you have studied the map, try to state the main point of the information shown on the map.

Global Positioning System (GPS)

Today, being lost could be a thing of the past for many people. Why? A system of satellites orbiting nearly 20,200 km above Earth can be used to pinpoint one's location anywhere on Earth as well as in the air.

Satellite
Each of two dozen GPS satellites continually sends out its current location and the exact time to receivers controlled by GPS users.

Location, Location, Location!

The Global Positioning System, or GPS, allows a user to locate his or her position anywhere on or above Earth to within a few meters or less. Hikers, drivers, boaters, and pilots use GPS to navigate. While its major use is navigation, GPS also has many scientific applications. Geologists use GPS to map some of the most rugged terrains on Earth. Points located with GPS can be entered into a computer and plotted to make maps. Archaeologists use GPS to map sites without disturbing ancient artifacts. Biologists can use the system to track threatened and endangered species.

Navigation
GPS systems aboard ships and boats have simplified navigation.

Keeping GPS on Track

GPS has become indispensable to surveyors and mappers, many types of scientists and engineers, and many ordinary people who need to know where they are. But like all technologies, GPS has limitations. To communicate with GPS satellites, receivers need an unobstructed view of the sky. Dense forests, tall buildings, and hazy conditions can prevent the receivers from picking up signals.

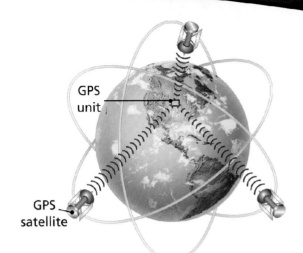

System of Satellites
At least three satellites must be above the horizon to pinpoint a location.

Receiver
GPS receivers are the size of a typical cellular phone. These devices receive and process satellite signals to determine the receiver's precise location.

Weigh the Impact

1. Identify the Need
Think about activities in which knowing one's precise location is important. Make a list of at least five activities.

2. Research
Research the activities you listed in Question 1 to find out if GPS has been applied to them.

3. Write
Choose one application of GPS mentioned in this feature. Or, propose an application of this guidance system that you think might be useful. Write one or two paragraphs to explain the application or how you think GPS might be applied to an activity.

Go Online
PHSchool.com

For: More on GPS
Visit: PHSchool.com
Web Code: cfh-2010

Topographic Maps

Reading Preview

Key Concepts
- How do mapmakers represent elevation, relief, and slope?
- How do you read a topographic map?
- What are some uses of topographic maps?

Key Terms
- topographic map
- contour line
- contour interval
- index contour

Target Reading Skill

Using Prior Knowledge Before you read, write what you know about topographic maps in a graphic organizer like the one below. As you read, write what you learn.

What You Know
1. Some maps show where mountains and plains are.
2.

What You Learned
1.
2.

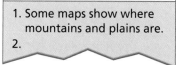

Lab zone Discover **Activity**

Can a Map Show Relief?

1. Carefully cut the corners off 8 pieces of cardboard so that they look rounded. Each piece should be at least 1 centimeter smaller than the one before.
2. Trim the long sides of the two largest pieces so that the long sides appear wavy. Don't cut more than 0.5 centimeter into the cardboard.
3. Trace the largest cardboard piece on a sheet of paper.
4. Trace the next largest piece inside the tracing of the first. Don't let any lines cross.
5. Trace the other cardboard pieces, from largest to smallest, one inside the other, on the same paper.
6. Stack the cardboard pieces beside the paper in the same order they were traced. Compare the stack of cardboard pieces with your drawing. How are they alike? How are they different?

Think It Over

Making Models If the cardboard pieces are a model of a landform, what do the lines on the paper represent?

An orienteering meet is not an ordinary race. Participants compete to see how quickly they can find a series of locations called control points. The control points are scattered over a large park or state forest. Orienteers choose a set number of control points, and then visit the points in any order. In this sport, your ability to read a map and use a compass is often more important than how fast you can run. In a major meet, there may be several hundred orienteers on dozens of teams.

At the start of an orienteering meet, you would need to consult your map. But the maps used in orienteering are different from road maps or maps in an atlas—they're topographic maps.

FIGURE 14
Orienteering
Orienteering helps people develop the skill of using a map and compass.

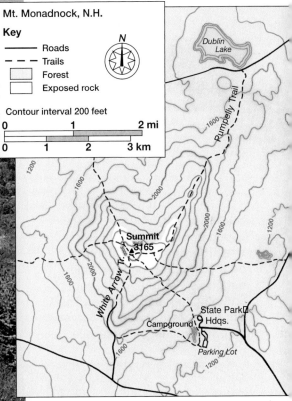

Mt. Monadnock, N.H.

Key

— Roads
--- Trails
Forest
Exposed rock

Contour interval 200 feet

0   1   2 mi
0   1   2   3 km

FIGURE 15
Contour Lines
The contour lines on a topographic map represent elevation and relief.
Comparing and Contrasting *What information does the topographic map provide that the photograph does not?*

Go **O**nline
active art

For: Topographic Map activity
Visit: PHSchool.com
Web Code: cfp-2014

Mapping Earth's Topography

A **topographic map** (tahp uh GRAF ik) is a map showing the surface features of an area. Topographic maps use symbols to portray the land as if you were looking down on it from above. Topographic maps provide highly accurate information on the elevation, relief, and slope of the ground surface.

Mapmakers use contour lines to represent elevation, relief, and slope on topographic maps. On a topographic map, a **contour line** connects points of equal elevation. In the United States, most topographic maps give contour intervals in feet rather than meters.

The change in elevation from contour line to contour line is called the **contour interval.** The contour interval for a given map is always the same. For example, the map in Figure 15 has a contour interval of 200 feet. If you start at one contour line and count up 10 contour lines, you have reached an elevation 2,000 feet above where you started. Usually, every fifth contour line, known as an index contour, is darker and heavier than the others. **Index contours** are labeled with the elevation in round units, such as 1,600 or 2,000 feet above sea level.

 Reading Checkpoint What do all the points connected by a contour line have in common?

Reading a Topographic Map

Looking at a topographic map with many squiggly contour lines, you may feel as if you are gazing into a bowl of spaghetti. But with practice, you can learn to read a topographic map like the one in Figure 16. **To read a topographic map, you must familiarize yourself with the map's scale and symbols and interpret the map's contour lines.**

Scale Topographic maps are usually large-scale maps. Large-scale maps show a close-up view of part of Earth's surface. In the United States, most topographic maps are at a scale of 1 : 24,000, or 1 centimeter equals 0.24 kilometers. At this scale, a map can show the details of elevation and features such as rivers and coastlines. Large buildings, airports, and major highways appear as outlines at the correct scale. Symbols are used to show houses and other small features.

FIGURE 16
Topographic Map
The different types of symbols on topographic maps provide data on elevation, relief, slopes, and human-made features. This United States Geological Survey map shows part of Tennessee.

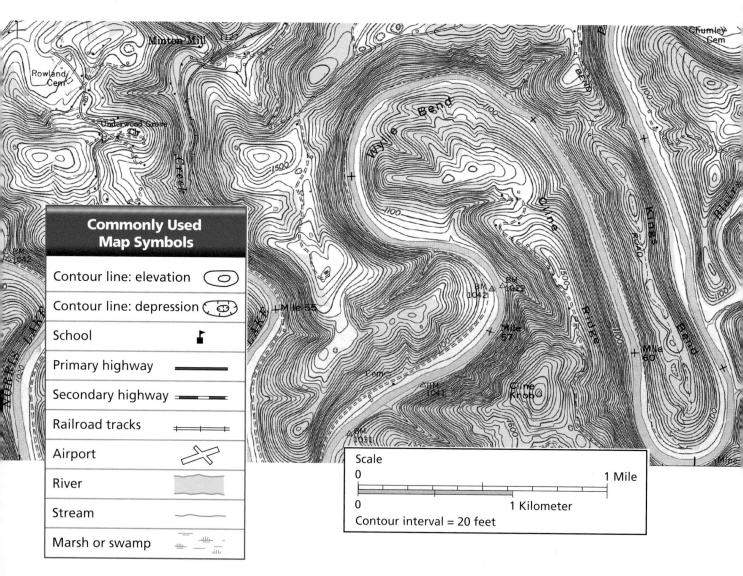

Commonly Used Map Symbols

Contour line: elevation	
Contour line: depression	
School	
Primary highway	
Secondary highway	
Railroad tracks	
Airport	
River	
Stream	
Marsh or swamp	

Scale
0 — 1 Mile
0 — 1 Kilometer
Contour interval = 20 feet

Mapping Elevation Data

The map shows the elevation data points on which the contour lines are based. Study the map and the map key, then answer the questions.

1. **Reading Maps** What is the contour interval on this map?

2. **Reading Maps** What color are the lowest points on the map? What range of elevations do these points represent?

3. **Reading Maps** What color are the highest points on the map? What range of elevations do these points represent?

4. **Applying Concepts** What is the elevation of the contour line labeled A?

5. **Inferring** Is the area between B and C a ridge or a valley? How can you tell?

6. **Interpreting Data** Describe how elevation changes along the trail from point D to point C.

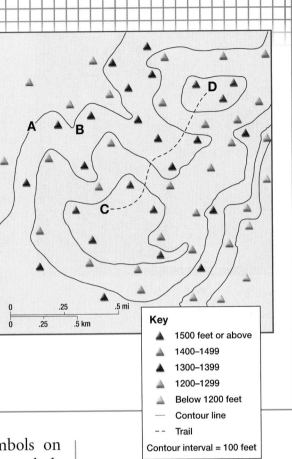

Key

▲	1500 feet or above
▲	1400–1499
▲	1300–1399
▲	1200–1299
▲	Below 1200 feet
—	Contour line
--	Trail

Contour interval = 100 feet

Symbols Mapmakers use a great variety of symbols on topographic maps. If you were drawing a map, what symbols would you use to represent a forest, a campground, an orchard, a swamp, or a school? Look at Figure 16 to see the symbols that are often used for these and other features.

Interpreting Contour Lines To find the elevation of a feature, begin at the labeled index contour, which is a heavier line than regular contour lines. Then, count the number of contour lines up or down to the feature.

Reading contour lines is the first step toward "seeing" an area's topography. Look at the topographic map in Figure 16. The closely spaced contour lines indicate steep slopes. The widely spaced contour lines indicate gentle slopes or relatively flat areas. A contour line that forms a closed loop with no other contour lines inside it indicates a hilltop. A closed loop with dashes inside indicates a depression, or hollow in the ground.

The shape of contour lines also help to show ridges and valleys. V-shaped contour lines pointing downhill indicate a ridge line. V-shaped contour lines pointing uphill indicate a valley. A stream in the valley flows toward the open end of the V.

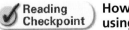 **Reading Checkpoint** How are hilltops and depressions represented using contour lines?

Interpreting Data

Study the topographic map in Figure 16. Where are the steepest slopes on the map found? How can you tell? What is the difference in elevation between the river and the top of Cline Knob?

Uses of Topographic Maps

Topographic maps have many uses in science and engineering, business, government, and everyday life. Suppose that you are an engineer planning a route for a highway over a mountain pass. Your design for the highway needs to solve several problems. To design a safe highway, you need a route that avoids the steepest slopes. To protect the area's water supply, the highway must stay a certain distance from rivers and lakes. You also want to find a route that avoids houses and other buildings. How would you solve these problems and find the best route for the highway? You would probably begin by studying topographic maps.

Businesses use topographic maps to help decide where to build new stores, housing, or factories. Local governments use them to decide where to build new schools and other public buildings. Topographic maps have recreational uses, too. If you were planning a bicycle trip, you could use a topographic map to see where your trip would be flat or hilly.

FIGURE 17
Using Topographic Maps
Topographic maps provide the data necessary for the planning of highways, bridges, and other large construction projects.

✓ **Reading Checkpoint** How do businesses use topographic maps?

Section 4 Assessment

🎯 **Target Reading Skill** Using Prior Knowledge Review your graphic organizer and revise it based on what you just learned in the section.

Reviewing Key Concepts

1. a. **Defining** What is a topographic map?
   b. **Explaining** How do topographic maps represent elevation and relief?
   c. **Calculating** If the contour interval on a topographic map is 50 meters, how much difference in elevation do 12 contour lines represent?

2. a. **Reviewing** What do you need to know about a topographic map in order to read it?
   b. **Comparing and Contrasting** Compare the way steep slopes are represented on a topographic map with the way gentle slopes are represented.
   c. **Inferring** Reading a map, you see V-shaped contour lines that point uphill. What land feature would you find in this area?

3. a. **Listing** What are four main uses of topographic maps?
   b. **Problem Solving** Suppose that your community needs a large, flat site for a new athletic field. How could you use a topographic map of your area to identify possible sites?

Writing in Science

Giving Directions Write a descriptive paragraph of a simple route from one point on the map on page 28 to another point. Your paragraph should provide the starting point, but not the end point. Include details such as distance, compass direction, and topography along the route. Share your paragraph with classmates to see if they can follow your directions.

A Map in a Pan

Problem

How can you make a topographic map?

Skills Focus

making models, interpreting maps

Materials

- deep-sided pan
- water
- marking pencil
- modeling clay
- clear, hard sheet of plastic
- metric ruler
- sheet of unlined white paper
- food coloring

Procedure

PART 1 Research and Investigate

1. Place a lump of clay on the bottom of a deep-sided pan. Shape the clay into a model of a hill.

2. Pour colored water into the pan to a depth of 1 centimeter to represent sea level.

3. Place a sheet of hard, clear plastic over the container.

4. Trace the outline of the pan on the plastic sheet with a marking pencil. Then, looking straight down into the pan, trace the outline the water makes around the edges of the clay model. Remove the plastic sheet from the pan.

5. Add another centimeter of water to the pan, bringing the depth of the water to 2 centimeters. Replace the plastic sheet exactly as before, then trace the water level again.

6. Repeat Step 5 several times. Stop when the next addition of water would completely cover your model.

7. Remove the plastic sheet. Trace the outlines that you drew on the plastic sheet onto a sheet of paper.

Analyze and Conclude

1. **Interpreting Maps** Looking at your topographic map, how can you tell which parts of your model hill have a steep slope? A gentle slope?

2. **Interpreting Maps** How can you tell from the map which point on the hill is the highest?

3. **Predicting** Where on your map would you be likely to find a stream? Explain.

4. **Applying Concepts** Is there any depression on your map where water would collect after it rained? What symbol should you use to identify this depression?

5. **Making Models** Compare your map with the clay landform. How are they alike? How are they different? How could you improve your map as a model of the landform?

More to Explore

Obtain a topographic map that includes an interesting landform such as a mountain, canyon, river valley, or coastline. After studying the contour lines on the map, make a sketch of what you think the landform looks like. Then build a scale model of the landform using clay or layers of cardboard or foamboard. How does your model landform compare with your sketch?

① Exploring Earth's Surface

Key Concepts

- The topography of an area includes the area's elevation, relief, and landforms.
- There are three main types of landforms: plains, mountains, and plateaus.

Key Terms

topography
elevation
relief
landform
plain
mountain
mountain range
plateau
landform region

② Models of Earth

Key Concepts

- Maps and globes are drawn to scale and use symbols to represent topography and other features on Earth's surface.
- Two of the lines that make up the grid, the equator and prime meridian, are the baselines for measuring distances on Earth's surface.
- The lines of latitude and longitude form a grid that can be used to find locations anywhere on Earth.
- Three common map projections are the Mercator projection, the equal-area projection, and the conic projection.

Key Terms

map
globe
scale
symbol
key
degree
equator
hemisphere
prime meridian
latitude
longitude
map projection

③ Maps and Computers

Key Concepts

- With computers, mapmakers can store, process, and display map data electronically.
- Computers produce maps using data from many sources, including satellites and the Global Positioning System.

Key Terms

surveying
digitizing
satellite image
pixel
Global Positioning System

④ Topographic Maps

Key Concepts

- Mapmakers use contour lines to represent elevation, relief, and slope on topographic maps.
- To read a topographic map, you must familiarize yourself with the map's scale and symbols and interpret the map's contour lines.
- Topographic maps have many uses in science and engineering, business, government, and everyday life.

Key Terms

topographic map
contour line
contour interval
index contour

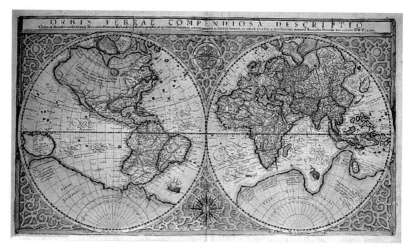

Review and Assessment

Go Online
PHSchool.com

For: Self-Assessment
Visit: PHSchool.com
Web Code: cfa-2010

Organizing Information

Concept Mapping Copy the concept map. Then complete the map to show the characteristics of the different types of landforms. (For more about concept mapping, see the Skills Handbook.)

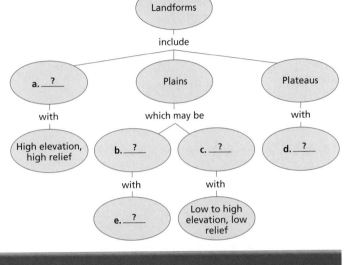

Reviewing Key Terms

Choose the letter of the best answer.

1. A landform that has high elevation but a mostly flat surface is a
   a. plain.
   b. mountain.
   c. mountain range.
   d. plateau.

2. Latitude is a measurement of distance north or south of the
   a. hemisphere.
   b. equator.
   c. index contour.
   d. prime meridian.

3. To show Earth's curved surface on a flat map, mapmakers choose different
   a. map projections.
   b. globes.
   c. scales.
   d. landform regions.

4. The digitized data on a computer map is made up of
   a. index contours.
   b. pixels.
   c. contour intervals.
   d. symbols.

5. On a topographic map, relief is shown using
   a. lines of latitude.
   b. lines of longitude.
   c. map projections.
   d. contour lines.

If the statement is true, write *true.* **If it is false, change the underlined word or words to make the statement true.**

6. <u>Relief</u> is a landform's height above sea level.

7. The <u>equator</u> is a half circle that extends from the North Pole to the South Pole.

8. If an airplane flew around Earth in a straight line from east to west, the airplane would cross lines of <u>longitude.</u>

9. An <u>index contour</u> is labeled to indicate the elevation along a contour line.

Writing in Science

Advertisement Suppose that you are a manufacturer of GPS tracking and mapping devices. Write an advertisement that describes as many uses for your device as you can think of.

Discovery CHANNEL SCHOOL

Mapping Earth's Surface
Video Preview
Video Field Trip
▶ Video Assessment

Review and Assessment

Checking Concepts

10. Compare the elevation of a coastal plain to that of an interior plain.

11. What is a mountain range?

12. What do geologists call an area where there is mostly one kind of topography?

13. The South Island of New Zealand lies at about 170° E. What hemisphere is it in?

14. What is one advantage of a Mercator projection? What is one disadvantage?

15. How do the contour lines on a topographic map indicate the slope of the land?

Math Practice

16. Scale and Ratios Earth's diameter is about 13,000 kilometers. If a globe has a diameter of 0.5 meter, write the globe's scale as a ratio. What distance on Earth would 1 centimeter on the globe represent?

Thinking Critically

17. Applying Concepts Which would be more likely to show a shallow, 1.5-meter-deep depression in the ground: a 1-meter contour interval or a 5-meter contour interval?

18. Interpreting Maps Use the map below to answer the question. What is the latitude and longitude of Point A? In which two hemispheres is Point A located?

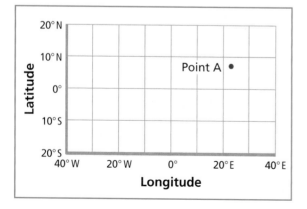

19. Problem Solving Your community has decided to build a zoo for animals from many regions of Earth. How could you use topographic maps of your area to help decide on the best location for the zoo?

Applying Skills

Use the map below to answer Questions 20–22.

This map shows part of Acadia National Park in Maine. The contour interval is 20 feet.

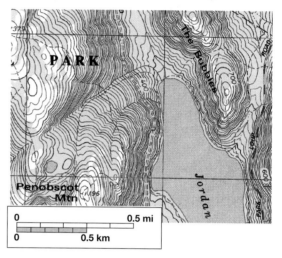

20. Interpreting Maps What is the elevation of the large lake? Which of the two Bubbles is higher?

21. Calculating Use the map scale to calculate the distance from the top of Penobscot Mountain to the large lake.

22. Inferring How can you tell whether the streams flow into or out of the large lake?

Lab zone Chapter **Project**

Performance Assessment Present your map to the class. What symbols did you use to represent the natural and physical features of your site? How did you measure and locate them on your map? How accurate is your map? Ask your classmates how you could improve your map. Write an evaluation of your map. What would you change about it? What would you keep the same? Does your map give others a clear idea of what the land looks like?

Standardized Test Prep

Choose the letter of the best answer.

1. On a map, what is the height above sea level of a point on Earth's surface?
   A topography   **B** relief
   C elevation   **D** latitude

2. You are an engineer preparing to build a new highway exit. You will need to look at details of the area where the new exit will be located. Which map scale would it be best to use, in order to see the needed topographic details?
   F 1 centimeter = 0.25 kilometers
   G 1 centimeter = 10.0 kilometers
   H 1 centimeter = 5.0 kilometers
   J 1 centimeter = 2.5 kilometers

Use the map below and your knowledge of science to answer Questions 3–4.

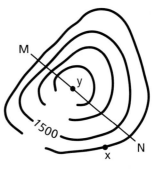

Contour interval = 15 meters

3. A topographic profile shows the shape or relief of the land along a given line. Along line M-N on the map, which of the following would the profile most closely resemble?

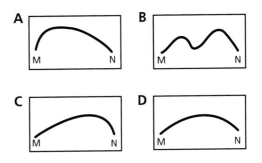

4. What is the elevation of the point marked *x* on the map?
   F 1400 meters   **G** 1500 meters
   H 1485 meters   **J** 1515 meters

5. How is longitude measured?
   A in degrees east or west of the prime meridian
   B in degrees east or west of the equator
   C in degrees north or south of the prime meridian
   D in kilometers east or west of the prime meridian

Constructed Response

6. Write a paragraph comparing a topographic map of an area with a satellite image of the same area. Assume that both are at the same scale. In your answer, explain how the topographic map and the satellite image are similar and how they are different.

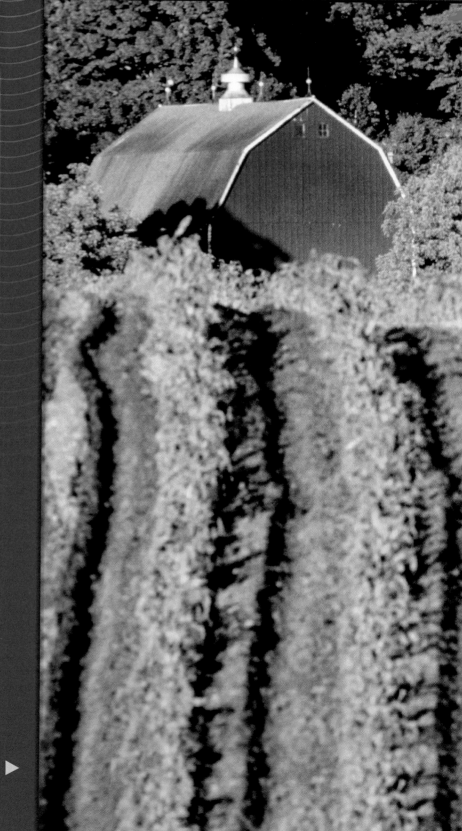

The rich soil on this farm is a ▶
valuable natural resource.

Lab zone Chapter **Project**

Soils for Seeds

The process of weathering affects all rocks exposed on Earth's surface. Weathering breaks rock into smaller and smaller particles. When the rock particles mix with other ingredients, such as leaves, the mixture is called soil. In this project you will test how soil and other growing materials affect the growth of plants.

Your Goal To determine how soil composition affects the growth of bean seeds

To complete this project, you must

● compare the particle size, shape, and composition of different growing materials

● compare how bean seeds grow in several different growing materials

● determine what type of soil or growing material is best for young bean plants

● follow the safety guidelines in Appendix A

Plan It! With your group, brainstorm what types of soil and other growing materials you will use in your experiment. What are the different variables that affect the growth of plants? How will you measure the growth of your bean plants? Plan your experiment and obtain your teacher's approval. As you carry out your experiment, observe and record the growth of your plants. Then present your results to your class.

Rocks and Weathering

Reading Preview

Key Concepts
- How do weathering and erosion affect Earth's surface?
- What are the causes of mechanical weathering and chemical weathering?
- What determines how fast weathering occurs?

Key Terms
- weathering
- erosion
- uniformitarianism
- mechanical weathering
- abrasion
- ice wedging
- chemical weathering
- oxidation
- permeable

Target Reading Skill

Relating Cause and Effect A cause makes something happen. An effect is what happens. As you read, identify the causes of chemical weathering. Write them in a graphic organizer like the one below.

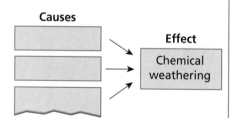

Causes

Effect

Chemical weathering

Lab zone Discover Activity

How Fast Can It Fizz?

1. Place a fizzing antacid tablet in a small beaker. Then grind up a second tablet and place it in another beaker. The whole tablet is a model of solid rock. The ground-up tablet is a model of rock fragments.

2. Add 100 mL of warm water to the beaker containing the whole tablet. Then stir with a stirring rod until the tablet dissolves completely. Use a stopwatch to time how long it takes.

3. Add 100 mL of warm water to the beaker containing the ground-up tablet. Then stir until all of the ground-up tablet dissolves. Time how long it takes.

Think It Over

Drawing Conclusions Which dissolved faster, the whole antacid tablet or the ground-up tablet? What variable affected how long it took each of them to dissolve?

Imagine a hike that lasts for months and covers hundreds of kilometers. Each year, many hikers go on such treks. They hike trails that run the length of America's great mountain ranges. For example, the John Muir Trail follows the Sierra Nevada mountains. The Sierras extend about 640 kilometers along the eastern side of California. In the east, the Appalachian Trail follows the Appalachian Mountains. The Appalachians stretch more than 2,000 kilometers from Alabama to Maine.

The two trails cross very different landscapes. The Sierras are rocky and steep, with many peaks rising 3,000 meters above sea level. The Appalachians are more rounded and gently sloping, and are covered with soil and plants. The highest peaks in the Appalachians are less than half the elevation of the highest peaks in the Sierras. Which mountain range do you think is older? The Appalachians formed more than 250 million years ago. The Sierras formed only within the last 10 million years. The forces that wear down rock on Earth's surface have had much longer to grind down the Appalachians.

Weathering and Erosion

The process of mountain building thrusts rock up to the surface of Earth. There, the rock is exposed to weathering. **Weathering** is the process that breaks down rock and other substances at Earth's surface. Heat, cold, water, and ice all contribute to weathering. So do the oxygen and carbon dioxide in the atmosphere. Repeated freezing and thawing, for example, can crack rock apart into smaller pieces. Rainwater can dissolve minerals that bind rock together. You don't need to go to the mountains to see examples of weathering. The forces that wear down mountains also cause bicycles to rust, paint to peel, sidewalks to crack, and potholes to form.

The forces of weathering break rocks into smaller and smaller pieces. Then the forces of erosion carry the pieces away. **Erosion** (ee ROH zhun) is the removal of rock particles by wind, water, ice, or gravity. **Weathering and erosion work together continuously to wear down and carry away the rocks at Earth's surface.** The weathering and erosion that geologists observe today also shaped Earth's surface millions of years ago. How do geologists know this? Geologists make inferences based on the principle of **uniformitarianism** (yoon uh fawrm uh TAYR ee un iz um). This principle states that the same processes that operate today operated in the past.

There are two kinds of weathering: mechanical weathering and chemical weathering. Both types of weathering act slowly, but over time they break down even the biggest, hardest rocks.

> **Reading Checkpoint** What is the difference between weathering and erosion?

FIGURE 1
Effects of Weathering
The jagged peaks of the Sierra Nevadas (bottom) formed within the last 10 million years. The more gently sloping Appalachians (top) have been exposed to weathering for 250 million years.
Inferring *How can you tell that the Sierra Nevadas formed much more recently than the Appalachians?*

FIGURE 2
Forces of Mechanical Weathering

Mechanical weathering affects all the rock on Earth's surface.

Forming Operational Definitions *Study the examples of mechanical weathering, then write a definition of each term in your own words.*

Freezing and Thawing
When water freezes in a crack in a rock, it expands and makes the crack bigger. The process of ice wedging also widens cracks in sidewalks and causes potholes in streets.

Release of Pressure
As erosion removes material from the surface of a mass of rock, pressure on the rock is reduced. This release of pressure causes the outside of the rock to crack and flake off like the layers of an onion.

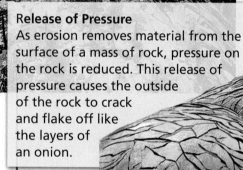

Animal Actions
Animals that burrow in the ground – including moles, gophers, prairie dogs, and some insects – loosen and break apart rocks in the soil.

Mechanical Weathering

If you hit a rock with a hammer, the rock may break into pieces. Like a hammer, some forces of weathering break rock into pieces. The type of weathering in which rock is physically broken into smaller pieces is called **mechanical weathering.** These smaller pieces of rock have the same composition as the rock they came from. If you have seen rocks that are cracked or split in layers, then you have seen rocks that are undergoing mechanical weathering. Mechanical weathering works slowly. But over very long periods of time, it does more than wear down rocks. Mechanical weathering eventually wears away whole mountains.

Abrasion
Sand and other rock particles that are carried by wind, water, or ice can wear away exposed rock surfaces like sandpaper on wood. Wind-driven sand helped shape the rocks shown here.

Plant Growth
Roots of trees and other plants enter cracks in rocks. As roots grow, they force the cracks farther apart. Over time, the roots of even small plants can pry apart cracked rocks.

The causes of mechanical weathering include freezing and thawing, release of pressure, plant growth, actions of animals, and abrasion. The term **abrasion** (uh BRAY zhun) refers to the grinding away of rock by rock particles carried by water, ice, wind, or gravity.

In cool climates, the most important force of mechanical weathering is the freezing and thawing of water. Water seeps into cracks in rocks and then freezes when the temperature drops. Water expands when it freezes. Ice therefore acts like a wedge that forces things apart. Wedges of ice in rocks widen and deepen cracks. This process is called **ice wedging.** When the ice melts, the water seeps deeper into the cracks. With repeated freezing and thawing, the cracks slowly expand until pieces of rock break off.

 Reading Checkpoint How does ice wedging weather rock?

Go Online
PHSchool.com

For: More on weathering
Visit: PHSchool.com
Web Code: cfd-2021

Chemical Weathering

In addition to mechanical weathering, another type of weathering attacks rock. **Chemical weathering** is the process that breaks down rock through chemical changes. **The causes of chemical weathering include the action of water, oxygen, carbon dioxide, living organisms, and acid rain.**

Each rock is made up of one or more minerals. Chemical weathering can produce new minerals as it breaks down rock. For example, granite is made up of several minerals, including feldspar, quartz, and mica. As a result of chemical weathering, granite eventually changes the feldspar minerals to clay minerals.

Chemical weathering creates holes or soft spots in rock, so the rock breaks apart more easily. Chemical and mechanical weathering often work together. As mechanical weathering breaks rock into pieces, more surface area becomes exposed to chemical weathering. The Discover activity at the beginning of this section shows how increasing the surface area increases the rate of a chemical reaction.

FIGURE 3
Weathering and Surface Area
As weathering breaks apart rock, the amount of surface area exposed to further weathering increases. Notice that the total volume of the rock stays the same even though the rock is broken into smaller and smaller pieces.
Predicting *What will happen to the surface area if each cube is again divided into four cubes?*

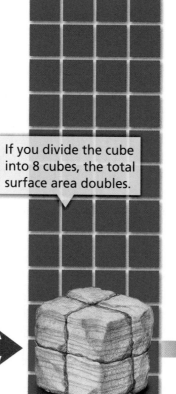

The surface area of a cube is equal to 6 times the area of each side.

If you divide the cube into 8 cubes, the total surface area doubles.

If you divide each of the 8 cubes into 64 cubes, the total surface area doubles again.

FIGURE 4
Effects of Chemical Weathering
Acid rain chemically weathered these stone gargoyles on the cathedral of Notre Dame in Paris, France.

Water Water is the most important cause of chemical weathering. Water weathers rock by dissolving it. When a rock or other substance dissolves in water, it mixes uniformly throughout the water to make a solution. Over time, many rocks will dissolve in water.

Oxygen The oxygen gas in air is an important cause of chemical weathering. If you have ever left a bicycle or metal tool outside in the rain, then you have seen how oxygen can weather iron. Iron combines with oxygen in the presence of water in a process called **oxidation.** The product of oxidation is rust. Rock that contains iron also oxidizes, or rusts. Rust makes rock soft and crumbly and gives it a red or brown color.

Carbon Dioxide Another gas found in air, carbon dioxide, also causes chemical weathering. Carbon dioxide dissolves in rainwater and in water that sinks through air pockets in the soil. The result is a weak acid called carbonic acid. Carbonic acid easily weathers rocks such as marble and limestone.

Living Organisms Imagine a seed landing on a rock face. As it sprouts, its roots push into cracks in the rock. As the plant's roots grow, they produce weak acids that slowly dissolve rock around the roots. Lichens—plantlike organisms that grow on rocks—also produce weak acids that chemically weather rock.

Acid Rain Over the past 150 years, people have been burning large amounts of coal, oil, and gas for energy. Burning these fuels can pollute the air with sulfur, carbon, and nitrogen compounds. Such compounds react chemically with the water vapor in clouds, forming acids. These acids mix with raindrops and fall as acid rain. Acid rain causes very rapid chemical weathering.

Reading Checkpoint How can plants cause chemical weathering?

Which Weathered Faster?

The graph shows the rate of weathering for two identical pieces of limestone that weathered in different locations.

1. **Reading Graphs** What does the *x*-axis of the graph represent?

2. **Reading Graphs** What does the *y*-axis of the graph represent?

3. **Reading Graphs** How much thickness did Stone A lose in 1,000 years? How much thickness did Stone B lose in the same period?

4. **Drawing Conclusions** Which stone weathered at a faster rate?

5. **Inferring** Since the two identical pieces of limestone weathered at different rates, what can you infer caused the difference in their rates of weathering?

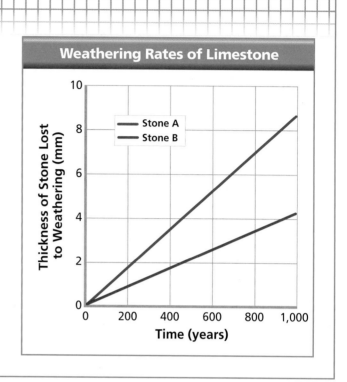

Weathering Rates of Limestone

Stone A
Stone B

Thickness of Stone Lost to Weathering (mm)

Time (years)

Rate of Weathering

Visitors to New England's historic cemeteries may notice a surprising fact. Slate tombstones carved in the 1700s are less weathered and easier to read than marble gravestones from the 1800s. Why is this so? Some kinds of rocks weather more rapidly than others. **The most important factors that determine the rate at which weathering occurs are the type of rock and the climate.**

Type of Rock The minerals that make up the rock determine how fast it weathers. Rock made of minerals that do not dissolve easily in water weathers slowly. Rock made of minerals that dissolve easily in water weathers faster.

Some rock weathers more easily because it is permeable. **Permeable** (PUR mee uh bul) means that a material is full of tiny, connected air spaces that allow water to seep through it. Permeable rock weathers chemically at a fast rate. Why? As water seeps through the spaces in the rock, it dissolves and removes material broken down by weathering.

Climate Climate refers to the average weather conditions in an area. Both chemical and mechanical weathering occur faster in wet climates. Rainfall provides the water needed for chemical changes as well as for freezing and thawing.

Granite

Marble

Chemical reactions occur faster at higher temperatures. That is why chemical weathering occurs more quickly where the climate is both hot and wet. Granite, for example, is a very hard rock that forms when molten material cools inside Earth. Granite weathers so slowly in cool climates that it is often used as a building stone. But in hot and wet climates, granite weathers more rapidly and eventually crumbles apart.

Reading Checkpoint How does rainfall affect the rate of weathering?

FIGURE 5
Which Rock Weathers Faster?
These two tombstones are about the same age and are in the same cemetery, yet one has weathered much less than the other.
Inferring *Which type of stone weathers faster, granite or marble? Explain.*

Section 1 Assessment

Target Reading Skill Relating Cause and Effect Refer to your graphic organizer about the causes of chemical weathering to help you answer Question 2 below.

Reviewing Key Concepts

1. a. **Defining** What is weathering?
   b. **Defining** What is erosion?
   c. **Predicting** Over millions of years, how do weathering and erosion change a mountain made of solid rock?
2. a. **Defining** What is chemical weathering?
   b. **Comparing and Contrasting** Compare and contrast mechanical weathering and chemical weathering.
   c. **Classifying** Classify each as chemical or mechanical weathering: freezing or thawing, oxidation, water dissolving chemicals in rock, abrasion, acid rain.
3. a. **Identifying** What are two factors that affect the rate of weathering?
   b. **Relating Cause and Effect** A granite monument is placed outside for 200 years in a region with a cool, dry climate. What would its rate of weathering be? Explain.

Lab zone At-Home **Activity**

Ice in a Straw Demonstrate one type of weathering for your family. Plug one end of a drinking straw with a small piece of clay. Fill the straw with water. Now plug the top of the straw with clay. Make sure that the clay plugs do not leak. Lay the straw flat in the freezer overnight. Remove the straw the next day. What happened to the clay plugs? What process produced this result? Be sure to dispose of the straw so that no one will use it for drinking.

Rock Shake

Problem

How will shaking and acid conditions affect the rate at which limestone weathers?

Skills Focus

interpreting data, calculating, drawing conclusions

Materials

- 300 mL of water
- balance
- paper towels
- masking tape
- 2 pieces of thin cloth
- marking pen or pencil
- 300 mL of vinegar, an acid
- plastic graduated cylinder, 250 mL
- 80 small pieces of water-soaked limestone
- 4 watertight plastic containers with screw-on caps, 500 mL

Procedure

PART 1 Day 1

1. Using masking tape, label the four 500-mL containers A, B, C, and D.

2. Separate the 80 pieces of limestone into four sets of 20.

3. Copy the data table in your notebook. Then place the first 20 pieces of limestone on the balance and record their mass in the data table. Place the rocks in container A.

4. Repeat Step 3 for the other sets of rocks and place them in containers B, C, and D.

5. Pour 150 mL of water into container A and container B. Put caps on both containers.

6. Pour 150 mL of vinegar into container C and container D. Put caps on both containers.

7. Predict the effect of weathering on the mass of the limestone pieces. Which will weather more: the limestone in water or the limestone in vinegar? (*Hint:* Vinegar is an acid.) Also predict the effect of shaking on the limestone in containers B and D. Record your predictions in your notebook.

8. Allow the pieces to soak overnight.

Data Table				
Container	Total Mass at Start	Total Mass Next Day	Change in Mass	Percent Change in Mass
A (water, no shaking)				
B (water, shaking)				
C (vinegar, no shaking)				
D (vinegar, shaking)				

PART 2 Day 2

9. Screw the caps tightly on containers B and D. Shake both containers for 10 to 15 minutes. Make sure that each container is shaken for exactly the same amount of time and at the same intensity. After shaking, set the containers aside. Do not shake containers A and C.

10. Open the top of container A. Place one piece of thin cloth over the opening of the container. Carefully pour all of the water out through the cloth into a waste container. Be careful not to let any of the pieces flow out with the water. Dry these pieces carefully and record their mass in your data table.

11. Next, determine how much limestone was lost through weathering in container A. (*Hint*: Subtract the mass of the limestone pieces remaining on Day 2 from the mass of the pieces on Day 1.)

12. Repeat Steps 10 and 11 for containers B, C, and D.

Analyze and Conclude

1. **Calculating** Calculate the percent change in mass of the 20 pieces for each container.

$$\% \text{ change} = \frac{\text{Change in mass} \times 100}{\text{Total mass at start}}$$

Record the results in the data table.

2. **Interpreting Data** Do your data show a change in mass of the 20 pieces in each of the four containers?

3. **Interpreting Data** Is there a greater change in total mass for the pieces in one container than for the pieces in another? Explain.

4. **Drawing Conclusions** How correct were your predictions of how shaking and acid would affect the weathering of limestone? Explain.

5. **Developing Hypotheses** If your data showed a greater change in the mass of the pieces in one of the containers, how might this change be explained?

6. **Drawing Conclusions** Based on your data, which variable do you think was more responsible for breaking down the limestone: the vinegar or the shaking? Explain.

7. **Communicating** Write a paragraph that explains why you allowed two of the containers to stand without shaking, and why you were careful to shake the other two containers for the same amount of time.

Design an Experiment

Would your results for this experiment change if you changed the variables? For example, you could soak or shake the pieces for a longer time, or test rocks other than limestone. You could also test whether adding more limestone pieces (30 rather than 20 in each set) would make a difference in the outcome. Design an experiment on the rate of weathering to test the effects of changing one of these variables. *Have your teacher approve your plan before you begin.*

How Soil Forms

Reading Preview

Key Concepts
- What is soil made of and how does it form?
- How do scientists classify soils?
- What is the role of plants and animals in soil formation?

Key Terms
- soil
- bedrock
- humus
- fertility
- loam
- soil horizon
- topsoil
- subsoil
- litter
- decomposer

Target Reading Skill
Building Vocabulary A definition states the meaning of a word or phrase by telling about its most important feature or function. Carefully read the definition of each Key Term and also read the neighboring sentences. Then write a definition of each Key Term in your own words.

Lab zone Discover **Activity**

What Is Soil?

1. Use a toothpick to separate a sample of soil into individual particles. With a hand lens, try to identify the different types of particles in the sample. Wash your hands when you are finished.
2. Write a "recipe" for the sample of soil, naming each of the "ingredients" that you think the soil contains. Include what percentage of each ingredient would be needed to make up the soil.
3. Compare your recipe with those of your classmates.

Think It Over
Forming Operational Definitions Based on your observations, how would you define *soil*?

A bare rock surface does not look like a spot where a plant could grow. But look more closely. In that hard surface is a small crack. Over many years, mechanical and chemical weathering will slowly enlarge the crack. Rain and wind will bring bits of weathered rock, dust, and dry leaves. The wind also may carry tiny seeds. With enough moisture, a seed will sprout and take root. Then, a few months later, the plant blossoms.

What Is Soil?

The crack in the rock seems to have little in common with a flower garden containing thick, rich soil. But soil is what the weathered rock and other materials in the crack have started to become. **Soil** is the loose, weathered material on Earth's surface in which plants can grow.

One of the main ingredients of soil comes from bedrock. **Bedrock** is the solid layer of rock beneath the soil. Once exposed at the surface, bedrock gradually weathers into smaller and smaller particles that are the basic material of soil.

Wildflowers in rocky soil ▶

Soil Composition Soil is more than just particles of weathered bedrock. **Soil is a mixture of rock particles, minerals, decayed organic material, water, and air.** Together, sand, silt, and clay make up the portion of soil that comes from weathered rock.

The decayed organic material in soil is called humus. **Humus** (HYOO mus) is a dark-colored substance that forms as plant and animal remains decay. Humus helps create spaces in soil for the air and water that plants must have. Humus also contains substances called nutrients, including nitrogen, sulfur, phosphorus, and potassium. Plants need nutrients in order to grow. As plants grow, they absorb nutrients from the soil.

Fertile soil is rich in the nutrients that plants need to grow. The **fertility** of soil is a measure of how well the soil supports plant growth. Soil that is rich in humus has high fertility. Sandy soil containing little humus has low fertility.

Soil Texture Sand feels coarse and grainy, but clay feels smooth and silky. These differences are differences in texture. Soil texture depends on the size of individual soil particles.

The particles of rock in soil are classified by size. As you can see in Figure 7, the largest soil particles are gravel. The smallest soil particles are clay. Clay particles are smaller than the period at the end of this sentence.

Soil texture is important for plant growth. Soil that is mostly clay has a dense, heavy texture. Some clay soils hold a lot of water, so plants grown in them may "drown" for lack of air. In contrast, sandy soil has a coarse texture. Water quickly drains through it, so plants may die for lack of water.

Soil that is made up of about equal parts of clay, sand, and silt is called **loam.** It has a crumbly texture that holds both air and water. Loam is best for growing most types of plants.

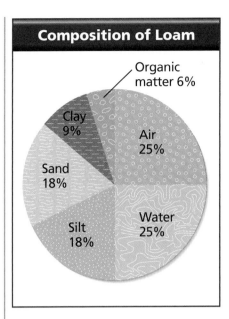

Composition of Loam

Organic matter 6%
Clay 9%
Air 25%
Sand 18%
Water 25%
Silt 18%

FIGURE 6
Loam, a type of soil, is made up of air, water, and organic matter as well as materials from weathered rock. **Interpreting Graphs** *What two materials make up the major portion of this soil?*

FIGURE 7
Soil particles range in size from gravel to clay particles too small to be seen by the unaided eye. The sand, silt, and clay shown here have been enlarged.

Soil Particle Size			
Clay	Silt	Sand	Gravel
Less than $\frac{1}{256}$ mm	Less than $\frac{1}{16}$ mm	Less than 2 mm	2 mm and larger

The Process of Soil Formation

Soil forms as rock is broken down by weathering and mixes with other materials on the surface. Soil is constantly being formed wherever bedrock is exposed. Soil formation continues over a long period of time.

Gradually, soil develops layers called horizons. A **soil horizon** is a layer of soil that differs in color and texture from the layers above or below it.

If you dug a hole in the ground about half a meter deep, you would see the different soil horizons. Figure 8 shows how soil scientists classify the soil into three horizons. The A horizon is made up of **topsoil,** a crumbly, dark brown soil that is a mixture of humus, clay, and other minerals. The B horizon, often called **subsoil,** usually consists of clay and other particles washed down from the A horizon, but little humus. The C horizon contains only partly weathered rock.

The rate at which soil forms depends on the climate and type of rock. Remember that weathering occurs most rapidly in areas with a warm, rainy climate. As a result, soil develops more quickly in these areas. In contrast, weathering and soil formation take place slowly in areas where the climate is cold and dry.

Some types of rock weather and form soil faster than others. For example, limestone, a type of rock formed from the shells and skeletons of once-living things, weathers faster than granite. Thus, soil forms more quickly from limestone than from granite.

Reading Checkpoint What factors affect the rate of soil formation?

Go **Online**
active art

For: Soil Horizons activity
Visit: PHSchool.com
Web Code: cfp-2022

FIGURE 8
Soil Layers
Soil horizons form in three steps.
Inferring *Which soil horizon is responsible for soil's fertility? Explain.*

❶ The C horizon forms as bedrock weathers and rock breaks up into soil particles.

❷ The A horizon develops as plants add organic material to the soil and plant roots weather pieces of rock.

❸ The B horizon develops as rainwater washes clay and minerals from the A horizon to the B horizon.

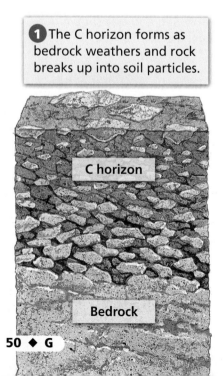

C horizon

Bedrock

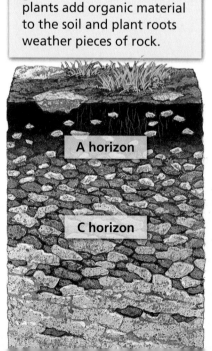

A horizon

C horizon

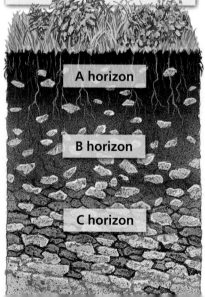

A horizon

B horizon

C horizon

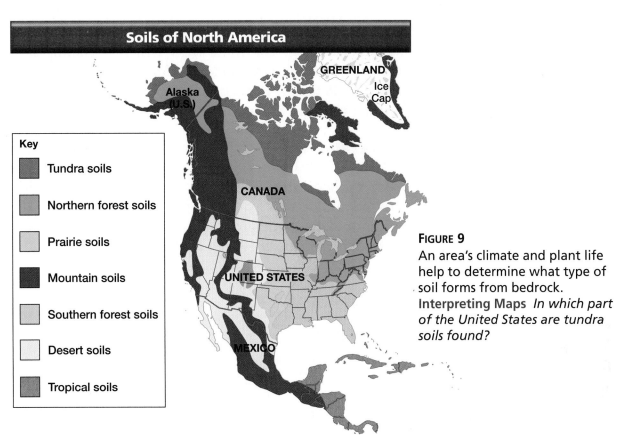

Soils of North America

Key
- Tundra soils
- Northern forest soils
- Prairie soils
- Mountain soils
- Southern forest soils
- Desert soils
- Tropical soils

GREENLAND
Ice Cap

Alaska (U.S.)

CANADA

UNITED STATES

MEXICO

FIGURE 9
An area's climate and plant life help to determine what type of soil forms from bedrock.
Interpreting Maps *In which part of the United States are tundra soils found?*

Soil Types

If you were traveling across the hills of north-central Georgia, you would see soils that seem to be made of red clay. In other parts of the country, soils can be black, brown, yellow, or gray. In the United States alone, there are thousands of different types of soil.

Scientists classify the different types of soil into major groups based on climate, plants, and soil composition. Fertile soil can form in regions with hot, wet climates, but rain may wash humus and minerals out of the A horizon. In mountains and polar regions with cold, dry climates, the soil is often very thin. The thickest, most fertile soil forms in climate regions with moderate temperatures and rainfall.

The most common plants found in a region are also used to help classify the soil. For example, grassland soils are very different from forest soils. In addition, scientists classify soil by its composition—whether it is rocky, sandy, or rich in clay. Other factors in the classification of soil include the type of bedrock and the amount of time the soil has been developing.

Major soil types found in North America include forest, prairie, desert, mountain, tundra, and tropical soils. Look at Figure 9 to see where each of the major soil types is found.

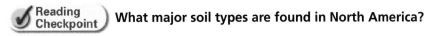
Reading Checkpoint What major soil types are found in North America?

Lab zone Try This Activity

A Square Meter of Soil
1. Outdoors, measure an area of one square meter. Mark your square with string.
2. Observe the color and texture of the soil at the surface and a few centimeters below the surface. Is it dry or moist? Does it contain sand, clay, or gravel? Are there plants, animals, or humus?
3. When you finish, leave the soil as you found it. Wash your hands.

Drawing Conclusions What can you conclude about the soil's fertility? Explain.

Living Organisms in Soil

If you look closely at soil, you can see that it is teeming with living things. **Some soil organisms make humus, the material that makes soil fertile. Other soil organisms mix the soil and make spaces in it for air and water.**

Forming Humus Plants contribute most of the organic remains that form humus. As plants shed leaves, they form a loose layer called **litter.** When plants die, their remains fall to the ground and become part of the litter. Plant roots also die and begin to decay underground. Although plant remains are full of stored nutrients, they are not yet humus.

FIGURE 10

Life in Soil

Every cubic meter of soil contains billions of organisms. All organ-isms that live in soil enrich humus with their remains or wastes. This illustration shows some of the organisms typically found in northern forest soil.
Relating Cause and Effect *Which organisms in the art help air and water to enter the soil?*

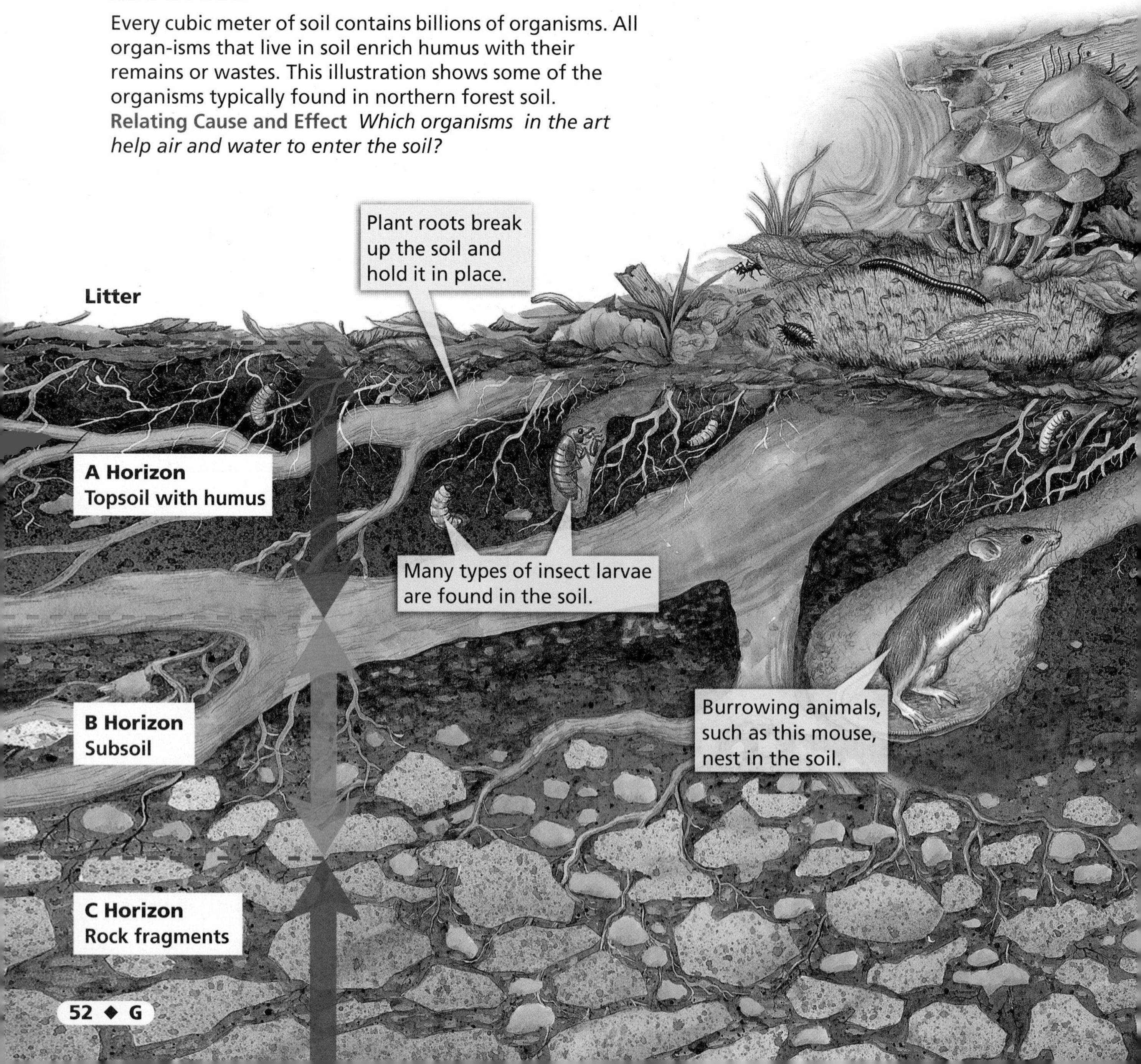

Litter

Plant roots break up the soil and hold it in place.

A Horizon
Topsoil with humus

Many types of insect larvae are found in the soil.

B Horizon
Subsoil

Burrowing animals, such as this mouse, nest in the soil.

C Horizon
Rock fragments

Humus forms in a process called decomposition. During decomposition, organisms that live in soil turn dead organic material into humus. These organisms are called decomposers. **Decomposers** are the organisms that break the remains of dead organisms into smaller pieces and digest them with chemicals.

Soil decomposers include fungi, bacteria, worms, and other organisms. Fungi are organisms such as molds and mushrooms. Fungi grow on, and digest, plant remains. Bacteria are microscopic decomposers that cause decay. Bacteria attack dead organisms and their wastes in soil. Very small animals, such as mites and worms, also decompose dead organic material and mix it with the soil.

Organisms such as snails and beetles feed on decaying organic material.

Chipmunks live in dens in the soil and search the litter for seeds and nuts.

The leaves, roots, and stems of plants are a major source of humus.

Ants are insects that live together in colonies in the soil.

Earthworms break up hard, compacted soil, making it easier for plant roots to spread and for air and water to enter the soil.

Bacteria are decomposers that break down animal and plant remains and wastes.

Fungi are decomposers that send out long, rootlike threads. From these threads, fungi release chemicals that digest plant remains.

FIGURE 11
Soil Mixers
Earthworms break up the soil, allowing in air and water. An earthworm eats its own weight in soil every day. **Predicting** *How fertile is soil that contains many earthworms likely to be? Explain.*

Mixing the Soil Earthworms do most of the work of mixing humus with other materials in soil. As earthworms eat their way through the soil, they carry humus down to the subsoil and subsoil up to the surface. Earthworms also pass out the soil they eat as waste. The waste soil is enriched with substances that plants need to grow, such as nitrogen.

Many burrowing mammals such as mice, moles, prairie dogs, and gophers break up hard, compacted soil and mix humus through it. These animals also add nitrogen to the soil when they produce waste. They add organic material when they die and decay.

Earthworms and burrowing animals also help to aerate, or mix air into, the soil. Plant roots need the oxygen that this process adds to the soil.

 Reading Checkpoint **Which animals are most important in mixing humus into the soil?**

Section 2 Assessment

Target Reading Skill
Building Vocabulary Use your definitions to help you answer the questions below.

Reviewing Key Concepts

1. **a. Describing** What five materials make up soil?
   b. Explaining How do soil horizons form?
   c. Sequencing Place these terms in the correct order starting from the surface: C horizon, subsoil, bedrock, topsoil.
2. **a. Reviewing** What are three main factors used to classify soils?
   b. Interpreting Maps Soil forms more rapidly in warm, wet areas than in cold, dry areas. Study the map in Figure 9. Which soil type on the map would you expect to form most slowly? Explain.

3. **a. Identifying** What are two main ways in which soil organisms contribute to soil formation?
   b. Describing Give examples of three types of decomposers and describe their effects on soil.
   c. Predicting What would happen to the fertility of a soil if all decomposers were removed? Explain.

Writing in Science

Product Label Write a product label for a bag of topsoil. Your label should give the soil a name that will make consumers want to buy it, state how and where the soil formed, give its composition, and suggest how it can be used.

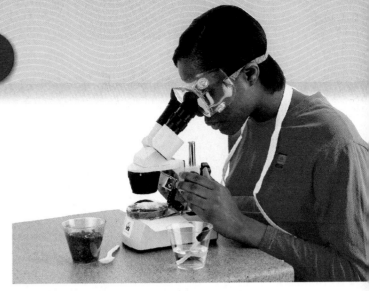

Comparing Soils

Problem

Which type of soil is better for growing flowers and vegetables?

Skills Focus

observing, inferring, developing hypotheses

Materials

- 20–30 grams of local soil
- 20–30 grams of bagged topsoil
- plastic spoon   • plastic dropper   • toothpick
- water   • stereomicroscope
- plastic petri dish or jar lid
- graph paper ruled with 1- or 2-mm spacing

Procedure 🧤 ✂️

1. Obtain a sample of local soil. As you observe the sample, record your observations in your lab notebook.

2. Spread half of the sample on the graph paper. Spread the soil thinly so that you can see the lines on the paper through the soil. Using the graph paper as a background, estimate the sizes of the particles that make up the soil.

3. Place the rest of the sample in the palm of your hand, rub it between your fingers, and squeeze it. Is it soft or gritty? Does it clump together or crumble when you squeeze it?

4. Place about half the sample in a plastic petri dish. Using the dropper, add water one drop at a time. Watch how the sample changes. Does any material in the sample float? As the sample gets wet, do you notice any odor? (*Hint:* If the wet soil has an odor or contains material that floats, it is likely to contain organic material.)

5. Look at some of the soil under the stereomicroscope. (*Hint:* Use the toothpick to separate the particles in the soil.) Sketch what you see. Label the particles, such as gravel, organic matter, or strangely shaped grains.

6. Repeat Steps 1–5 with the topsoil. Be sure to record your observations.

7. Clean up and dispose of your samples as directed by your teacher. **CAUTION:** *Wash your hands when you finish handling soil.*

Analyze and Conclude

1. **Observing** Did you observe any similarities between the local soil sample and the top-soil? Any differences?

2. **Inferring** What can you infer about the composition of both types of soil from the different sizes of their particles? From your observations of texture? From how the samples changed when water was added?

3. **Inferring** Do you think that both types of soil were formed in the same way? Explain.

4. **Developing Hypotheses** Based on your observations and study of the chapter, develop a hypothesis about which soil would be better for growing flowers and vegetables.

5. **Communicating** Write a report for consumers that summarizes your analysis of the two soil samples. Be sure to describe what factors you analyzed and give a suggestion for which soil consumers should use for growing flowers and vegetables.

Design an Experiment

In Question 4 you developed a hypothesis about which soil would be better for growing flowers and vegetables. Design an experiment that would test this hypothesis. Be sure to indicate how you would control variables. *After you receive your teacher's approval, carry out your experiment.*

Soil Conservation

Reading Preview

Key Concepts
- Why is soil a valuable resource?
- How can soil lose its value?
- What are some ways that soil can be conserved?

Key Terms
- sod • natural resource
- Dust Bowl • soil conservation
- contour plowing
- conservation plowing
- crop rotation

⟳ Target Reading Skill

Previewing Visuals Before you read, preview Figure 13, The Dust Bowl. Then write two questions that you have about the photo and map in a graphic organizer like the one below. As you read, answer your questions.

The Dust Bowl

Q.	Where was the Dust Bowl?
A.	
Q.	

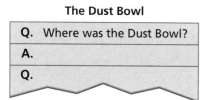
Prairie grasses and wildflowers ▼

How Can You Keep Soil From Washing Away?

1. Pour about 500 mL of soil into a pie plate, forming a pile.
2. Devise a way to keep the soil from washing away when water is poured over it. To protect the pile of soil, you may use craft sticks, paper clips, pebbles, modeling clay, strips of paper, or other materials approved by your teacher.
3. After arranging your materials to protect the soil, hold a container filled with 200 mL of water about 20 cm above the center of the soil. Slowly pour the water in a stream onto the pile of soil.
4. Compare your pan of soil with those of your classmates.

Think It Over
Observing Based on your observations, what do you think is the best way to prevent soil on a slope from washing away?

Suppose you were a settler traveling west in the mid 1800s. Much of your journey would have been through vast, open grasslands called prairies. After the forests and mountains of the East, the prairies were an amazing sight. Grass taller than a person rippled and flowed in the wind like a sea of green.

The prairie soil was very fertile. It was rich with humus because of the tall grass. The **sod**—the thick mass of tough roots at the surface of the soil—kept the soil in place and held onto moisture.

The prairies covered a vast area. They included Iowa and Illinois, as well as the eastern parts of Kansas, Nebraska, and North and South Dakota. Today, farms growing crops such as corn, soybeans, and wheat have replaced the prairies. But prairie soils are still among the most fertile in the world.

The Value of Soil

A **natural resource** is anything in the environment that humans use. **Soil is one of Earth's most valuable natural resources because everything that lives on land, including humans, depends directly or indirectly on soil.** Plants depend directly on the soil to live and grow. Humans and animals depend on plants—or on other animals that depend on plants—for food.

Fertile soil is valuable because there is a limited supply. Less than one eighth of the land on Earth has soils that are well suited for farming. Soil is also in limited supply because it takes a long time to form. It can take hundreds of years for just a few centimeters of soil to form. The thick, fertile soil of the prairies took many thousands of years to develop.

Discovery CHANNEL SCHOOL

Weathering and Soil Formation

Video Preview
▶ Video Field Trip
Video Assessment

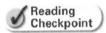 **Reading Checkpoint** Why is the soil in many areas unsuitable for farming?

Soil Damage and Loss

Human activities and changes in the environment can affect the soil. **The value of soil is reduced when soil loses its fertility and when topsoil is lost due to erosion.**

Loss of Fertility Soil can be damaged when it loses its fertility. Soil that has lost its fertility is said to be exhausted. This type of soil loss occurred in large parts of the South in the late 1800s. Soils in which only cotton had been grown were exhausted. Many farmers abandoned their farms. Early in the 1900s in Alabama, a scientist named George Washington Carver developed new crops and farming methods that helped to restore soil fertility in the South. Peanuts were one crop that helped make the soil fertile again. Peanut plants are legumes. Legumes have small lumps on their roots that contain nitrogen-fixing bacteria. These bacteria make nitrogen, an important nutrient, available in a form that plants can use.

FIGURE 12
Restoring Soil Fertility
George Washington Carver (1864–1943) taught new methods of soil conservation. He also developed new varieties of peanut plants, which helped restore soil fertility. **Applying Concepts** *What nutrient do peanut plants add to the soil?*

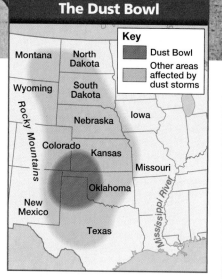

The Dust Bowl

Key
- Dust Bowl
- Other areas affected by dust storms

Montana
North Dakota
Wyoming
South Dakota
Nebraska
Iowa
Rocky Mountains
Colorado
Kansas
Missouri
Oklahoma
New Mexico
Texas
Mississippi River

FIGURE 13
The Dust Bowl
The Dust Bowl ruined farmland in western Oklahoma and parts of the surrounding states. Wind blew dry particles of soil into great clouds of dust that traveled thousands of kilometers.

Go Online
SCi LINKS
NSTA

For: Links on soil conservation
Visit: www.SciLinks.org
Web Code: scn-0723

Loss of Topsoil Whenever soil is exposed, water and wind can quickly erode it. Plant cover can protect soil from erosion. Plants break the force of falling rain, and plant roots hold the soil together. Wind is another cause of soil loss. Wind erosion is most likely in areas where farming methods are not suited to dry conditions. For example, wind erosion contributed to the Dust Bowl on the Great Plains.

Soil Loss in the Dust Bowl Toward the end of the 1800s, farmers settled the Great Plains. The soil of the Great Plains is fertile. But rainfall decreases steadily from east to west across the Great Plains. The region also has droughts—years when rainfall is scarce. Plowing removed the grass from the Great Plains and exposed the soil. In times of drought, the topsoil quickly dried out, turned to dust, and blew away.

By 1930, almost all of the Great Plains had been turned into farms or ranches. Then, a long drought turned the soil on parts of the Great Plains to dust. The wind blew the soil east in great, black clouds that reached Chicago and New York City. The erosion was most serious in the southern Plains states. This area, shown in Figure 13, was called the **Dust Bowl.** The Dust Bowl helped people appreciate the value of soil. With government support, farmers in the Great Plains and throughout the country began to take better care of their land. They adopted methods of farming that helped save the soil. Some methods were new. Others had been practiced for hundreds of years.

✓ **Reading Checkpoint** What caused the Dust Bowl?

Soil Conservation

Since the Dust Bowl, farmers have adopted modern methods of soil conservation. **Soil conservation** is the management of soil to prevent its destruction. **Soil can be conserved through contour plowing, conservation plowing, and crop rotation.**

In **contour plowing,** farmers plow their fields along the curves of a slope. This helps slow the runoff of excess rainfall and prevents it from washing the soil away.

In **conservation plowing,** farmers disturb the soil and its plant cover as little as possible. Dead weeds and stalks of the previous year's crop are left in the ground to help return soil nutrients, retain moisture, and hold soil in place. This method is also called low-till or no-till plowing.

In **crop rotation,** a farmer plants different crops in a field each year. Different types of plants absorb different amounts of nutrients from the soil. Some crops, such as corn and cotton, absorb large amounts of nutrients. The year after planting these crops, the farmer plants crops that use fewer soil nutrients, such as oats, barley, or rye. The year after that the farmer sows legumes such as alfalfa or beans to restore the nutrient supply.

Reading Checkpoint How does conservation plowing help conserve soil?

FIGURE 14
Soil Conservation Methods
This farm's fields show evidence of contour plowing and crop rotation. **Predicting** *How might contour plowing affect the amount of topsoil?*

Section 3 Assessment

Target Reading Skill Previewing Visuals Compare your questions and answers about Figure 13 with those of a partner.

Reviewing Key Concepts

1. **a. Defining** What is a natural resource?
   b. Explaining Why is soil valuable as a natural resource?
2. **a. Listing** What are two ways in which the value of soil can be reduced?
   b. Explaining Explain how topsoil can be lost.
   c. Relating Cause and Effect What caused the Dust Bowl?
3. **a. Defining** What is soil conservation?
   b. Listing What are three methods by which farmers can conserve soil?
   c. Problem Solving A farmer growing corn wants to maintain soil fertility and reduce erosion. What conservation methods could the farmer try? Explain.

Writing in Science

Public Service Announcement
A severe drought in a farming region threatens to produce another Dust Bowl. Write a paragraph about soil conservation to be read as a public service announcement on radio stations. The announcement should identify the danger of soil loss due to erosion. It should also describe the steps farmers can take to conserve the soil.

① Rocks and Weathering

Key Concepts

● Weathering and erosion work together continuously to wear down and carry away the rocks at Earth's surface.

● The causes of mechanical weathering include freezing and thawing, release of pressure, plant growth, actions of animals, and abrasion.

● The causes of chemical weathering include the action of water, oxygen, carbon dioxide, living organisms, and acid rain.

● The most important factors that determine the rate at which weathering occurs are the type of rock and the climate.

Key Terms

weathering
erosion
uniformitarianism
mechanical weathering
abrasion
ice wedging
chemical weathering
oxidation
permeable

② How Soil Forms

Key Concepts

● Soil is a mixture of rock particles, minerals, decayed organic material, water, and air.

● Soil forms as rock is broken down by weathering and mixes with other materials on the surface. Soil is constantly being formed wherever bedrock is exposed.

● Scientists classify the different types of soil into major groups based on climate, plants, and soil composition.

● Some soil organisms make humus, the material that makes soil fertile. Other soil organisms mix the soil and make spaces in it for air and water.

Key Terms

soil
bedrock
humus
fertility
loam
soil horizon
topsoil
subsoil
litter
decomposer

③ Soil Conservation

Key Concepts

● Soil is one of Earth's most valuable natural resources because everything that lives on land, including humans, depends directly or indirectly on soil.

● The value of soil is reduced when soil loses its fertility and when topsoil is lost due to erosion.

● Soil can be conserved through contour plowing, conservation plowing, and crop rotation.

Key Terms

sod
natural resource
Dust Bowl
soil conservation
contour plowing
conservation plowing
crop rotation

Review and Assessment

Go Online
PHSchool.com
For: Self-Assessment
Visit: PHSchool.com
Web Code: cfa-2020

Organizing Information

Sequencing Fill in the flowchart to show how soil horizons form. (For more information on flowcharts, see the Skills Handbook.)

Soil Horizons

Bedrock begins to weather.

↓

a. _____ ? _____

↓

b. _____ ? _____

↓

c. _____ ? _____

Reviewing Key Terms

Choose the letter of the best answer.

1. The process that splits rock through freezing and thawing is called
   a. erosion.
   b. chemical weathering.
   c. ice wedging.
   d. abrasion.

2. Acid rain results in
   a. chemical weathering.
   b. abrasion.
   c. oxidation.
   d. mechanical weathering.

3. Soil that is made up of roughly equal parts of clay, sand, and silt is called
   a. sod.
   b. loam.
   c. tropical soil.
   d. subsoil.

4. The B horizon consists of
   a. subsoil.
   b. topsoil.
   c. litter.
   d. bedrock.

5. The humus in soil is produced by
   a. mechanical weathering.
   b. bedrock.
   c. chemical weathering.
   d. decomposers.

If the statement is true, write *true*. If it is false, change the underlined word or words to make the statement true.

6. <u>Mechanical weathering</u> is the removal of rock particles by gravity, wind, water, or ice.

7. Rock that is <u>permeable</u> weathers easily because it is full of tiny air spaces.

8. The decayed organic material in soil is called <u>loam</u>.

9. The layer of plant remains at the surface of the soil is called <u>litter</u>.

10. In <u>contour plowing</u>, farmers conserve soil fertility by leaving dead stalks and weeds in the ground.

Writing in Science

Journal Entry You are a farmer on the tall grass prairie in the midwestern United States. Write a journal entry describing prairie soil. Include the soil's composition, how it formed, and how animals helped it develop.

Discovery CHANNEL SCHOOL™

Weathering and Soil Formation
Video Preview
Video Field Trip
▶ Video Assessment

Review and Assessment

Checking Concepts

11. What is the principle of uniformitarianism?

12. Explain how plants can act as agents of both mechanical and chemical weathering.

13. What is the role of gases such as oxygen and carbon dioxide in chemical weathering?

14. Briefly describe how soil is formed.

15. Which contains more humus, topsoil or subsoil? Which has higher fertility? Explain.

16. What organism does most of the work in mixing humus into soil?

17. What role did grass play in conserving the soil of the prairies?

18. How do conservation plowing and crop rotation contribute to soil conservation?

Thinking Critically

19. **Predicting** If mechanical weathering breaks a rock into pieces, how would this affect the rate at which the rock weathers chemically?

20. **Comparing and Contrasting** Compare the layers in the diagram below in terms of their composition and humus content.

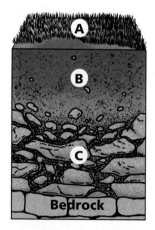

21. **Classifying** Classify as mechanical or chemical weathering: cracks in a sidewalk next to a tree; limestone with holes like Swiss cheese; a rock that slowly turns reddish brown.

Applying Skills

Use the following information to answer Questions 22–24.

You have two samples of soil. One is mostly sand and one is mostly clay.

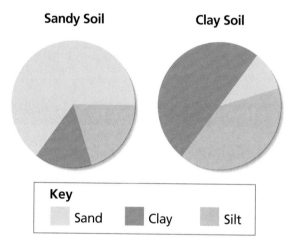

22. **Developing Hypotheses** Which soil sample would lose water more quickly? Why?

23. **Designing Experiments** Design an experiment to test how quickly water passes through each soil sample.

24. **Posing Questions** You are a farmer who wants to grow soybeans in one of these two soils. What questions would you need to answer before choosing where to plant your soybeans?

Lab zone Chapter **Project**

Performance Assessment You are ready to present your data and conclusions about what type of material is best for growing bean plants. How did your group's results compare with those of the other groups in your class?

In your journal, describe how well the results of your experiment matched your predictions. What have you learned from this project about soil characteristics that help plants to grow? How could you improve your experiment?

Standardized Test Prep

Choose the letter of the best answer.

1. Which of the following is a type of mechanical weathering?
   A abrasion
   B freezing and thawing
   C plant growth
   D all of the above

2. You are designing an experiment to test the resistance to weathering of various types of materials. What weathering process could be modeled using sandpaper?
   F acid rain
   G freezing and thawing
   H abrasion
   J all of the above

3. In what type of climate would soil form fastest from limestone bedrock?
   A a cold, dry climate   **B** a cold, wet climate
   C a hot, dry climate   **D** a hot, wet climate

Use the data table below and your knowledge of science to answer Questions 4–5.

Soil Erosion by State			
	tons/acre/year		
State	Water Erosion	Wind Erosion	Total Erosion
Montana	1.08	3.8	4.9
Wyoming	1.57	2.4	3.97
Texas	3.47	14.9	18.4
New Mexico	2.00	11.5	13.5
Colorado	2.5	8.9	11.4
Tennessee	14.12	0.0	14.12
Hawaii	13.71	0.0	13.71

4. Of the states listed in the table, which two have the greatest amount of erosion by water?
   F Texas and Tennessee
   G Texas and Hawaii
   H New Mexico and Colorado
   J Tennessee and Hawaii

5. What state in the table has the greatest soil erosion?
   A Texas
   B Hawaii
   C Tennessee
   D New Mexico

Constructed Response

6. Two rocks, each in a different location, have been weathering for the same amount of time. Mature soil has formed from one rock, but only immature soil has formed from the other. What factors might have caused this difference in rate of soil formation? In your answer, include examples of both mechanical and chemical weathering.

Chapter

3

Erosion and Deposition

Chapter Preview

❶ Changing Earth's Surface
Discover *How Does Gravity Affect Materials on a Slope?*
Skills Activity *Making Models*
Skills Lab *Sand Hills*

❷ Water Erosion
Discover *How Does Moving Water Wear Away Rocks?*
Try This *Raindrops Falling*
Skills Lab *Streams in Action*

❸ The Force of Moving Water
Discover *How Are Sediments Deposited?*
Skills Activity *Developing Hypotheses*
Analyzing Data *Sediment on the Move*

❹ Glaciers
Discover *How Do Glaciers Change the Land?*

❺ Waves
Discover *What Can Be Learned From Beach Sand?*
Skills Activity *Calculating*

❻ Wind
Discover *How Does Moving Air Affect Sediment?*
At-Home Activity *Desert Pavement*

Water erosion formed the Grand Canyon, viewed here from Toroweap Point. ▶

Discovery
CHANNEL
SCHOOL™

Erosion and Deposition

▶ Video Preview
Video Field Trip
Video Assessment

▶Lab zone™ Chapter **Project**

Design and Build a Dam

Dams on major rivers are among the most spectacular works of engineering. These structures serve many purposes. Dams help to control flooding, generate power, and store water for drinking and watering crops. Dams can be constructed out of a variety of materials—wood, concrete, and even soil.

Your Goal To build a dam using various types of soil. To complete this project, you must

- conduct an experiment to determine the permeability of different soils
- investigate how readily the different soils erode when water passes over them
- design and build a dam
- test the dam and redesign if time allows
- follow the safety guidelines in Appendix A

Plan It! You will use a combination of three different soils to build the dam. First, you will need to test the permeability of each type of soil. Then develop an experiment to test how easily water erodes the soil. The results of the two experiments will provide you with information about the soils you tested. As you design your dam, think about what layers or combinations of materials will make the most effective dam. When you have tested your dam, present your conclusions to your class.

Changing Earth's Surface

Reading Preview

Key Concepts
- What processes wear down and build up Earth's surface?
- What causes the different types of mass movement?

Key Terms
- erosion • sediment
- deposition • mass movement

Target Reading Skill

Comparing and Contrasting As you read, compare and contrast the different types of mass movement by completing a table like the one below.

Mass Movement

Type of Mass Movement	Speed	Slope
Landslide		

Lab zone Discover **Activity**

How Does Gravity Affect Materials on a Slope?

1. Place a small board flat on your desk. Place a marble on the board and slowly tip one end of the board up slightly. Observe what happens.
2. Place a block of wood on the board. Slowly lift one end of the board and observe the result.
3. Next, cover the board and the wood block with sandpaper and repeat Step 2.

Think It Over

Developing Hypotheses How do the results of each step compare? Develop a hypothesis to explain the differences in your observations.

The ground you stand on is solid. But under certain conditions, solid earth can quickly change to thick, soupy mud. For example, high rains soaked into the soil and triggered the devastating mudflow in Figure 1. A river of mud raced down the mountainside, burying homes and cars. Several lives were lost. In moments, the mudflow moved a huge volume of soil mixed with water and rock downhill.

Wearing Down and Building Up

A mudflow is a spectacular example of erosion. **Erosion** is the process by which natural forces move weathered rock and soil from one place to another. You may have seen water carrying soil and gravel down a driveway after it rains. That's an example of erosion. A mudflow is a very rapid type of erosion. Other types of erosion move soil and rock more slowly. Gravity, running water, glaciers, waves, and wind are all causes, or agents, of erosion. In geology, an agent is a force or material that causes a change in Earth's surface.

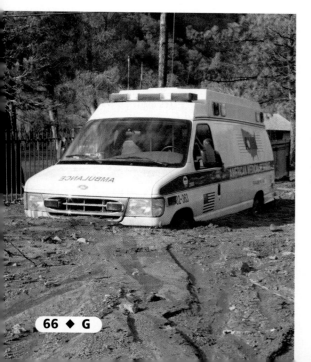

FIGURE 1
Mudflow
A mudflow caused by heavy rains in San Bernardino, California, brought this ambulance to a stop.

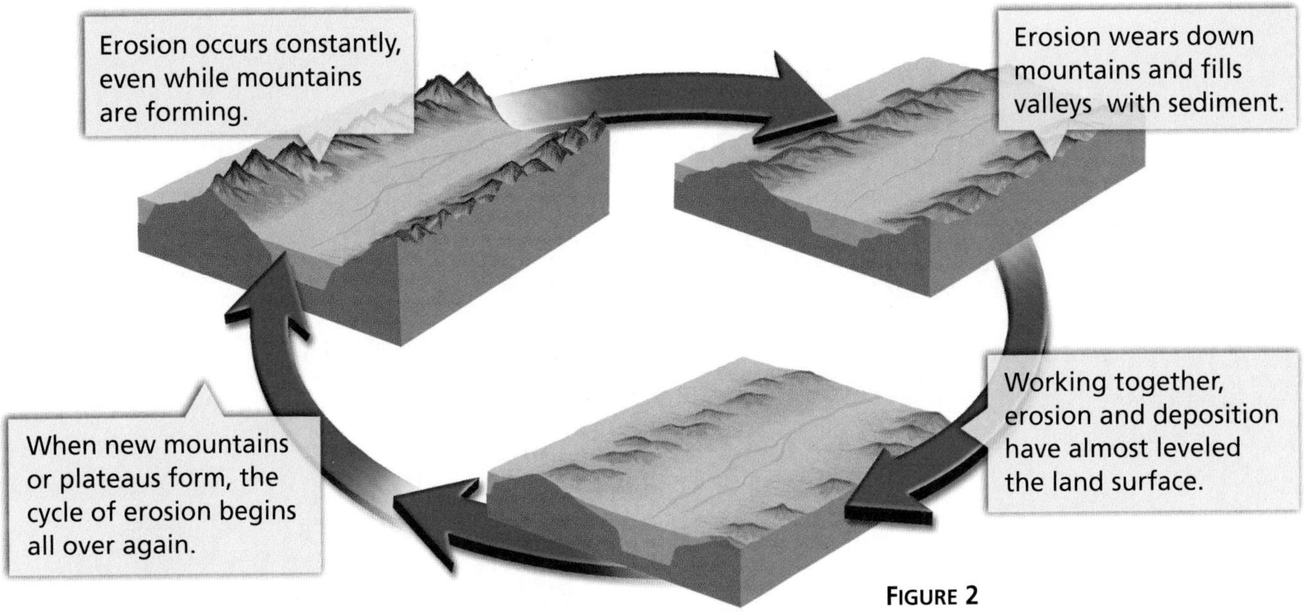

Erosion occurs constantly, even while mountains are forming.

Erosion wears down mountains and fills valleys with sediment.

When new mountains or plateaus form, the cycle of erosion begins all over again.

Working together, erosion and deposition have almost leveled the land surface.

FIGURE 2
Cycle of Erosion and Deposition
Over millions of years, erosion gradually wears away mountains while deposition fills in valleys with sediment.
Predicting *What would happen to the surface of the land if uplift did not occur?*

The material moved by erosion is **sediment.** Sediment may consist of pieces of rock or soil or the remains of plants and animals. Both weathering and erosion produce sediment. **Deposition** occurs where the agents of erosion, deposit, or lay down, sediment. Deposition changes the shape of the land. You may have watched a playing child who picked up several toys, carried them across a room, and then put them down. This child was acting something like an agent of erosion and deposition.

Weathering, erosion, and deposition act together in a cycle that wears down and builds up Earth's surface. Erosion and deposition are at work everywhere on Earth. As a mountain wears down in one place, new landforms build up in other places. The cycle of erosion and deposition is never-ending.

Reading Checkpoint What is sediment?

Mass Movement

Imagine that you are sitting on a bicycle at the top of a hill. With only a slight push, you can coast down the hill. If the slope of the hill is very steep, you will reach a high speed before reaching the bottom. The force that pulls you and your bicycle downward is gravity. Gravity pulls everything toward the center of Earth.

Gravity is the force that moves rock and other materials downhill. Gravity causes **mass movement,** any one of several processes that move sediment downhill. The different types of mass movement include landslides, mudflows, slump, and creep. Mass movement can be rapid or slow.

Lab zone **Skills Activity**

Making Models

You can make a model of mass movement. Design a plan to model one of the types of mass movement using sand, pebbles, and water. With your teacher's approval, make and test your model.

How well did your model represent the type of mass movement you chose? How could you improve your model?

Landslide

Slump

FIGURE 3
Mass Movement
In addition to mudflows, types of mass movement include landslides, slump, and creep.
Making Judgments *Which form of mass movement produces the most drastic change in the surface?*

Landslides The most destructive kind of mass movement is a landslide, which occurs when rock and soil slide quickly down a steep slope. Some landslides contain huge masses of rock. But many landslides contain only a small amount of rock and soil. Some landslides occur where road builders have cut highways through hills or mountains. Figure 3 shows an example of a landslide.

Mudflows A mudflow is the rapid downhill movement of a mixture of water, rock, and soil. The amount of water in a mudflow can be as high as 60 percent. Mudflows often occur after heavy rains in a normally dry area. In clay soils with a high water content, mudflows may occur even on very gentle slopes. Under certain conditions, clay soils suddenly turn to liquid and begin to flow. An earthquake can trigger both mudflows and landslides. Mudflows can be very dangerous.

Slump If you slump your shoulders, the entire upper part of your body drops down. In the type of mass movement known as slump, a mass of rock and soil suddenly slips down a slope. Unlike a landslide, the material in slump moves down in one large mass. It looks as if someone pulled the bottom out from under part of the slope. Slump often occurs when water soaks the bottom of soil that is rich in clay.

Creep

Go Online
active art

For: Mass Movement activity
Visit: PHSchool.com
Web Code: cfp-2031

Creep Creep is the very slow downhill movement of rock and soil. It can even occur on gentle slopes. Creep often results from the freezing and thawing of water in cracked layers of rock beneath the soil. Like the movement of an hour hand on a clock, creep is so slow you can barely notice it. But you can see the effects of creep in objects such as telephone poles, gravestones, and fenceposts. Creep may tilt these objects at spooky angles. Landscapes affected by creep may have the eerie, out-of-kilter look of a funhouse in an amusement park.

 Reading Checkpoint **What is the main difference between slump and a landslide?**

Section 1 Assessment

Target Reading Skill Comparing and Contrasting Use the information in your table to help you answer Question 2 below.

Reviewing Key Concepts

1. **a. Listing** What are five agents of erosion?
   b. Defining In your own words, write a definition of *deposition.*
   c. Predicting Over time, how will erosion and deposition affect a mountain range? Explain.
2. **a. Listing** What are the four types of mass movement?
   b. Relating Cause and Effect What force causes all types of mass movement?
   c. Inferring A fence runs across a steep hillside. The fence is tilted downhill and forms a curve rather than a straight line. What can you infer happened to the fence? Explain.

Lab zone **At-Home Activity**

Evidence of Erosion After a rainstorm, take a walk with an adult family member around your neighborhood. Look for evidence of erosion. Try to find areas where there is loose soil, sand, gravel, or rock. **CAUTION:** *Stay away from any large pile of loose sand or soil—it may slide without warning.* Which areas have the most erosion? The least erosion? How does the slope of the ground affect the amount of erosion? Sketch or take photographs of the areas showing evidence of erosion.

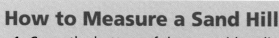
Sand Hills

Problem

What is the relationship between the height and width of a sand hill?

Skills

developing hypotheses, interpreting data, predicting

Materials

- dry sand, 500 mL • cardboard tube
- tray (about 15 cm × 45 cm × 60 cm)
- wooden barbecue skewer • masking tape
- spoon • ruler • pencil or crayon
- several sheets of white paper

Procedure

1. Begin by observing how gravity causes mass movement. To start, place the cardboard tube vertically in the center of the tray.

2. Using the spoon, fill the cardboard tube with the dry sand. Take care not to spill the sand around the outside of the tube.

3. Carefully lift the sand-filled tube straight up so that all the sand flows out. As you lift the tube, observe the sand's movement.

4. Develop a hypothesis explaining how you think the width of the sand pile is related to its height for different amounts of sand.

5. Empty the sand in the tray back into a container. Then set up your system for measuring the sand hill.

6. Copy the data table into your lab notebook.

Data Table					
Test	1	2	3	4	5
Width					
Height					

7. Following Steps 1 through 3, make a new sand hill.

8. Measure and record the sand hill's height and width for Test 1. (See the instructions on the bottom of the page to help you accurately measure the height and width.)

How to Measure a Sand Hill

1. Cover the bottom of the tray with unlined white paper and tape it firmly in place.

2. Mark off points 0.5 cm apart along one side of the paper in the tray.

3. Carefully draw the sand hill's outline on the paper. The line should go completely around the base of the hill.

4. Now measure the width of the hill against the marks you made along the edge of the paper.

5. Measure the sand hill's height by inserting a barbecue skewer through its center. Make a mark on the skewer at the top of the hill.

6. Remove the skewer and use the ruler to measure how much of the skewer was buried in the hill. Try not to disturb the sand.

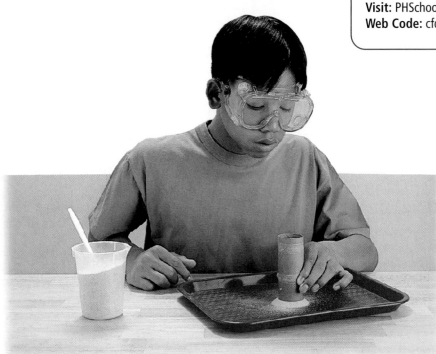

9. Now test what happens when you add more sand to the sand hill. Place your cardboard tube vertically at the center of the sand hill. Be careful not to push the tube down into the sand hill! Using the spoon, fill the tube with sand as before.

10. Carefully raise the tube and observe the sand's movement.

11. Measure and record the sand hill's height and width for Test 2.

12. Repeat Steps 9 through 11 at least three more times. After each test, record your results. Be sure to number each test.

Analyze and Conclude

1. **Graphing** Make a graph showing how the sand hill's height and width changed with each test. (Hint: Use the x-axis of the graph for height. Use the y-axis of the graph for width.)

2. **Interpreting Data** What does your graph show about the relationship between the sand hill's height and width?

3. **Drawing Conclusions** Does your graph support your hypothesis about the sand hill's height and width? Why or why not?

4. **Developing Hypotheses** How would you revise your original hypothesis after examining your data? Give reasons for your answer.

5. **Predicting** Predict what would happen if you continued the experiment for five more tests. Extend your graph with a dashed line to show your prediction. How could you test your prediction?

6. **Communicating** Write a paragraph in which you discuss how you measured your sand hill. Did any problems you had in making your measurements affect your results? How did you adjust your measurement technique to solve these problems?

Design an Experiment

Do you think the use of different materials, such as wet sand or gravel, would produce different results from those using dry sand? Make a new hypothesis about the relationship between slope and width in hills made of materials other than dry sand. Design an experiment in which you test how these different materials form hills. *Obtain your teacher's approval before you try the experiment.*

Chapter 3 G ◆ 71

Reading Preview

Key Concepts
- What process is mainly responsible for shaping the surface of the land?
- What features are formed by water erosion and deposition?
- What causes groundwater erosion?

Key Terms
- runoff • rill • gully • stream
- tributary • flood plain
- meander • oxbow lake
- alluvial fan • delta
- groundwater • stalactite
- stalagmite • karst topography

Target Reading Skill

Previewing Visuals Before you read, preview Figure 10. Then write two questions that you have about the illustration in a graphic organizer like the one below. As you read, answer your questions.

The Course of a River

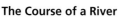

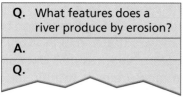

Q.	What features does a river produce by erosion?
A.	
Q.	

Discover Activity

How Does Moving Water Wear Away Rocks?

1. Obtain two bars of soap that are the same size and brand.
2. Open a faucet just enough to let the water drip out very slowly. How many drops of water does the faucet release per minute?
3. Place one bar of soap in a dry place. Place the other bar of soap under the faucet. Predict the effect of the dripping water droplets on the soap.
4. Let the faucet drip for 10 minutes.
5. Turn off the faucet and observe both bars of soap. What difference do you observe between them?

Think It Over
Predicting What would the bar of soap under the dripping faucet look like if you left it there for another 10 minutes? For an hour? How could you speed up the process? Slow it down?

Walking in the woods in summer, you can hear the racing water of a stream before you see the stream itself. The water roars as it foams over rock ledges and boulders. When you reach the stream, you see water rushing by. Sand and pebbles tumble along the bottom of the stream. As it swirls downstream, the water also carries twigs, leaves, and bits of soil. In sheltered pools, insects such as water striders skim the water's calm surface. Beneath the surface, a rainbow trout swims in the clear water.

In winter, the stream freezes. Chunks of ice scrape and grind away at the stream's bed and banks. In spring, the stream floods. Then the flow of water may be strong enough to move large rocks. But throughout the year, the stream continues to erode its small part of Earth's surface.

▼ A stream in summer

Runoff and Erosion

Moving water is the major agent of the erosion that has shaped Earth's land surface. Erosion by water begins with the splash of rain. Some rainfall sinks into the ground. Some evaporates or is taken up by plants. The force of a falling raindrop can loosen and pick up soil particles. As water moves over the land, it carries these particles with it. This moving water is called runoff. **Runoff** is water that moves over Earth's surface. When runoff flows in a thin layer over the land, it may cause a type of erosion called sheet erosion.

Amount of Runoff The amount of runoff in an area depends on five main factors. The first factor is the amount of rain an area receives. A second factor is vegetation. Grasses, shrubs, and trees reduce runoff by absorbing water and holding soil in place. A third factor is the type of soil. Some types of soils absorb more water than others. A fourth factor is the shape of the land. Land that is steeply sloped has more runoff than flatter land. Finally, a fifth factor is how people use the land. For instance, a paved parking lot absorbs no water, so all the rain that falls on it becomes runoff. Runoff also increases when a farmer cuts down crops, since this removes vegetation from the land.

Generally, more runoff means more erosion. In contrast, factors that reduce runoff will reduce erosion. Even though deserts have little rainfall, they often have high runoff and erosion because they have few plants. In wet areas, runoff and erosion may be low because there are more plants to protect the soil.

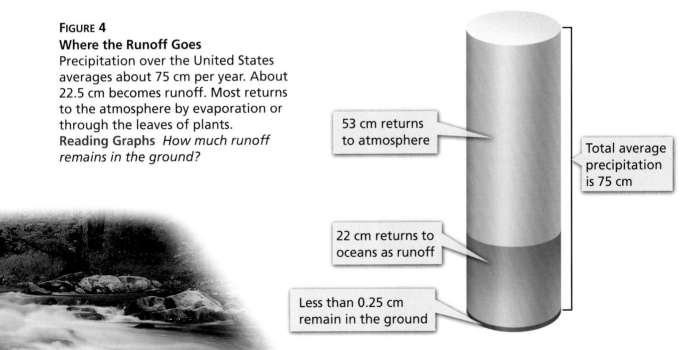

FIGURE 4
Where the Runoff Goes
Precipitation over the United States averages about 75 cm per year. About 22.5 cm becomes runoff. Most returns to the atmosphere by evaporation or through the leaves of plants.
Reading Graphs *How much runoff remains in the ground?*

53 cm returns to atmosphere

Total average precipitation is 75 cm

22 cm returns to oceans as runoff

Less than 0.25 cm remain in the ground

Raindrops Falling

Find out how the force of falling raindrops affects soil.

1. Fill a petri dish with fine-textured soil to a depth of about 1 cm. Make sure the soil has a smooth flat surface, but do not pack it firmly in the dish.
2. Place the dish in the center of a newspaper.
3. Fill a dropper with water. Squeeze a large water drop from a height of 1 m onto the surface of the soil. Repeat 4 times.
4. Use a meter stick to measure the distance the soil splashed from the dish. Record your observations.
5. Repeat Steps 1 through 4, this time from a height of 2 m.

Drawing Conclusions Which test produced the greater amount of erosion? Why?

Rills and Gullies Because of gravity, runoff and the material it contains move downhill. As runoff travels, it forms tiny grooves in the soil called **rills.** As many rills flow into one another, they grow larger, forming gullies. A **gully** is a large groove, or channel, in the soil that carries runoff after a rainstorm. As water flows through gullies, it moves soil and rocks with it, thus enlarging the gullies through erosion. Gullies contain water only after it rains.

Streams and Rivers Gullies join together to form a larger channel called a stream. A **stream** is a channel along which water is continually flowing down a slope. Unlike gullies, streams rarely dry up. Small streams are also called creeks or brooks. As streams flow together, they form larger and larger bodies of flowing water. A large stream is often called a river.

Tributaries A stream grows into a larger stream or river by receiving water from tributaries. A **tributary** is a stream or river that flows into a larger river. For example, the Missouri and Ohio rivers are tributaries of the Mississippi River. A drainage basin, or watershed, is the area from which a river and its tributaries collect their water.

Reading Checkpoint What is a tributary?

FIGURE 5
Runoff, Rills, and Gullies
Water flowing across the land runs together to form rills, gullies, and streams.
Predicting What will happen to the land between the gullies as they grow wider?

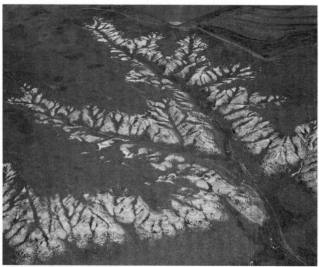

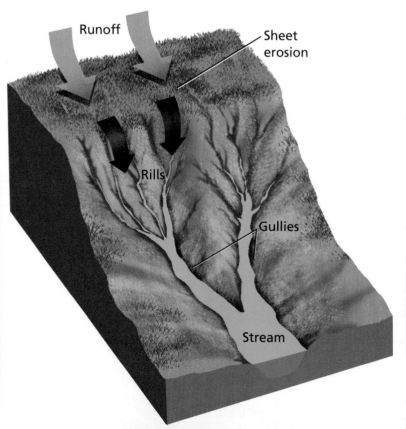

Runoff

Sheet erosion

Rills

Gullies

Stream

Erosion by Rivers

As a river flows from the mountains to the sea, the river forms a variety of features. **Through erosion, a river creates valleys, waterfalls, flood plains, meanders, and oxbow lakes.**

Rivers often form on steep mountain slopes. Near its source, a river is often fast flowing and generally follows a straight, narrow course. The steep slopes along the river erode rapidly. The result is a deep, **V**-shaped valley.

Waterfalls Waterfalls may occur where a river meets an area of rock that is very hard and erodes slowly. The river flows over this rock and then flows over softer rock downstream. As you can see in Figure 6, the softer rock wears away faster than the harder rock. Eventually a waterfall develops where the softer rock was removed. Areas of rough water called rapids also occur where a river tumbles over hard rock.

Flood Plain Lower down on its course, a river usually flows over more gently sloping land. The river spreads out and erodes the land, forming a wide river valley. The flat, wide area of land along a river is a **flood plain.** A river often covers its flood plain when it overflows its banks during floods. On a wide flood plain, the valley walls may be kilometers away from the river itself.

FIGURE 6
How a Waterfall Forms
A waterfall forms where a flat layer of tough rock lies over a layer of softer rock that erodes easily. When the softer rock erodes, pieces of the harder rock above break off, creating the waterfall's sharp drop.

Harder rock layers eventually break off.

Softer rock layers erode first.

Rapids are areas of turbulence below the falls where water rushes over rocks.

FIGURE 7

Meanders and Oxbow Lakes
Erosion often forms meanders and oxbow lakes where a river winds across its floodplain.

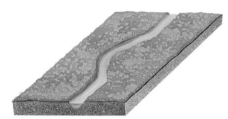

1 A small obstacle creates a slight bend in the river.

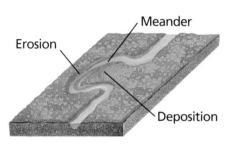

2 As water erodes the outer edge of a meander, the bend becomes bigger. Deposition occurs along the inner edge.

Meander

Erosion

Deposition

3 Eventually, the meander curves back on itself.

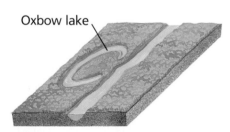

Oxbow lake

4 The river breaks through and takes a new course. An oxbow lake remains.

Meanders A river often develops meanders where it flows through easily eroded rock or sediment. A **meander** is a loop-like bend in the course of a river. As the river winds from side to side, it tends to erode the outer bank and deposit sediment on the inner bank of a bend. Over time, the meander becomes more and more curved.

When the gently sloping part of a river flows through an area of sediment or soft rock, it can erode a very wide flood plain. Along this part of a river's course, its channel is deep and wide. Meanders are common. The southern stretch of the Mississippi River is one example of a river that meanders on a wide, gently sloping flood plain.

Oxbow Lakes Sometimes a meandering river forms a feature called an oxbow lake. As Figure 7 shows, an **oxbow lake** is a meander that has been cut off from the river. An oxbow lake may form when a river floods. During the flood, high water finds a straighter route downstream. As the flood waters fall, sediments dam up the ends of a meander. The meander has become an oxbow lake.

Reading Checkpoint How does an oxbow lake form?

Deposits by Rivers

As water moves, it carries sediments with it. Any time moving water slows down, it drops, or deposits, some of the sediment. As the water slows down, fine particles fall to the river's bed. Larger stones quit rolling and sliding. **Deposition creates landforms such as alluvial fans and deltas. It can also add soil to a river's flood plain.** In Figure 8 on pages 78–79, you can see these and other features shaped by rivers and streams.

Alluvial Fans Where a stream flows out of a steep, narrow mountain valley, the stream suddenly becomes wider and shallower. The water slows down. Here sediments are deposited in an alluvial fan. An **alluvial fan** is a wide, sloping deposit of sediment formed where a stream leaves a mountain range. As its name suggests, this deposit is shaped like a fan. You can see an alluvial fan in Figure 8.

Deltas A river ends its journey when it flows into a still body of water, such as an ocean or a lake. Because the river water is no longer flowing downhill, the water slows down. At this point, the sediment in the water drops to the bottom. Sediment deposited where a river flows into an ocean or lake builds up a landform called a **delta.** Deltas can be a variety of shapes. Some are arc shaped, others are triangle shaped. The delta of the Mississippi River, shown in Figure 9, is an example of a type of delta called a "bird's foot" delta.

Soil on Flood Plains Deposition can also occur during floods. Then heavy rains or melting snow cause a river to rise above its banks and spread out over its flood plain. When the flood water finally retreats, it deposits sediment as new soil. Deposition of new soil over a flood plain is what makes a river valley fertile. Dense forests can grow in the rich soil of a flood plain. The soil is also perfect for growing crops.

 Reading Checkpoint How can a flood be beneficial?

FIGURE 8
Alluvial Fan
This alluvial fan in Death Valley, California, was formed from deposits by streams from the mountains.

FIGURE 9
Mississippi Delta
This satellite image shows the part of the Mississippi River delta where the river empties into the Gulf of Mexico.
Observing *What happens to the Mississippi River as it flows through its delta? Can you find the river's main channel?*

Waterfalls and Rapids
Waterfalls and rapids are common where the river passes over harder rock.

V-Shaped Valley
Near its source, the river flows through a deep, V-shaped valley. As the river flows, it cuts the valley deeper.

Flood Plain
A flood plain forms where the river's power of erosion widens its valley rather than deepening it.

Meanders
Where the river flows across easily eroded sediment, its channel bends from side to side in a series of meanders.

Beaches
Sand carried downstream by the river spreads along the coast to form beaches.

FIGURE 10

The Course of a River

The slope and size of a river, as well as the land through which it flows, determine how a river shapes the land. **Classifying** *Which features along the river result from erosion? Which result from deposition?*

Tributary
The river receives water and sediment from a tributary—a smaller river or stream that flows into it.

Oxbow Lake
An oxbow lake is a meander cut off from the river by deposition of sediment.

Valley Widening
As the river approaches sea level, it meanders more and develops a wider valley and broader flood plain.

Bluffs
Erosion forms cliffs called bluffs along the edge of a flood plain.

Delta
Where the river flows into the ocean, it deposits sediment, forming a delta.

Go Online
PHSchool.com

For: More on erosion
Visit: PHSchool.com
Web Code: cfd-2032

Groundwater Erosion

When rain falls and snow melts, not all of the water evaporates or becomes runoff. Some water soaks into the ground. There it fills the openings in the soil and trickles into cracks and spaces in layers of rock. **Groundwater** is the term geologists use for this underground water. Like running water on the surface, groundwater affects the shape of the land.

Groundwater can cause erosion through a process of chemical weathering. When water sinks into the ground, it combines with carbon dioxide to form a weak acid, called carbonic acid. Carbonic acid can break down limestone. Groundwater containing carbonic acid flows into any cracks in the limestone. Then some of the limestone changes chemically and is carried away in a solution of water. This process gradually hollows out pockets in the rock. Over time, these pockets develop into large holes underground, called caves or caverns.

Cave Formations The action of carbonic acid on limestone can also result in deposition. Inside limestone caves, deposits called stalactites and stalagmites often form. Water containing carbonic acid and calcium from limestone drips from a cave's roof. As the water evaporates, it leaves behind a deposit of calcite. A deposit that hangs like an icicle from the roof of a cave is known as a **stalactite** (stuh LAK tyt). Slow dripping builds up a cone-shaped **stalagmite** (stuh LAG myt) from the cave floor.

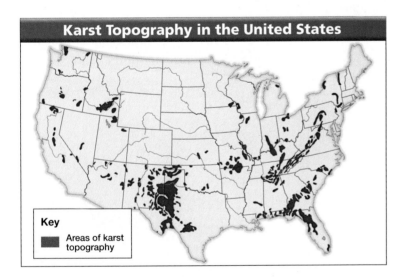

Karst Topography in the United States

Key
■ Areas of karst topography

FIGURE 11
Karst topography is found in many parts of the United States where the bedrock is made up of thick layers of limestone.

Karst Topography In rainy regions where there is a layer of limestone near the surface, groundwater erosion can significantly change the shape of the land. Streams are rare, because water easily sinks down into the weathered limestone. Deep valleys and caverns are common. If the roof of a cave collapses because of the erosion of the underlying limestone, the result is a depression called a sinkhole. This type of landscape is called **karst topography** after a region in Eastern Europe. In the United States, regions of karst topography are found in Florida, Texas, and many other states.

 Reading Checkpoint How does deposition occur in a limestone cave?

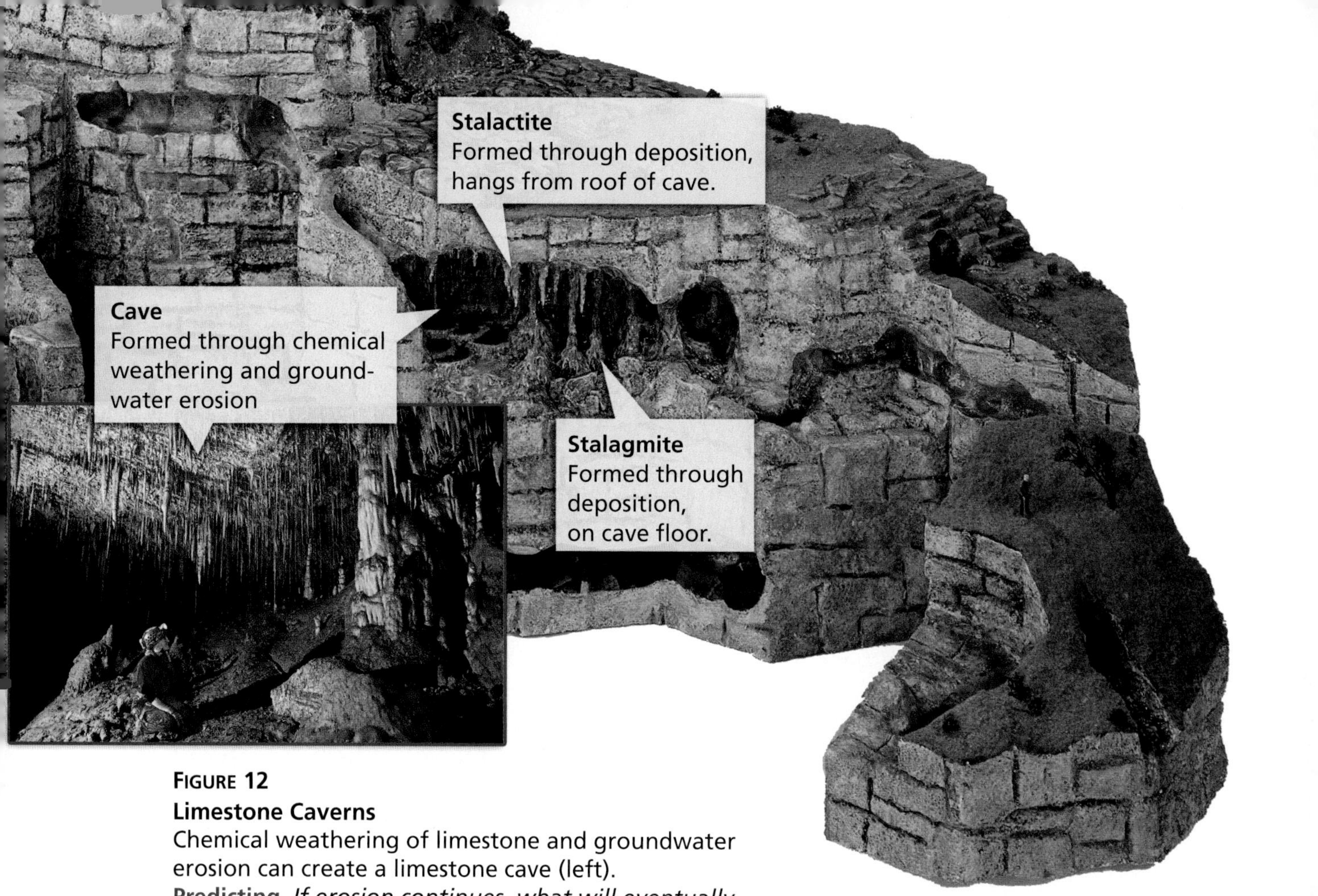

Stalactite
Formed through deposition, hangs from roof of cave.

Cave
Formed through chemical weathering and ground-water erosion

Stalagmite
Formed through deposition, on cave floor.

FIGURE 12
Limestone Caverns
Chemical weathering of limestone and groundwater erosion can create a limestone cave (left).
Predicting *If erosion continues, what will eventually happen to the cave that lies just beneath the surface?*

Section 2 Assessment

Target Reading Skill Previewing Visuals Refer to your questions and answers about Figure 10 to help you answer Question 2 below.

Reviewing Key Concepts

1. a. **Reviewing** What is the major agent of erosion on Earth's surface?
   b. **Sequencing** List these in order of size: tributary, stream, rill, gully, runoff, river.
   c. **Predicting** Where would gullies be more likely to form: a field with plowed soil and no plants, or a field covered with thick grass? Explain.
2. a. **Listing** What are five features that erosion forms along a river?
   b. **Listing** What are three features that result from deposition along a river?
   c. **Relating Cause and Effect** Why does a delta often form where a river empties into the ocean?

3. a. **Identifying** What process is the cause of groundwater erosion?
   b. **Explaining** How do groundwater erosion and deposition produce a limestone cave?

Lab zone At-Home **Activity**

Erosion Cube In a small dish, build a cube out of 27 small sugar cubes. Your cube should be three sugar cubes on a side. Fold a square piece of paper towel to fit the top of the cube. Wet the paper towel, place it on the cube, and let it stand for 15 or 20 minutes. Every few minutes, sprinkle a few drops of water on the paper towel to keep it wet. Then remove the paper towel. What happened to your cube? How is the effect of water on a sugar cube similar to groundwater eroding limestone? How is it different?

Streams in Action

Problem

How do rivers and streams erode the land?

Skills Focus

making models, observing

Materials 🥽 👕 ✂️

- diatomaceous earth
- plastic measuring cup
- spray bottle
- hand lens
- watch or clock
- water
- 1 metal spoon
- plastic foam cup
- blue food coloring
- liquid detergent
- scissors
- 2 wood blocks about 2.5 cm thick
- bucket to hold 2–3 L of water or a source of tap water
- plastic stirrers, 10–12 cm long, with two small holes each
- wire, 13–15 cm long, 20 gauge

Procedure

PART 1 Creating Streams Over Time

1. Your teacher will give you a plastic tub containing diatomaceous earth that has been soaked with water. Place the tub on a level surface. **CAUTION:** *Dry diatomaceous earth produces dust that may be irritating if inhaled.* To keep the diatomaceous earth from drying out, spray it lightly with water.

2. One end of the tub will contain more diatomaceous earth. Use a block of wood to raise this end of the tub 2.5 cm.

3. Place the cup at the upper end of the slope with the notches pointing to the left and right.

4. Press the cup firmly down into the earth to secure its position.

5. Start the dripper (see Step 6 in the box below). Allow the water to drip to the right onto the diatomaceous earth.

6. Allow the dripper to drip for 5 minutes. (*Hint:* When you need to add more water, be careful not to disturb the dripper.)

Making the Dripper

1. Insert the wire into one of the two holes in a plastic stirrer. The ends of the wire should protrude from the stirrer.

2. Gently bend the stirrer into a **U** shape. Be careful not to make any sharp bends. This is the dripper.

3. With scissors, carefully cut two small notches on opposite sides of the top of the foam cup.

4. Fill the cup to just below the notches with water colored with two drops of blue food coloring. Add more food coloring later as you add more water to the cup.

5. Add one drop of detergent to keep air bubbles out of the dripper and increase flow.

6. To start the dripper, fill it with water. Then quickly tip it and place it in one of the notches in the cup, as shown above.

7. Adjust the flow rate of the dripper to about 2 drips per 1 second. (*Hint:* Bend the dripper into more of a **U** shape to increase flow. Lessen the curve to reduce flow.)

5. Replace the cup and restart the dripper, placing it in the notch on the left side of the cup. Allow the dripper to drip for 5 minutes. Notice any changes in the new stream bed.

6. At the end of 5 minutes, remove the dripper.

7. Draw the new stream bed in your lab notebook. Label it "Increased Angle."

8. Follow your teacher's instructions for clean-up after this activity. Wash your hands when you have finished.

Analyze and Conclude

1. **Observing** Compare the 5-minute stream with the 10-minute stream. How did the length of time that the water flowed affect erosion along the stream bed?

2. **Drawing Conclusions** Were your predictions about the effects of increasing the angle of slope correct? Explain your answer.

3. **Observing** What happened to the eroded material that was carried downstream?

4. **Making Models** What features of streams were you able to observe using the stream table model? How could you modify the model to observe additional features?

5. **Controlling Variables** What other variables besides time and angle of slope might affect the way rivers and streams erode the land?

6. **Communicating** Describe an example of water erosion that you have seen, such as water flowing down a hillside or street after a heavy rain. Include in your answer details such as the slope of the land, the color of the water, and the effects of the erosion.

Design an Experiment

Design a stream table experiment to measure how the amount of sediment carried by a river changes as the volume of flow of the river increases. *Obtain your teacher's approval before you try the experiment.*

7. Observe the flow of water and the changes it makes. Use the hand lens to look closely at the stream bed.

8. After 5 minutes, remove the dripper.

9. In your lab notebook, draw a picture of the resulting stream and label it "5 minutes."

10. Now switch the dripper to the left side of the cup. Restart the dripper and allow it to drip for 10 minutes. Then remove the dripper.

11. Draw a picture and label it "10 minutes."

PART 2 **Changing the Angle of Slope**

1. Remove the cup from the stream table.

2. Save the stream bed on the right side of the tub. Using the bowl of the spoon, smooth out the diatomaceous earth on the left side.

3. To increase the angle of slope of your stream table, raise the end of the tub another 2.5 cm.

4. In your lab notebook, predict the effects of increasing the angle of slope.

Protecting Homes in Flood Plains

At least ten million American households are located in flood plains. Living near a river is tempting. Riverside land is often flat and easy to build on. Because so many people now live in flood plains, the cost of flood damage has been growing. Communities along rivers want to limit the cost of flooding. They want to know how they can protect the people and buildings already in flood plains. They also want to know how to discourage more people from moving into flood plains.

The Issues

Should the Government Insure People Against Flood Damage?

The United States government offers insurance to households in flood plains. The insurance pays part of the cost of repairs after a flood. Government flood insurance is available only to towns and cities that take steps to reduce flood damage. Cities must allow new building only on high ground. The insurance will not pay to rebuild homes that are badly damaged by flood water. Instead, these people must use the money to find a home somewhere else.

Critics say that insurance just encourages development in areas that flood. Another problem with the insurance is cost. It is very expensive. Only 17 percent of people who live in flood plains buy the government insurance. Supporters say insurance rewards towns and cities that make rules to control building on flood plains. Over time, this approach would mean fewer homes and other buildings on flood plains—and less damage from flooding.

▼ Flooded homes in Davenport, Iowa.

Floodwater Rising
Rain from Hurricane Isabel caused this flooding in Alexandria, Virginia in 2003

How Much of the Flood Plain Should Be Protected?

Government flood insurance is available only in areas where scientists expect flooding about once in 100 years, or once in 500 years. But such figures are just estimates. Three floods occurred in only 12 years in a government flood insurance area near Sacramento, California.

Should the Government Tell People Where They Can Live?

Some programs of flood control forbid all new building. Other programs may also encourage people to move to safer areas. The 1997 flood on the Red River in Grand Forks, North Dakota, is one example. After the flood, the city of Grand Forks offered to buy all the damaged buildings near the river. The city wants to build high walls of earth to protect the rest of the town.

The Grand Forks plan might prevent future damage, but is it fair? Supporters say that since the government has to pay for flood damage, it has the right to make people leave flood plains. Critics of such plans say that people should be free to live where they want, even in risky areas.

Who should decide in which neighborhood no new houses can be built? Who decides which people should be asked to move away from a flood plain? Experts disagree over whether local, state, or United States government officials should decide which areas to include. Some believe scientists should make the decision.

Weigh the Impact

1. Identify the Problem
In your own words, describe the controversy surrounding flood plains and housing.

2. Analyze the Options
List several steps that could be taken to reduce the damage done to buildings in flood plains. For each step, include who would benefit from the step and who would pay the costs.

3. Find a Solution
Your town has to decide what to do about a neighborhood damaged by the worst flood in 50 years. Write a speech that argues for your solution.

For: More on protecting homes in flood plains
Visit: PHSchool.com
Web Code: cfh-2030

The Force of Moving Water

Reading Preview

Key Concepts
- What enables water to do work?
- How does sediment enter rivers and streams?
- What factors affect a river's ability to erode and carry sediment?

Key Terms
- energy • potential energy
- kinetic energy • abrasion
- load • friction • turbulence

Target Reading Skill
Building Vocabulary A definition states the meaning of a word or phrase by telling about its most important feature or function. Carefully read the definition of each Key Term and also read the neighboring sentences. Then write a definition of each Key Term in your own words.

Lab zone Discover **Activity**

How Are Sediments Deposited?

1. Put on your goggles.
2. Obtain a clear plastic jar or bottle with a top. Fill the jar about two-thirds full with water.
3. Fill a plastic beaker with 200 mL of fine and coarse sand, soil, clay, and small pebbles.
4. Pour the mixture into the jar of water. Screw on the top tightly and shake for two minutes. Be sure to hold onto the jar firmly.
5. Set the jar down and observe it for 10 to 15 minutes.

Think It Over
Inferring In what order are the sediments in the jar deposited? What do you think causes this pattern?

The Merrimack River in New Hampshire and Massachusetts is only 180 kilometers long. But the Merrimack does a great deal of work as it runs from the mountains to the sea. The river's waters fall 82 meters through many rapids and waterfalls. During the 1800s, people harnessed this falling water to run machines that could spin thread and weave cloth.

Work and Energy

A river's water has energy. **Energy** is the ability to do work or cause change. There are two kinds of energy. **Potential energy** is energy that is stored and waiting to be used later. The Merrimack's waters begin with potential energy due to their position above sea level. **Kinetic energy** is the energy an object has due to its motion. **As gravity pulls water down a slope, the water's potential energy changes to kinetic energy that can do work.**

When energy does work, the energy is transferred from one object to another. Along the Merrimack River, the kinetic energy of the moving water was transferred to the spinning machines. It became mechanical energy harnessed for making cloth. But all along a river, moving water has other effects. A river is always moving sediment from the mountains to the sea. At the same time, a river is also eroding its banks and valley.

FIGURE 13
Water Power
Dams like this one on the Merrimack River in Lowell, Massachusetts, help to harness the power of flowing water.

How Water Erodes

Gravity causes the movement of water across Earth's land surface. But how does water cause erosion? In the process of water erosion, water picks up and moves sediment. Sediment includes soil, rock, clay, and sand. Sediment can enter rivers and streams in a number of ways. **Most sediment washes or falls into a river as a result of mass movement and runoff. Other sediment erodes from the bottom or sides of the river.** Wind may also drop sediment into the water.

Abrasion is another process by which a river obtains sediment. **Abrasion** is the wearing away of rock by a grinding action. Abrasion occurs when particles of sediment in flowing water bump into the streambed again and again. Abrasion grinds down sediment particles. For example, boulders become smaller as they are moved down a stream bed. Sediments also grind and chip away at the rock of the stream bed, deepening and widening the stream's channel.

The amount of sediment that a river carries is its **load.** Gravity and the force of the moving water cause the sediment load to move downstream. Most large sediment falls to the bottom and moves by rolling and sliding. Fast-moving water actually lifts sand and other, smaller sediment and carries it downstream. Water dissolves some sediment completely. The river carries these dissolved sediments in solution. Figure 14 shows other ways in which water can carry sediment. For example, grains of sand or small stones can move by bouncing.

 Reading Checkpoint What causes the sediment in a river to move downstream?

Lab zone Skills Activity

Developing Hypotheses

A geologist is comparing alluvial fans. One alluvial fan is composed of gravel and small boulders. The other fan is composed of sand and silt. Propose a hypothesis to explain the difference in the size of the particles in the two fans. (*Hint:* Think of the characteristics of the streams that formed each alluvial fan.)

FIGURE 14
Movement of Sediment
Rivers and streams carry sediment in several ways.
Predicting *How would a boulder in a stream be likely to move?*

Direction of flow

Dissolved sediment

Suspended sediment

Larger particles pushed or rolled along streambed

Smaller particles move by bouncing

For: More on river erosion
Visit: PHSchool.com
Web Code: cfd-2033

Erosion and Sediment Load

The power of a river to cause erosion and carry sediment depends on several factors. **A river's slope, volume of flow, and the shape of its stream bed all affect how fast the river flows and how much sediment it can erode.**

A fast-flowing river carries more and larger particles of sediment. When a river slows down, it drops its sediment load. The larger particles of sediment are deposited first.

Slope Generally, if a river's slope increases, the water's speed also increases. A river's slope is the amount the river drops toward sea level over a given distance. If a river's speed increases, its sediment load and power to erode may increase. But other factors are also important in determining how much sediment the river erodes and carries.

Volume of Flow A river's flow is the volume of water that moves past a point on the river in a given time. As more water flows through a river, its speed increases. During a flood, the increased volume of water helps the river to cut more deeply into its banks and bed. When a river floods, its power to erode may increase by a hundredfold A flooding river can carry huge amounts of sand, soil, and other sediments. It may move giant boulders as if they were pebbles.

FIGURE 15
The Slope of a River
A river's slope is usually greatest near the river's source. As a river approaches its mouth, its slope lessens.
Inferring *Where would you expect the water in this river to have the greatest amount of potential energy?*

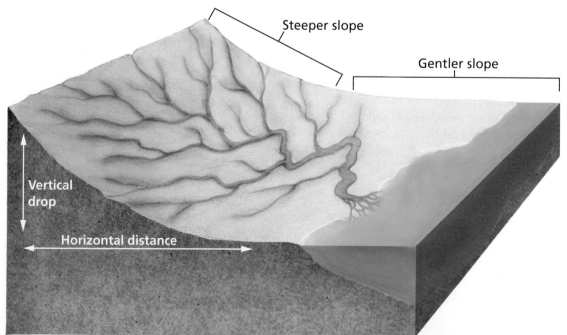

Stream Bed Shape A stream bed's shape affects the amount of friction between the water and the stream bed. **Friction** is the force that opposes the motion of one surface as it moves across another surface. Friction, in turn, affects a river's speed. Where a river is deep, less water comes in contact with the stream bed. The reduced friction allows the river to flow faster. In a shallow river, much of the water comes in contact with the stream bed. Therefore friction increases, reducing the river's speed.

A stream bed is often full of boulders and other obstacles. This roughness prevents the water from flowing smoothly. Roughness thus increases friction and reduces the river's speed. Instead of moving downstream, the water moves every which way in a type of movement called **turbulence.** For example, a stream on a steep slope may flow at a slower speed than a large river on a gentle slope. Friction and turbulence slow the stream's flow. But a turbulent stream or river may have great power to erode.

FIGURE 16
Turbulence
The turbulent flow of this stream increases the stream's power to cause erosion.

Math ▸ Analyzing Data

Sediment on the Move

The speed, or velocity, of a stream affects the size of the sediment particles the stream can carry. Study the graph, then answer the questions below.

1. **Reading Graphs** What variable is shown on the x-axis of the graph?

2. **Reading Graphs** What variable is shown on the y-axis of the graph?

3. **Interpreting Data** What is the speed at which a stream can move fine sand? Small pebbles? Large boulders?

4. **Predicting** A stream's speed increases to about 600 cm per second during a flood. What are the largest particles the stream can move?

5. **Developing Hypotheses** Write a hypothesis that states the relationship between the speed of a stream and the size of the sediment particles it can move.

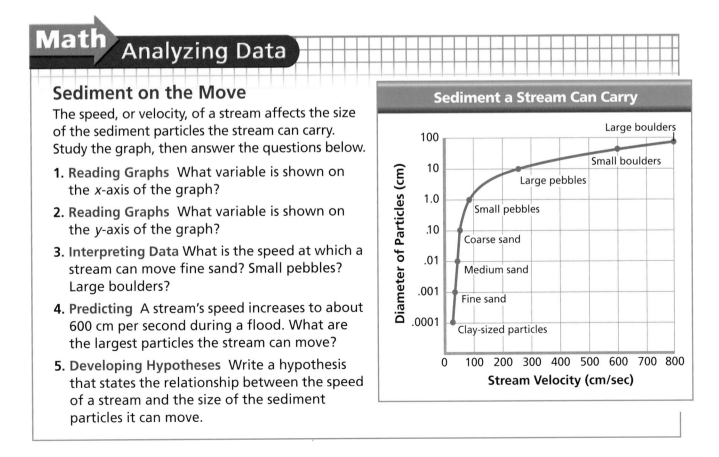

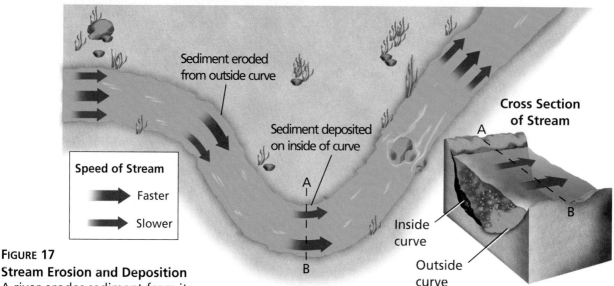

FIGURE 17
Stream Erosion and Deposition
A river erodes sediment from its banks on the outside curve and deposits sediment on the inside curve.
Relating Cause and Effect *Why does a river deposit sediment on the inside of a curve?*

Factors Affecting Erosion and Deposition Whether a river flows in a straight line or a curved line affects the way it erodes and deposits sediment. Where a river flows in a straight line, the water flows faster near the center of the river than along its sides. Deposition occurs along the sides of the river, where the water moves more slowly.

If a river curves, the water moves fastest along the outside of the curve. There, the river tends to cut into its bank, causing erosion. Sediment is deposited on the inside curve, where the water speed is slowest. You can see this process in Figure 17.

Reading Checkpoint Where a stream curves, in what part of the stream does the water flow fastest?

Section 3 Assessment

Target Reading Skill Building Vocabulary
Use your definitions to help answer the questions.

Reviewing Key Concepts

1. a. Defining What is energy?
  b. Explaining How is a river's potential energy changed into kinetic energy?
  c. Relating Cause and Effect What are two effects produced by flowing water in a river?
2. a. Reviewing What are two main sources of the sediment that rivers and streams carry?
  b. Describing Describe a process by which a stream can erode its stream bed.
  c. Predicting Near a stream's source, a stream erodes a piece of rock from its stream bed. As the rock is carried down the stream, how will its size and shape change? Explain.

3. a. Identifying What three factors affect how fast a river flows?
  b. Interpreting Diagrams Study Figure 17 above. Over time, what will happen to the river's bank at B? Why?

Writing in Science

Comparison Paragraph A river transports sediment particles of four different sizes from its source to its mouth: tiny clay particles, grains of sand, pebbles, and boulders. Write a paragraph that compares clay particles and pebbles in terms of how they move, how fast they travel, and how their potential energy changes during the journey.

Glaciers

Reading Preview

Key Concepts
- What are the two kinds of glaciers?
- How does a valley glacier form and move?
- How do glaciers cause erosion and deposition?

Key Terms
- glacier • continental glacier
- ice age• valley glacier
- plucking • till • moraine • kettle

Target Reading Skill

Asking Questions Before you read, preview the red headings. In a graphic organizer like the one below, ask a *what, how,* or *where* question for each heading. As you read, answer your questions.

Glaciers

Question	Answer
What kinds of glaciers are there?	Valley glaciers and . . .

Discover **Activity**

How Do Glaciers Change the Land?

1. Put some sand in a small plastic container.
2. Fill the container with water and place the container in a freezer until the water turns to ice.
3. Remove the block of ice from the container. Hold the ice with a paper towel.
4. Rub the ice, sand side down, over a bar of soap. Observe what happens to the surface of the soap.

Think It Over

Inferring Based on your observations, how do you think moving ice could change the surface of the land?

You are on a boat trip near the coast of Alaska. You sail by vast evergreen forests and snow-capped mountains. Then, as your boat rounds a point of land, you see an amazing sight. A great mass of ice winds like a river between rows of mountains. Suddenly you hear a noise like thunder. Where the ice meets the sea, a giant chunk of ice breaks off and plunges into the water. Carefully, the pilot steers your boat around the iceberg and toward the mass of ice. It towers over your boat. You see that it is made up of solid ice that is deep blue and green as well as white. What is this river of ice?

▼ **The Hubbard Glacier in Alaska winds downhill between high mountains.**

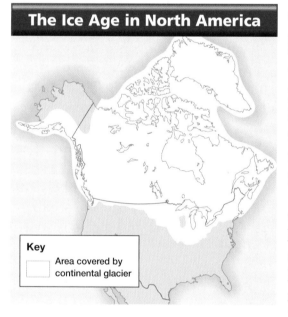

FIGURE 18
Continental Glaciers
Today, huge icebergs form where a continental glacier (above) meets the ocean. During the last ice age (below), a continental glacier covered most of northern North America.

The Ice Age in North America

Key
☐ Area covered by continental glacier

Huge icebergs form where Antartica's continental glacier meets the ocean.

How Glaciers Form and Move

Geologists define a **glacier** as any large mass of ice that moves slowly over land. **There are two kinds of glaciers—continental glaciers and valley glaciers.**

Continental Glaciers A **continental glacier** is a glacier that covers much of a continent or large island. They can spread out over millions of square kilometers. Today, continental glaciers cover about 10 percent of Earth's land. They cover Antarctica and most of Greenland. The glacier covering Antarctica is over 2 kilometers thick! Continental glaciers can flow in all directions as they move. Continental glaciers spread out much as pancake batter spreads out in a frying pan.

Many times in the past, continental glaciers have covered larger parts of Earth's surface. These times are known as **ice ages.** For example, about 2.5 million years ago, continental glaciers covered about one third of Earth's land. The glaciers advanced and retreated, or melted back, several times. They finally retreated about 10,000 years ago.

Valley Glaciers A **valley glacier** is a long, narrow glacier that forms when snow and ice build up high in a mountain valley. The sides of mountains keep these glaciers from spreading out in all directions. Instead, they usually move down valleys that have already been cut by rivers. Valley glaciers are found on many high mountains. Although they are much smaller than continental glaciers, valley glaciers can be tens of kilometers long.

High in mountain valleys, temperatures seldom rise above freezing. Snow builds up year after year. The weight of more and more snow compacts the snow at the bottom into ice. **Glaciers can form only in an area where more snow falls than melts. Once the depth of snow and ice reaches more than 30 to 40 meters, gravity begins to pull the glacier downhill.**

Valley glaciers flow at a rate of a few centimeters to a few meters per day. But sometimes a valley glacier slides down more quickly in what is called a surge. A surging glacier can flow as much as 6 kilometers a year.

 Reading Checkpoint On what type of landform are valley glaciers found?

How Glaciers Shape the Land

The movement of a glacier changes the land beneath it. Although glaciers work slowly, they are a major force of erosion. **The two processes by which glaciers erode the land are plucking and abrasion.**

Glacial Erosion As a glacier flows over the land, it picks up rocks in a process called **plucking.** Beneath a glacier, the weight of the ice can break rocks apart. These rock fragments freeze to the bottom of the glacier. When the glacier moves, it carries the rocks with it. Figure 19 shows plucking by a glacier. Plucking can move even huge boulders.

Many rocks remain on the bottom of the glacier, and the glacier drags them across the land. This process, called abrasion, gouges and scratches the bedrock. You can see the results of erosion by glaciers in Figure 19.

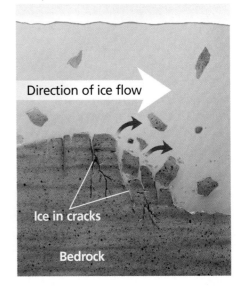

FIGURE 19
Glacial Erosion
As a glacier moves (above), plucking breaks pieces of bedrock from the ground. Erosion by glaciers (below) can carve a mountain peak into a sharp horn and grind out a **V**-shaped valley to form a **U**-shaped valley.
Observing *What other changes did the glacier produce in this landscape?*

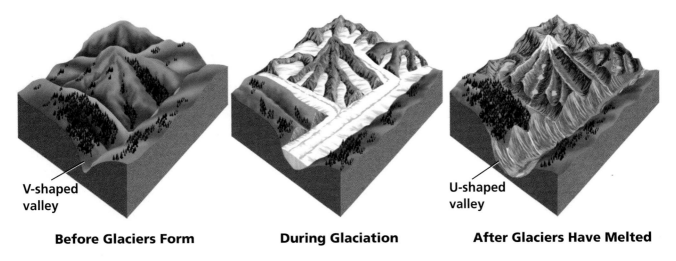

V-shaped valley

U-shaped valley

Before Glaciers Form   **During Glaciation**   **After Glaciers Have Melted**

Horn
When glaciers carve away the sides of a mountain, the result is a horn, a sharpened peak.

Cirque
A cirque is a bowl-shaped hollow eroded by a glacier.

Arête
An arête is a sharp ridge separating two cirques.

Fiord
A fiord forms when the level of the sea rises, filling a valley once cut by a glacier.

FIGURE 20
Glacial Landforms
As glaciers advance and retreat, they sculpt the landscape by erosion and deposition.
Classifying *Classify these glacial features according to whether they result from erosion or deposition: drumlin, horn, cirque, moraine, U-shaped valley.*

Go Online
SciLINKS NSTA

For: Links on glaciers
Visit: www.SciLinks.org
Web Code: scn-0734

Glacial Deposition A glacier gathers a huge amount of rock and soil as it erodes the land in its path. **When a glacier melts, it deposits the sediment it eroded from the land, creating various landforms.** These landforms remain for thousands of years after the glacier has melted.

The mixture of sediments that a glacier deposits directly on the surface is called **till.** Till is made up of particles of many different sizes. Clay, silt, sand, gravel, and boulders can all be found in till.

The till deposited at the edges of a glacier forms a ridge called a **moraine.** A terminal moraine is the ridge of till at the farthest point reached by a glacier. Long Island in New York is a terminal moraine from the continental glaciers of the last ice age.

Retreating glaciers also create features called kettles. A **kettle** is a small depression that forms when a chunk of ice is left in glacial till. When the ice melts, the kettle remains. The continental glacier of the last ice age left behind many kettles. Kettles often fill with water, forming small ponds or lakes called kettle lakes. Such lakes are common in areas, such as Minnesota, that were covered with ice.

Reading Checkpoint **What is a terminal moraine?**

U-Shaped Valley
A flowing glacier scoops out a U-shaped valley.

Glacial Lake
Glaciers may leave behind large lakes in long basins.

Moraine
A moraine forms where a glacier deposits mounds or ridges of till.

Drumlin
A drumlin is a long mound of till that is smoothed in the direction of the glacier's flow.

Kettle Lake
A kettle lake forms when a depression left in till by melting ice fills with water.

Section 4 Assessment

Target Reading Skill Asking Questions Use the answers to the questions you wrote about the headings to help you answer the questions below.

Reviewing Key Concepts

1. **a. Defining** What is a continental glacier?
   b. Defining What is a valley glacier?
   c. Comparing and Contrasting How are the two types of glaciers similar? How are they different?
2. **a. Reviewing** What condition is necessary for a glacier to form?
   b. Explaining How does a glacier move?
   c. Relating Cause and Effect Why does the snow that forms a glacier change to ice?
3. **a. Identifying** What are two ways in which glaciers erode Earth's surface?
   b. Describing How does glacial deposition occur?

Writing in Science

Travel Brochure A travel agency wants people to go on a tour of a mountain region with many glaciers. Write a paragraph for a travel brochure describing what people will see on the tour. In your answer, include features formed by glacial erosion and deposition.

Waves

Reading Preview

Key Concepts
- What gives waves their energy?
- How do waves erode a coast?
- What features result from deposition by waves?

Key Terms
- headland • beach
- longshore drift • spit

Target Reading Skill

Identifying Main Ideas As you read Erosion by Waves, write the main idea in a graphic organizer like the one below. Then write three supporting details that further explain the main idea.

Main Idea

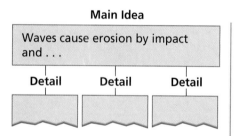

Waves cause erosion by impact and . . .		
Detail	Detail	Detail

▼ **Waves on the Oregon coast**

What Is Sand Made Of?

1. Collect a spoonful of sand from each of two different beaches.
2. Examine the first sample of beach sand with a hand lens.
3. Record the properties of the sand grains, for example, color and shape. Are the grains smooth and rounded or angular and rough?
4. Examine the second sample and repeat Step 3. How do the two samples compare?

Think It Over

Posing Questions What questions do you need to answer to understand beach sand? Use what you know about erosion and deposition to help you think of questions.

Ocean waves contain energy—sometimes a great deal of energy. Created by ocean winds, they carry energy vast distances across the Pacific Ocean. Acting like drills or buzz saws, the waves erode the solid rock of the coast into cliffs and caves. Waves also carry sediment that forms features such as beaches.

How Waves Form

The energy in waves comes from wind that blows across the water's surface. As the wind makes contact with the water, some of its energy transfers to the water. Large ocean waves are the result of powerful storms far out at sea. But ordinary breezes can produce waves in lakes or small ponds.

The energy that water picks up from the wind causes water particles to move up and down as the wave goes by. But the water particles themselves don't move forward.

A wave changes as it approaches land. In deep water, a wave only affects the water near the surface. But as it approaches shallow water, the wave begins to drag on the bottom. The friction between the wave and the bottom causes the wave to slow down. Now the water actually does move forward with the wave. This forward-moving water provides the force that shapes the land along the shoreline.

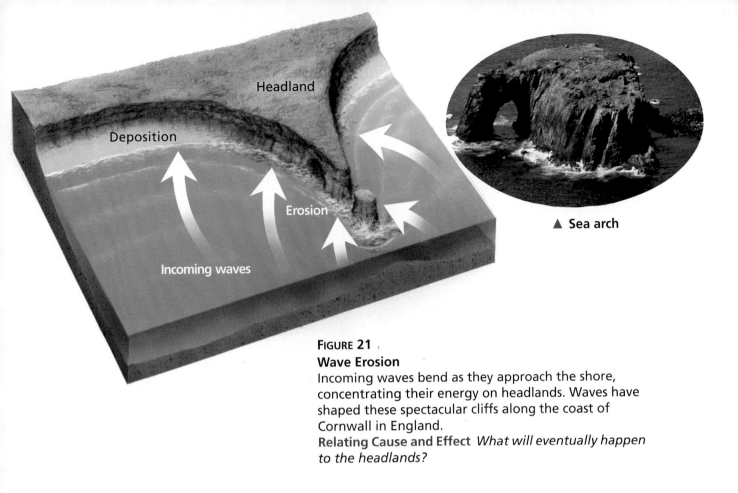

Headland

Deposition

Erosion

Incoming waves

▲ Sea arch

FIGURE 21
Wave Erosion
Incoming waves bend as they approach the shore, concentrating their energy on headlands. Waves have shaped these spectacular cliffs along the coast of Cornwall in England.
Relating Cause and Effect *What will eventually happen to the headlands?*

Erosion by Waves

Waves are the major force of erosion along coasts. **Waves shape the coast through erosion by breaking down rock and transporting sand and other sediment.**

How Waves Erode One way waves erode the land is by impact. Large waves can hit rocks along the shore with great force. This energy in waves can break apart rocks. Over time, waves can make small cracks larger. Eventually, the waves cause pieces of rock to break off.

Waves also erode by abrasion. As a wave approaches shallow water, it picks up sediment, including sand and gravel. This sediment is carried forward by the wave. When the wave hits land, the sediment wears away rock like sandpaper wearing away wood.

Waves coming to shore gradually change direction. The change in direction occurs as different parts of a wave begin to drag on the bottom. Notice how the waves in Figure 21 change direction as they approach the shore. The energy of these waves is concentrated on headlands. A **headland** is a part of the shore that sticks out into the ocean. Headlands stand out from the coast because they are made of harder rock that resists erosion by the waves. But, over time, waves erode the headlands and even out the shoreline.

Go Online
SciLINKS
NSTA

For: Links on waves
Visit: www.SciLinks.org
Web Code: scn-0735

Erosional Features

Wave-cut cliff

Sea cave
Formed as wave action hollows out the cliff

Headland

Sea arch
Formed when sea caves on either side of a headland join

Sea stack
Left standing when a sea arch collapses

FIGURE 22
The Changing Coast
Erosion and deposition create a variety of features along a coast. **Predicting** *What will eventually happen to the sea arch?*

Landforms Created by Wave Erosion When waves hit a steep, rocky coast, they strike the area again and again. Think of an ax striking the trunk of a tree. The cut gets bigger and deeper with each strike of the blade. Finally the tree falls. In a similar way, ocean waves erode the base of the land along a steep coast. Where the rock is softer, the waves erode the land faster. Over time the waves may erode a hollow area in the rock called a sea cave.

Eventually, waves may erode the base of a cliff so much that the rock above collapses. The result is a wave-cut cliff. You can see an example of such a cliff in Figure 22.

Another feature created by wave erosion is a sea arch. A sea arch forms when waves erode a layer of softer rock that underlies a layer of harder rock. If an arch collapses, the result might be a sea stack, a pillar of rock rising above the water.

Reading Checkpoint **Over a long period of time, what effect do waves have on a steep, rocky coast?**

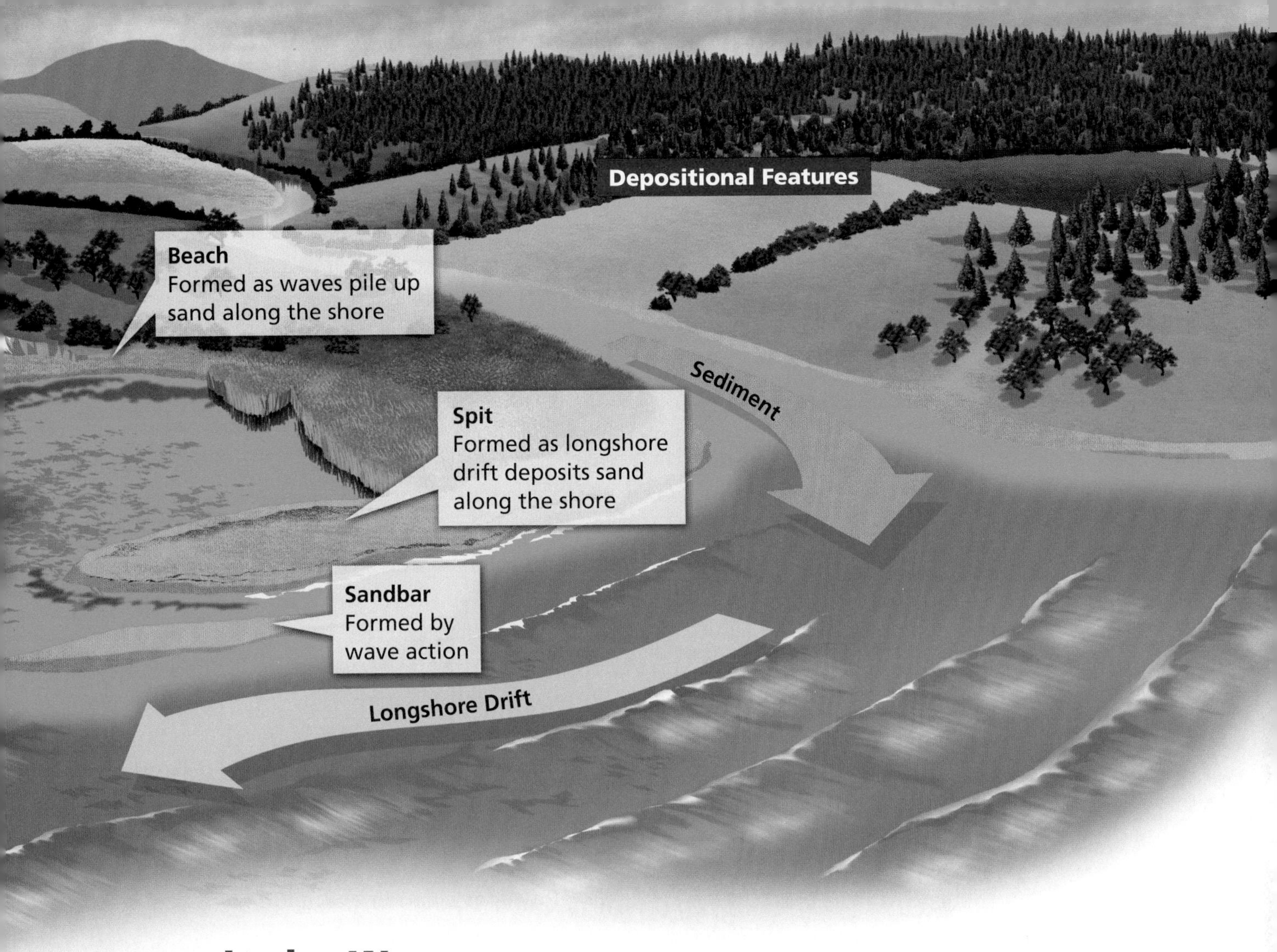

Depositional Features

Beach
Formed as waves pile up sand along the shore

Sediment

Spit
Formed as longshore drift deposits sand along the shore

Sandbar
Formed by wave action

Longshore Drift

Deposits by Waves

Waves shape a coast when they deposit sediment, forming coastal features such as beaches, spits, and barrier beaches. Deposition occurs when waves slow down, causing the water to drop its sediment. This process is similar to the deposition that occurs on a river delta when the river slows down and drops its sediment load.

Beaches As waves reach the shore, they drop the sediment they carry, forming a beach. A **beach** is an area of wave-washed sediment along a coast. The sediment deposited on beaches is usually sand. Most sand comes from rivers that carry eroded particles of rock into the ocean. But not all beaches are made of sand. Some beaches are made of small fragments of coral or sea shells piled up by wave action. Florida has many such beaches.

The sediment on a beach usually moves down the beach after it has been deposited. Waves usually hit the beach at an angle instead of straight on. These angled waves create a current that runs parallel to the coastline. As waves repeatedly hit the beach, some of the beach sediment moves down the beach with the current, in a process called **longshore drift.**

Lab zone Skills Activity

Calculating A sandy coast erodes at a rate of 1.25 m per year. But a severe storm can erode an additional 3.75 m from the shore. If 12 severe storms occur during a 50-year period, how much will the coast erode? If you wish, you may use an electronic calculator to find the answer.

Spits One result of longshore drift is the formation of a spit. A **spit** is a beach that projects like a finger out into the water. Spits form as a result of deposition by longshore drift. Spits occur where a headland or other obstacle interrupts longshore drift, or where the coast turns abruptly.

FIGURE 23
Spits
This aerial photograph shows how longshore drift can carry sand and deposit it to form a spit.
Observing *How many spits can you find in this image?*

Sandbars and Barrier Beaches Incoming waves carrying sand may build up sandbars, long ridges of sand parallel to the shore. A barrier beach is similar to a sandbar. A barrier beach forms when storm waves pile up large amounts of sand above sea level forming a long, narrow island parallel to the coast. Barrier beaches are found in many places along the Atlantic coast of the United States, such as the Outer Banks of North Carolina. People have built homes on many of these barrier beaches. But the storm waves that build up the beaches can also wash them away. Barrier beach communities must be prepared for the damage that hurricanes and other storms can bring.

Reading Checkpoint How does a barrier beach form?

Section 5 Assessment

Target Reading Skill Identifying Main Ideas Use your graphic organizer to help you answer Question 2 below.

Reviewing Key Concepts

1. **a. Explaining** What is the source of the energy in ocean waves?
   b. Describing How does an ocean wave change when it reaches shallow water?
   c. Inferring Does an ocean wave possess potential energy or kinetic energy? Explain.
2. **a. Identifying** What are two results of wave erosion along a coast?
   b. Describing What are two ways in which waves erode rock?
   c. Sequencing Place these features in the order in which they would probably form: sea stack, sea cave, headland, cliff, sea arch.
3. **a. Listing** What are three features formed by wave deposition?
   b. Relating Cause and Effect Beginning with the source of sand, explain the process by which a spit forms.

Writing in Science

Explaining a Process Suppose that you live in a coastal area that has a barrier beach. Write a paragraph in which you explain the processes that formed the barrier beach. Also describe how the forces might change it over time.

Wind

Reading Preview

Key Concepts
- How does wind cause erosion?
- What features result from deposition by wind?

Key Terms
- sand dune
- deflation
- loess

Target Reading Skill
Sequencing As you read, make a flowchart like the one below that shows the process of wind erosion and deposition. Write each step of the process in a separate box in the flowchart in the order in which it occurs.

Wind Erosion

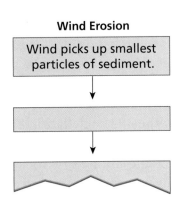

Wind picks up smallest particles of sediment.

Wind erosion constantly shapes the giant sand dunes in the Namib Desert of southwestern Africa. ▼

Discover Activity

How Does Moving Air Affect Sediment?

1. Cover the bottom of a pan with a flat layer of cornmeal 1–2 cm deep.
2. Gently blow over the layer of cornmeal using a straw to direct your breath. Observe what happens. **CAUTION:** *Do not blow the cornmeal in the direction of another student.*

Think It Over
Observing What changes did the wind you created make in the flat layer of cornmeal?

Imagine a landscape made almost entirely of sand. One such place is the Namib Desert. The desert stretches 1,900 kilometers along the coast of Namibia in Africa. In the southern half of the Namib are rows of giant sand dunes. A **sand dune** is a deposit of wind-blown sand. Some sand dunes in the Namib are more than 200 meters high and 15 kilometers long. Much of the sand in the dunes originally came from the nearby Orange River. Over thousands of years, wind has swept the sand across the desert, piling up huge, ever-changing dunes.

How Wind Causes Erosion

Wind by itself is the weakest agent of erosion. Water, waves, moving ice, and even mass movement have more effect on the land. Yet wind can be a powerful force in shaping the land in areas where there are few plants to hold the soil in place. For example, few plants grow in deserts, so wind can easily move the grains of dry sand. **Wind causes erosion by deflation and abrasion.**

FIGURE 24
Wind Erosion
Wind erosion moves sediment particles of different sizes in the three ways shown at right.
Comparing and Contrasting *Compare the movement of sediment by wind with the movement of sediment by water in Figure 14 on page 87. How are the processes similar? How are they different?*

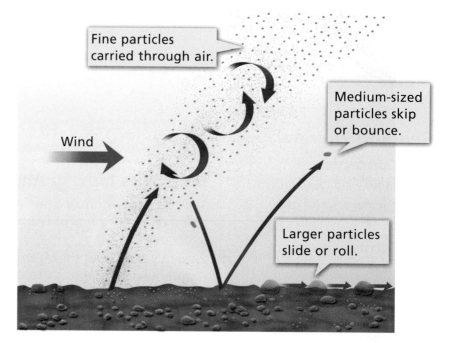

Fine particles carried through air.

Medium-sized particles skip or bounce.

Wind

Larger particles slide or roll.

FIGURE 25
Desert Pavement
Wind erosion formed this desert pavement in the Arizona desert. Wind-driven sand may polish and shape individual stones.

Deflation The main way that wind causes erosion is by deflation. Geologists define **deflation** as the process by which wind removes surface materials. When wind blows over the land, it picks up the smallest particles of sediment. This sediment is made of bits of clay and silt. The stronger the wind, the larger the particles that it can pick up. Slightly heavier particles, such as sand, might skip or bounce for a short distance. But sand soon falls back to the ground. Strong winds can even roll heavier sediment particles over the ground. Figure 24 shows how wind erodes by deflation.

Deflation does not usually have a great effect on land. However, in parts of the Great Plains in the 1930s, deflation caused the loss of about 1 meter of topsoil in just a few years. In deserts, deflation can sometimes create an area of rock fragments called desert pavement. You can see an area of desert pavement in Figure 25. There, wind has blown away the smaller sediment. All that remains are rocky materials that are too heavy to be moved. Where there is already a slight depression in the ground, deflation can produce a bowl-shaped hollow called a blowout.

Abrasion Abrasion by wind-carried sand can polish rock, but it causes little erosion. At one time, geologists thought that the sediment carried by wind cut the stone shapes seen in deserts. But now evidence shows that most desert landforms are the result of weathering and water erosion.

Reading Checkpoint Where would you be most likely to see evidence of wind erosion?

Wind Deposition

All the sediment picked up by wind eventually falls to the ground. This happens when the wind slows down or some obstacle, such as a boulder or a clump of grass, traps the windblown sand sediment. **Wind erosion and deposition may form sand dunes and loess deposits.** When the wind strikes an obstacle, the result is usually a sand dune. Sand dunes can be seen on beaches and in deserts where wind-blown sediment has built up.

Sand Dunes Sand dunes come in many shapes and sizes. Some are long, with parallel ridges, while others are **U**-shaped. They can also be very small or very large—some sand dunes in China have grown to heights of 500 meters. Sand dunes move over time. Little by little, the sand shifts with the wind from one side of the dune to the other. This process is shown in Figure 26. Sometimes plants begin growing on a dune. Plant roots can help to anchor the dune in one place.

Loess Deposits Sediment that is finer than sand, such as particles of clay and silt, is sometimes deposited in layers far from its source. This fine, wind-deposited sediment is **loess** (LES). Large loess deposits are found in central China and in such states as Nebraska, South Dakota, Iowa, Missouri, and Illinois. Loess helps to form fertile soil. Many areas with thick loess deposits are valuable farmlands.

Wind direction

FIGURE 26
Movement of Sand Dunes
Wind direction is one factor that helps determine the shape and size of sand dunes.

Section 6 Assessment

Target Reading Skill Sequencing Refer to your flowchart as you answer the questions below.

Reviewing Key Concepts

1. a. **Reviewing** What are two kinds of wind erosion?
   b. **Explaining** Explain how sediment particles of different sizes move during wind erosion.
   c. **Predicting** In a desert, soil containing a mixture of sand and small rocks is exposed to wind erosion. Over time, how would the land surface change? Explain.
2. a. **Relating Cause and Effect** What causes wind to deposit sand or other sediment?
   b. **Identifying** What are two types of features that result from wind deposition?
   c. **Problem Solving** How could sand dunes be held in place to keep them from drifting onto a parking lot?

Lab zone At-Home **Activity**

Desert Pavement To model desert pavement, put a few coins in a shallow pan. Sprinkle enough flour over the coins to cover them. Then blow air gently through a straw across the surface of the flour. Be careful not to draw in any flour through the straw. Be certain the blown flour will not get in your or anyone else's eyes. Ask your family to predict what would happen if the "wind" blew for a long time.

① Changing Earth's Surface

Key Concepts

- Weathering, erosion, and deposition act together in a cycle that wears down and builds up Earth's surface.
- Gravity causes mass movement, including landslides, mudflows, slump, and creep.

Key Terms

erosion	deposition
sediment	mass movement

② Water Erosion

Key Concepts

- Moving water is the major agent of the erosion that has shaped Earth's land surface.
- Through erosion, a river creates valleys, water–falls, flood plains, meanders, and oxbow lakes.
- Deposition creates alluvial fans and deltas. It can also add soil to a river's flood plain.
- Groundwater can cause erosion through a process of chemical weathering.

Key Terms

- runoff • rill • gully • stream • tributary
- flood plain • meander • oxbow lake
- alluvial fan • • delta • groundwater
- stalactite • stalagmite • karst topography

③ The Force of Moving Water

Key Concepts

- As gravity pulls water down a slope, the water's potential energy changes to kinetic energy.
- Most sediment washes or falls into river as a result of mass movement and runoff.
- A river's slope, volume of flow, and the shape of its stream bed all affect how fast the river flows and how much sediment it can erode.

Key Terms

energy	load
potential energy	friction
kinetic energy	turbulence
abrasion	

④ Glaciers

Key Concepts

- There are two kinds of glaciers—continental glaciers and valley glaciers.
- Glaciers can form only in an area where more snow falls than melts.
- The two processes by which glaciers erode the land are plucking and abrasion.
- When a glacier melts, it deposits the sediment it eroded from the land, creating various landforms.

Key Terms

glacier	plucking
continental glacier	till
ice age	moraine
valley glacier	kettle

⑤ Waves

Key Concepts

- The energy in waves comes from wind that blows across the water's surface.
- Waves shape the coast through erosion by breaking down rock and transporting sand and other sediment.
- Waves shape a coast when they deposit sediment, forming coastal features such as beaches, spits, and barrier beaches.

Key Terms

headland	longshore drift
beach	spit

⑥ Wind

Key Concepts

- Wind causes erosion by deflation and abrasion.
- Wind erosion and deposition may form sand dunes and loess deposits.

Key Terms

sand dune	deflation	loess

Review and Assessment

Go Online
PHSchool.com
For: Self-Assessment
Visit: PHSchool.com
Web Code: cfa-2030

Organizing Information

Flowcharts Copy the flowchart about stream formation onto a separate sheet of paper. Then complete it and add a title. (For more on flowcharts, see the Skills Handbook).

Stream Formation

Raindrops strike ground.

↓

Runoff forms.

↓

a. _____ ? _____

↓

b. _____ ? _____

↓

c. _____ ? _____

↓

d. _____ ? _____

Reviewing Key Terms

Choose the letter of the best answer.

1. The eroded materials carried by water or wind are called
   a. stalactites.
   b. desert pavement.
   c. sediment.
   d. moraines.

2. The downhill movement of eroded materials is known as
   a. mass movement.
   b. abrasion.
   c. deposition.
   d. deflation.

3. Where a stream bed is rough, the stream flows more slowly because of
   a. sediment.
   b. friction.
   c. deposition.
   d. potential energy.

4. A mass of rock and soil deposited directly by a glacier is called
   a. load.   b. till.
   c. loess.   d. erosion.

5. The erosion of sediment by wind is
   a. deposition.   b. deflation.
   c. plucking.   d. glaciation.

If the statement is true, write *true*. If it is false, change the underlined word or words to make the statement true.

6. The process by which sediment in water settles in new locations is <u>mass movement</u>.

7. <u>Groundwater</u> that flows in a thin layer over the land causes sheet erosion.

8. Because it is moving, flowing water has a type of energy called <u>kinetic energy</u>.

9. A looplike bend in the river is a <u>meander</u>.

10. The sediment deposited at the edge of a glacier forms a ridge called a <u>kettle</u>.

Writing in Science

Article Suppose that you have just returned from a visit to a limestone cave, such as Mammoth Cave in Kentucky. Write an article describing your visit to the cave. Include how the cave formed, what you saw during your visit, and how features inside the cave developed.

Discovery CHANNEL **SCHOOL**™

Erosion and Deposition
Video Preview
Video Field Trip
▶ Video Assessment

Review and Assessment

Checking Concepts

11. What agents of erosion are assisted by the force of gravity?

12. How do a river's slope and volume of flow affect the river's sediment load?

13. What is turbulence? How does it affect the speed of a river and the river's power to cause erosion?

14. Where is the speed of the flowing water in a river the slowest? Explain.

15. What are ice ages?

16. How does a kettle lake form?

17. How does a loess deposit form?

Thinking Critically

18. **Comparing and Contrasting** Compare and contrast landslides and mudflows.

19. **Applying Concepts** Under what conditions would you expect abrasion to cause the most erosion of a riverbed?

20. **Making Judgments** A salesperson offers to sell your family a new house right on a riverbank for very little money. Why might your family hesitate to buy this house?

21. **Relating Cause and Effect** What caused the features labeled A, B, and C in the diagram below to form? Explain.

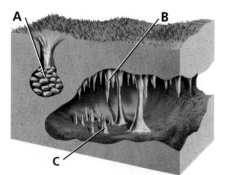

22. **Problem Solving** Suppose you are a geologist studying a valley glacier. What method could you use to tell if it is advancing or retreating?

23. **Inferring** You see a sandy beach along a coastline. Where did the sand come from?

Applying Skills

Use the table below to answer Questions 24–26.

The table shows how a river's volume of flow and sediment load change over six months.

Month	Volume of Flow (cubic meters/ second)	Sediment Load (metric tons/day)
January	1.5	200
February	1.7	320
March	2.6	725
April	4.0	1,600
May	3.2	1,100
June	2.8	900

24. **Graphing** Make one graph with the month on the x-axis and the volume of flow on the y-axis. Make a second graph with the sediment load on the y-axis. Compare your two graphs. When were the river's volume of flow and load the greatest? The lowest?

25. **Developing Hypotheses** Use your graphs to develop a hypothesis about the relationship between volume of flow and sediment load.

26. **Relating Cause and Effect** What may have occurred in the river's drainage basin in April to cause the changes in volume of flow and sediment load? Explain.

Lab zone Chapter **Project**

Performance Assessment Now you are ready to present to your class. Explain which types of soil you chose and why you chose them. Discuss the design of your dam, the tests you conducted, and the results. In your journal, write about the easiest and hardest parts of this project. How would you design your dam differently if you did the project again?

Standardized Test Prep

Choose the letter of the best answer.

1. As a stream flows from a mountainous area to a flatter area, what happens to the size of the sediment the stream normally carries?
   A The sediment size does not change.
   B The sediment size carried by the stream increases.
   C The sediment size carried by the stream decreases.
   D The stream drops all the sediment it was carrying.

2. How does wind carry sediment particles?
   F as fine particles carried through the air
   G as particles that bounce along the ground
   H as larger particles that slide or roll along the ground
   J all of the above

Use the diagram below and your knowledge of science to answer Questions 3–4.

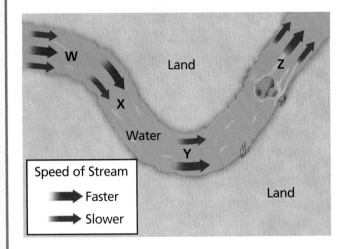

3. What is the erosional feature in the diagram?
   A a meander
   B a delta
   C a flood plain
   D karst topography

4. In the diagram, where is the speed of the stream the greatest?
   F at Y
   G at X
   H at W
   J at Z

5. What is the process by which weathered rock, sediment, and soil is moved from place to place?
   A erosion
   B delta formation
   C running water
   D runoff

Constructed Response

6. Describe how gravity is involved in the erosion of Earth's surface by mass movement, running water, and glaciers. Be sure to first explain what erosion is.

Interactive Textbook

A paleontologist examines a fossilized dinosaur skeleton in the Denver Natural History Museum.

Lab zone Chapter **Project**

A Journey Back in Time

This chapter will take you on a journey through geologic time. You will learn how fossils reveal the history of life on Earth. To guide you on your journey, you and your classmates will make a timeline showing the many periods of geologic time.

Your Goal To become an expert on one geologic time period and assist in constructing a timeline

To complete this project, you must

- research a geologic time period of your choice
- create a travel brochure that shows what life was like in this time period
- illustrate your time period for the timeline
- follow the safety guidelines in Appendix A

Plan It! Begin by selecting a time period you would like to investigate. Check with your teacher to be sure that all the time periods will be covered by members of your class. Then, collect information on your time period's animals, plants, and environment. Use this information to write a travel brochure about your time period. Create illustrations that depict your time period and place them on the timeline. Use the travel brochure to present your geologic time period to your classmates.

Fossils

Reading Preview

Key Concepts
- How do fossils form?
- What are the different kinds of fossils?
- What does the fossil record tell about organisms and environments of the past?

Key Terms
- fossil
- sedimentary rock
- mold
- cast
- petrified fossil
- carbon film
- trace fossil
- paleontologist
- scientific theory
- evolution
- extinct

Target Reading Skill

Using Prior Knowledge Before you read, look at the section headings and visuals to see what this section is about. Then write what you know about fossils in a graphic organizer like the one below. As you read, write what you learn.

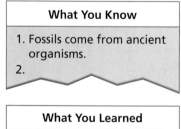

What You Know
1. Fossils come from ancient organisms.
2.

What You Learned
1.
2.

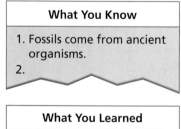

Lab zone **Discover Activity**

What's in a Rock?

1. Use a hand lens to carefully observe the rock sample provided by your teacher. You may also study the photograph of limestone below.
2. Make a drawing of any shapes you see in the rock. Include as many details as you can. Beneath your drawing, write a description of what you see.

Think It Over

Inferring What do you think the rock contains? How do you think the shapes you observed in the rock got there?

Millions of years ago, a fish died and sank to the bottom of a lake. Before the fish could decay completely, layers of sediment covered it. Minerals in the sediment seeped into the fish's bones. Slowly, pressure changed the sediment into solid rock. Inside the rock, the fish became a fossil.

Fossils are the preserved remains or traces of living things. Fossils like the ancient fish in Figure 1 provide evidence of how life has changed over time. Fossils can also help scientists infer how Earth's surface has changed. Fossils are clues to what past environments were like.

How a Fossil Forms

Most fossils form when living things die and are buried by sediments. The sediments slowly harden into rock and preserve the shapes of the organisms. Fossils are usually found in sedimentary rock. **Sedimentary rock** is the type of rock that is made of hardened sediment. Recall that sediment is the material removed by erosion. Sediment is made up of rock particles or the remains of living things. Sandstone, limestone, and coal are examples of sedimentary rocks. Most fossils form from animals or plants that once lived in or near quiet water such as swamps, lakes, or shallow seas where sediments build up. In Figure 1, you can see how a fossil might form.

FIGURE 1
How a Fossil Forms
A fossil may form when sediment quickly covers an animal's body. **Classifying** *In what type of rock would this fossil be found?*

An animal dies and sinks into shallow water.

Sediment covers the animal.

The sediment becomes rock, preserving parts of the animal.

Weathering and erosion eventually expose the fossil at the surface.

When an organism dies, its soft parts often decay quickly or are eaten by animals. That is why only hard parts of an organism generally leave fossils. These hard parts include bones, shells, teeth, seeds, and woody stems. It is rare for the soft parts of an organism to become a fossil.

For a fossil to form, the remains or traces of an organism must be protected from decay. Then several processes may cause a fossil to form. **Fossils found in rock include molds and casts, petrified fossils, carbon films, and trace fossils. Other fossils form when the remains of organisms are preserved in substances such as tar, amber, or ice.**

Molds and Casts The most common fossils are molds and casts. Both copy the shape of ancient organisms. A **mold** is a hollow area in sediment in the shape of an organism or part of an organism. A mold forms when the hard part of the organism, such as a shell, is buried in sediment.

Later, water carrying dissolved minerals and sediment may seep into the empty space of a mold. If the water deposits the minerals and sediment there, the result is a cast. A **cast** is a copy of the shape of an organism. A cast is the opposite of its mold. Both the mold and cast preserve details of the animal's structure. Figure 1 shows a process that could form a mold and cast fossil.

Go Online

SC_i NSTA
L_{INKS}

For: Links on fossils
Visit: www.SciLinks.org
Web Code: scn-0741

FIGURE 2
Kinds of Fossils

In addition to petrified fossils, fossils may be molds and casts, carbon films, trace fossils, or preserved remains.
Classifying *You split apart a rock and find the imprint of a seashell on one half of the rock. What type of fossil have you found?*

Petrified Fossils A fossil may form when the remains of an organism become petrified. The term *petrified* means "turning into stone." **Petrified fossils** are fossils in which minerals replace all or part of an organism. The fossil tree trunks shown in Figure 2 are examples of petrified wood. These fossils formed after sediment covered the wood. Then water rich in dissolved minerals seeped into spaces in the plant's cells. Over time, the water evaporated, leaving the hardened minerals behind. Some of the original wood remains, but the minerals have hardened and preserved it.

Carbon Films Another type of fossil is a **carbon film,** an extremely thin coating of carbon on rock. How does a carbon film form? Remember that all living things contain carbon. When sediment buries an organism, some of the materials that make up the organism evaporate, or become gases. These gases escape from the sediment, leaving carbon behind. Eventually, only a thin film of carbon remains. This process can preserve the delicate parts of plant leaves and insects.

Trace Fossils Most types of fossils preserve the shapes of ancient animals and plants. In contrast, **trace fossils** provide evidence of the activities of ancient organisms. A fossilized footprint is one example of a trace fossil. A dinosaur made the fossil footprint shown in Figure 2. The mud or sand that the animal stepped in was buried by layers of sediment. Slowly the sediment became solid rock, preserving the footprint for millions of years.

▲ **Petrified Fossils**
These petrified tree trunks in Arizona were formed 200 million years ago, yet look as if they were just cut down.

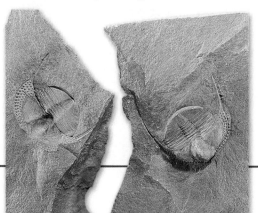

Molds and Casts
The fossil mold (left) clearly shows the shape of the animal called *Cryptolithus*. So does the fossil cast (right). *Cryptolithus* lived in the oceans about 450 million years ago. ▼

▲ **Carbon Films**
This carbon film fossil of insects is between 5 million and 23 million years old.

Fossil footprints provide clues about an animal's size and behavior. Did the animal walk on two or four legs? Did it live alone or with others of its kind? A scientist can infer the answers to such questions by looking at fossil footprints.

Other examples of trace fossils include the trails that animals followed or the burrows that they lived in. A trail or burrow can give clues about the size and shape of the organism, where it lived, and how it obtained food.

Preserved Remains Some processes preserve the remains of organisms with little or no change. For example, some remains are preserved when organisms become trapped in tar. Tar is sticky oil that seeps from Earth's surface. Many fossils preserved in tar have been found at the Rancho La Brea tar pits in Los Angeles, California. Thousands of years ago, animals came to drink the water that covered these pits. Somehow, they became stuck in the tar and then died. The tar soaked into their bones, preserving the bones from decay.

Ancient organisms also have been preserved in amber. Amber is the hardened resin, or sap, of evergreen trees. First, an insect is trapped on sticky resin. After the insect dies, more resin covers it, sealing it from air and protecting its body from decay.

Freezing is another way in which remains can be preserved. The frozen remains of woolly mammoths, huge ancient relatives of elephants, have been found in very cold regions of Siberia and Alaska. Freezing has preserved even the mammoths' hair and skin.

Reading Checkpoint What are three ways in which the remains of an organism can be preserved with little change?

▲ **Dinosaur Footprint**

◄ **Trace Fossils**
These students are measuring a dinosaur footprint in Zilker Park in Austin, Texas.

Amber
A fossil preserved in amber provides a window into the history of past life on Earth. Body parts, including the hairlike bristles on an insect's legs, its antennae, and its delicate wings, are often perfectly preserved. ▼

FIGURE 3

Fossil Clues to Past Environments

Fossils of many different kinds of organisms were formed in this ancient lakeshore environment. *Inferring How do you think the fossil of the bat was preserved?*

Change Over Time

Scientists who study fossils are called **paleontologists** (pay lee un TAHL uh jists). Paleontologists collect fossils from sedimentary rocks all over the world. They use this information to determine what past life forms were like. They want to learn what these organisms ate, what ate them, and in what kind of environment they lived.

Paleontologists also classify organisms. They group similar organisms together. They arrange organisms in the order in which they lived, from earliest to latest. Together, all the information that paleontologists have gathered about past life is called the fossil record. **The fossil record provides evidence about the history of life and past environments on Earth. The fossil record also shows that different groups of organisms have changed over time.**

Icaronycteris (bat)

Cattails

Crocodilian

Bat

Sunfish

Gar

Gar fossil

Herring

Sequoia

Frigate birds

Sycamore leaves

Sycamores

Uintatherium

Hyracotherium

Coryphodon

Phenacodus

Palms

Fossils and Past Environments Paleontologists use fossils to build up a picture of Earth's past environments. The fossils found in an area tell whether the area was a shallow bay, an ocean bottom, or a freshwater swamp.

Fossils also provide evidence about the past climate of a region. For example, coal has been found in Antarctica. But coal only forms from the remains of plants that grow in warm, swampy regions. As you probably know, thick layers of ice and snow now cover Antarctica. The presence of coal shows that the climate of Antarctica was once much warmer than it is today.

Scientists can use fossils to learn about changes in Earth's surface. For example, the fossils in Figure 3 are about 50 million years old. They were found in a region of dry plains and plateaus in the state of Wyoming. From these fossils, scientists have inferred that back then the region had many shallow lakes and swamps. Lush forests with many different kinds of plants and animals flourished in a warm, subtropical climate.

DISCOVERY
CHANNEL
SCHOOL

A Trip Through Geologic Time

Video Preview
▶ Video Field Trip
Video Assessment

FIGURE 4
Ancestry of the Elephant
From fossils, scientists have reconstructed the paleomastodon (left). This animal had a short trunk and short tusks on both upper and lower jaws. The paleomastodon is an ancestor of the modern elephant (right).
Inferring *Why is the paleomastodon only known from its fossils?*

Change and the Fossil Record The fossil record reveals a surprising fact: Fossils occur in a particular order. Older rocks contain fossils of simpler organisms. Younger rocks contain fossils of more complex organisms. In other words, the fossil record shows that life on Earth has evolved, or changed over time. Simple, one-celled organisms have given rise to complex plants and animals.

The fossil record provides evidence to support the theory of evolution. A **scientific theory** is a well-tested concept that explains a wide range of observations. **Evolution** is the gradual change in living things over long periods of time.

The fossil record shows that millions of types of organisms have evolved. But many others have become extinct. A type of organism is **extinct** if it no longer exists and will never again live on Earth.

Reading Checkpoint What is a scientific theory?

Section 1 Assessment

Target Reading Skill **Using Prior Knowledge** Review your graphic organizer and revise it based on what you just learned in the section.

Reviewing Key Concepts

1. a. Defining What is a fossil?
  b. Summarizing In general, how does a fossil form?
  c. Relating Cause and Effect Which parts of an organism are most likely to be preserved as fossils? Why?

2. a. Listing What are the five different kinds of fossils?
  b. Explaining How does a carbon film fossil form?
  c. Comparing and Contrasting How are petrified fossils similar to preserved remains? How are they different?

3. a. Reviewing What are two things that scientists can learn from the fossil record?
  b. Making Generalizations What does the fossil record show about how life has changed over time?

Lab zone **At-Home Activity**

Family Fossils A fossil is something old that has been preserved. With your parents' permission, look around your house for the oldest object you can find. Interview family members to determine how old the object is, why it has been preserved, and how it may have changed since it was new. Make a drawing of the object and bring it to class. Tell your class the story of this "fossil."

The Relative Age of Rocks

Reading Preview

Key Concepts
- What is the law of superposition?
- How do geologists determine the relative age of rocks?
- How are index fossils useful to geologists?

Key Terms
- relative age • absolute age
- law of superposition
- extrusion • intrusion • fault
- unconformity • index fossil

Target Reading Skill

Asking Questions Before you read, preview the red headings. In a graphic organizer like the one below, ask a *what* or *how* question for each heading. As you read, write answers to your questions.

Relative Age

Question	Answer
What does the position of rock layers reveal?	The position of rock layers shows . . .

Lab zone Discover **Activity**

Which Layer Is the Oldest?

1. Make a stack of different-colored layers of clay. Each layer should be about the size and thickness of a pancake. If these flat layers are sediments, which layer of sediment was deposited first? (*Hint:* This is the oldest layer.)

2. Now form the stack into a dome by pressing it over a small rounded object, such as a small bowl. With a cheese-slicer or plastic knife, carefully cut off the top of the dome. Look at the layers that you have exposed. Which layer is the oldest?

Think It Over
Inferring If you press the stack into a small bowl and trim away the clay that sticks above the edge, where will you find the oldest layer?

As sedimentary rock forms, the remains of organisms in the sediment may become fossils. Millions of years later, if you split open the rock, you might see the petrified bones of an extinct reptile or insect.

Your first question about a new fossil might be, "What is it?" Your next question would probably be, "How old is it?" Geologists have two ways to express the age of a rock and any fossil it contains. The **relative age** of a rock is its age compared to the ages of other rocks. You have probably used the idea of relative age when comparing your age with someone else's age. For example, if you say that you are older than your brother but younger than your sister, you are describing your relative age.

The relative age of a rock does not provide its absolute age. The **absolute age** of a rock is the number of years since the rock formed. It may be impossible to know a rock's absolute age exactly. But sometimes geologists can determine a rock's absolute age to within a certain number of years.

◀ The age of each family member could be given as relative age or absolute age.

The Position of Rock Layers

Have you ever seen rock layers of different colors on a cliff beside a road? What are these layers, and how did they form? The sediment that forms sedimentary rocks is deposited in flat layers one on top of the other. Over time, the sediment hardens and changes into sedimentary rock. These rock layers provide a record of Earth's geologic history.

It can be difficult to determine the absolute age of a rock. So geologists use a method to find a rock's relative age. Geologists use the **law of superposition** to determine the relative ages of sedimentary rock layers. **According to the law of superposition, in horizontal sedimentary rock layers the oldest layer is at the bottom. Each higher layer is younger than the layers below it.**

The walls of the Grand Canyon in Arizona illustrate the law of superposition. You can see some of the rock layers found in the Grand Canyon in Figure 5. The deeper down you go in the Grand Canyon, the older the rocks.

Reading Checkpoint **Why do sedimentary rocks have layers?**

FIGURE 5
The Grand Canyon
More than a dozen rock layers make up the walls of the Grand Canyon. You can see five layers clearly in the photograph. **Applying Concepts** *In which labeled layers would you find the oldest fossils? Explain.*

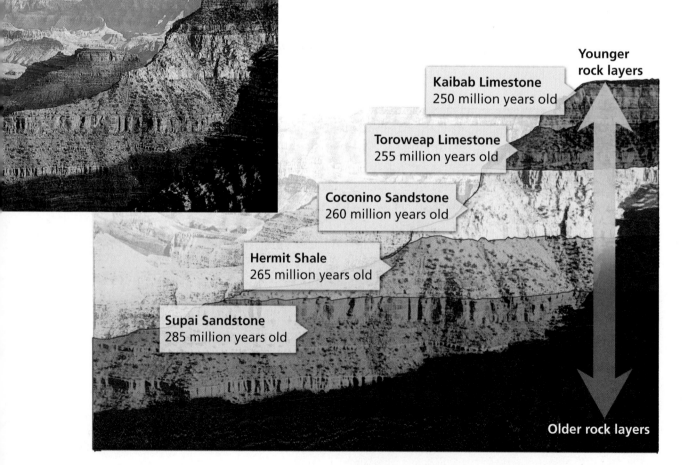

Younger rock layers

Kaibab Limestone
250 million years old

Toroweap Limestone
255 million years old

Coconino Sandstone
260 million years old

Hermit Shale
265 million years old

Supai Sandstone
285 million years old

Older rock layers

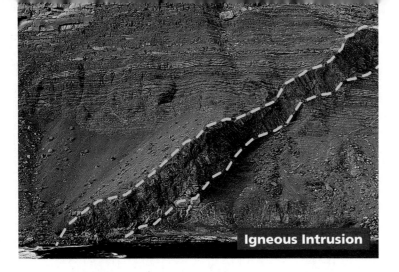

Igneous Intrusion

Fault

FIGURE 6
Intrusions and Faults
Intrusions and faults give clues to the relative ages of rocks. An intrusion (left) cuts through rock layers. Rock layers are broken and shifted along a fault (right).

Determining Relative Age

There are other clues besides the position of rock layers to the relative ages of rocks. **To determine relative age, geologists also study extrusions and intrusions of igneous rock, faults, and gaps in the geologic record.**

Clues From Igneous Rock Igneous rock forms when magma or lava hardens. Magma is molten material beneath Earth's surface. Magma that flows onto the surface is called lava.

Lava that hardens on the surface is called an **extrusion.** An extrusion is always younger than the extrusion below it.

Beneath the surface, magma may push into bodies of rock. There, the magma cools and hardens into a mass of igneous rock called an **intrusion.** An intrusion is always younger than the rock layers around and beneath it. Figure 6 shows an intrusion. Geologists study where intrusions and extrusions formed in relation to other rock layers. This helps geologists understand the relative ages of the different types of rock.

Clues From Faults More clues come from the study of faults. A **fault** is a break in Earth's crust. Forces inside Earth cause movement of the rock on opposite sides of a fault.

A fault is always younger than the rock it cuts through. To determine the relative age of a fault, geologists find the relative age of the most recent rock layer through which the fault slices.

Movements along faults can make it harder for geologists to determine the relative ages of rock layers. You can see in Figure 6 how the rock layers no longer line up because of movement along the fault.

Lab zone Try This **Activity**

Sampling a Sandwich
Your teacher will give you a sandwich that represents rock layers in Earth's crust.

1. Use a round, hollow, uncooked noodle as a coring tool. Push the noodle through the layers of the sandwich.

2. Pull the noodle out of the sandwich. Break the noodle gently to remove your core sample.

3. Draw a picture of what you see in each layer of the core.

Making Models Which layer of your sandwich is the "oldest"? The "youngest"? Why do you think scientists study core samples?

1 Sedimentary rocks form in horizontal layers.

2 Folding tilts the rock layers.

3 The surface is eroded.

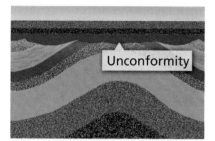

Unconformity

4 New sediment is deposited, forming rock layers above the unconformity.

FIGURE 7
Unconformity
An unconformity occurs where erosion wears away layers of sedimentary rock. Other rock layers then form on top.
Sequencing *What two processes must take place before an unconformity can form?*

Gaps in the Geologic Record The geologic record of sedimentary rock layers is not always complete. Deposition slowly builds layer upon layer of sedimentary rock. But some of these layers may erode away, exposing an older rock surface. Then deposition begins again, building new rock layers.

The surface where new rock layers meet a much older rock surface beneath them is called an **unconformity**. An unconformity is a gap in the geologic record. An unconformity shows where some rock layers have been lost because of erosion. Figure 7 shows how an unconformity forms.

✔ **Reading Checkpoint**   **What is an unconformity?**

Using Fossils to Date Rocks

To date rock layers, geologists first give a relative age to a layer of rock at one location. Then they can give the same age to matching layers of rock at other locations.

Certain fossils, called index fossils, help geologists match rock layers. To be useful as an **index fossil,** a fossil must be widely distributed and represent a type of organism that existed only briefly. A fossil is considered widely distributed if it occurs in many different areas. Geologists look for index fossils in layers of rock. **Index fossils are useful because they tell the relative ages of the rock layers in which they occur.**

Geologists use particular types of organisms as index fossils—for example, certain types of ammonites. Ammonites (AM uh nyts) were a group of hard-shelled animals. Ammonites evolved in shallow seas more than 500 million years ago and became extinct about 65 million years ago.

Ammonite fossils make good index fossils for two reasons. First, they are widely distributed. Second, many different types of ammonites evolved and then become extinct after a few million years.

Geologists can identify the different types of ammonites through differences in the structure of their shells. Based on these differences, geologists can identify the rock layers in which a particular type of ammonite fossil occurs.

You can use index fossils to match rock layers. Look at Figure 8, which shows rock layers from four different locations. Notice that two of the fossils are found in only one of these rock layers. These are the index fossils.

✔ **Reading Checkpoint**   **What characteristics must a fossil have to be useful as an index fossil?**

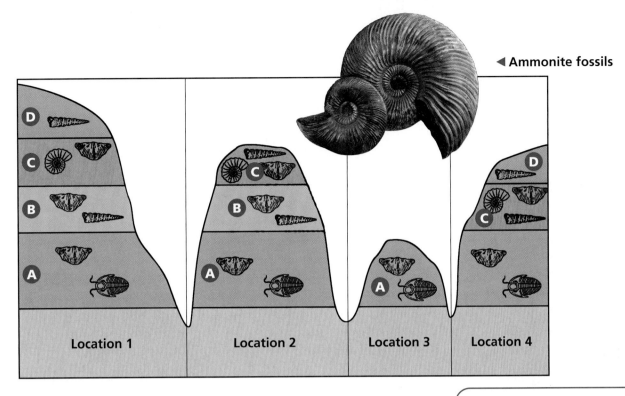

◀ Ammonite fossils

FIGURE 8
Using Index Fossils
Scientists use index fossils to match up rock layers at locations that may be far apart. The ammonites in layer C are index fossils. *Interpreting Diagrams Can you find another index fossil in the diagram? (Hint: Look for a fossil that occurs in only one time period, but in several different locations.)*

Location 1 Location 2 Location 3 Location 4

Go Online
active art

For: Index Fossil activities
Visit: PHSchool.com
Web Code: cfp-2042

Section 2 Assessment

🔵 **Target Reading Skill** **Asking Questions** Use the answers to the questions you wrote about the headings to help you answer the questions below.

Reviewing Key Concepts

1. a. **Defining** In your own words, define the terms *relative age* and *absolute age*.
   b. **Explaining** What is the law of superposition?
   c. **Inferring** A geologist finds a cliff where the edges of several different rock layers can be seen. Which layer is the oldest? Explain.

2. a. **Reviewing** Besides the law of superposition, what are three types of clues to the relative age of rock layers?
   b. **Comparing and Contrasting** Compare and contrast extrusions and intrusions.
   c. **Sequencing** An intrusion crosses an extrusion. Which layer is the older? Explain.

3. a. **Defining** What is an index fossil?

   b. **Applying Concepts** The fossil record shows that horseshoe crabs have existed with very little change for about 200 million years. Would horseshoe crabs be useful as an index fossil? Explain why or why not.

Lab zone **At-Home Activity**

Drawer to the Past Collect ten items out of a drawer full of odds and ends such as keys, coins, receipts, photographs, and souvenirs. Have your family members put them in order from oldest to newest. What clues will you use to determine their relative ages? How can you determine the oldest object of all? List the ten items in order of their relative age. Do you know the absolute age of any of the items?

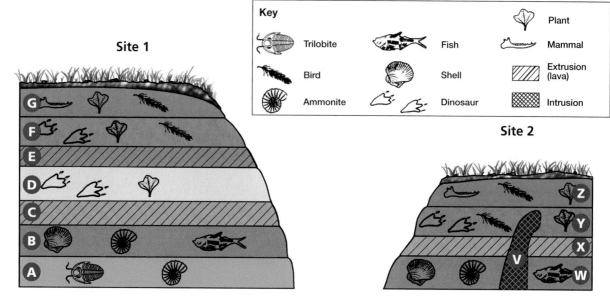

Site 1

Key

Trilobite	Fish	Plant
Bird	Shell	Extrusion (lava)
Ammonite	Dinosaur	Intrusion

Site 2

Finding Clues to Rock Layers

Problem

How can you use fossils and geologic features to interpret the relative ages of rock layers?

Skills Focus

interpreting data, drawing conclusions

Procedure

1. Study the rock layers at Sites 1 and 2. Write down the similarities and differences between the layers at the two sites.

2. List the kinds of fossils that are found in each rock layer of Sites 1 and 2.

Analyze and Conclude

Site 1

1. **Interpreting Data** What "fossil clues" in layers A and B indicate the kind of environment that existed when these rock layers were formed? How did the environment change in layer D?

2. **Drawing Conclusions** Which layer is the oldest? How do you know?

3. **Drawing Conclusions** Which of the layers formed most recently? How do you know?

4. **Inferring** Why are there no fossils in layers C and E?

5. **Observing** What kind of fossils are found in layer F?

Site 2

6. **Inferring** Which layer at Site 1 might have formed at the same time as layer W at Site 2?

7. **Relating Cause and Effect** What clues show an unconformity or gap in the horizontal rock layers? Which rock layers are missing? What might have happened to these rock layers?

8. **Interpreting Data** Which is older, intrusion V or layer Y? How do you know?

9. **Communicating** Write a journal entry describing how the environment at Site 2 changed over time. Starting with the earliest layer, describe the types of organisms, their environment, and how the environment changed.

More to Explore

Draw a sketch similar to Site 2 and include a fault that cuts across the intrusion. Have a partner then identify the relative age of the fault, the intrusion, and the layers cut by the fault.

Radioactive Dating

Reading Preview

Key Concepts
- What happens during radioactive decay?
- What can be learned from radioactive dating?

Key Terms
- atom • element
- radioactive decay • half-life

🎯 Target Reading Skill

Identifying Main Ideas As you read the Determining Absolute Ages section, write the main idea in a graphic organizer like the one below. Then write three supporting details that give examples of the main idea.

Main Idea

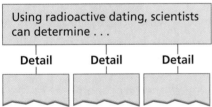

Using radioactive dating, scientists can determine . . .

Detail	Detail	Detail

Lab zone • Discover **Activity**

How Long Till It's Gone?

1. Make a small cube—about 5 cm × 5 cm × 5 cm —from modeling clay.
2. Carefully use a knife to cut the clay in half. Put one half of the clay aside.
3. Cut the clay in half two more times. Each time you cut the clay, put one half of it aside.

Think It Over
Predicting How big will the remaining piece of clay be if you repeat the process several more times?

In Australia, scientists have found sedimentary rocks that contain some of the world's oldest fossils. These are fossils of stromatolites (stroh MAT uh lyts). Stromatolites are the remains of reefs built by organisms similar to present-day bacteria. Sediment eventually covered these reefs. As the sediment changed to rock, so did the reefs. Using absolute dating, scientists have determined that some stromatolites are more than 3 billion years old. To understand absolute dating, you need to learn more about the chemistry of rocks.

FIGURE 9
Stromatolites
Scientists think that these ancient stromatolites in Australia (right) were formed by organisms similar to blue-green bacteria (above).

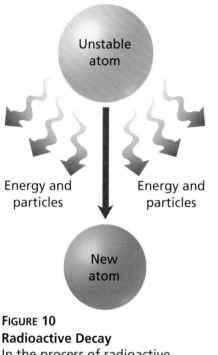

FIGURE 10
Radioactive Decay
In the process of radioactive decay, an atom releases energy and particles as it changes to a new kind of atom.

Radioactive Decay

Rocks are a form of matter. All the matter you see, including rocks, is made of tiny particles called **atoms.** When all the atoms in a particular type of matter are the same, the matter is an **element.** Carbon, oxygen, iron, lead, and potassium are just some of the more than 110 currently known elements.

Most elements are stable. They do not change under normal conditions. But some elements exist in forms that are unstable. Over time, these elements break down, or decay, by releasing particles and energy in a process called **radioactive decay.** These unstable elements are said to be radioactive. **During radioactive decay, the atoms of one element break down to form atoms of another element.**

Radioactive elements occur naturally in igneous rocks. Scientists use the rate at which these elements decay to calculate the rock's age. You calculate your age based on a specific day—your birthday. What's the "birthday" of a rock? For an igneous rock, that "birthday" is when it first hardens to become rock. As a radioactive element within the igneous rock decays, it changes into another element. So the composition of the rock changes slowly over time. The amount of the radioactive element goes down. But the amount of the new element goes up.

The rate of decay of each radioactive element is constant—it never changes. This rate of decay is the element's half-life. The **half-life** of a radioactive element is the time it takes for half of the radioactive atoms to decay. You can see in Figure 11 how a radioactive element decays over time.

✓ **Reading Checkpoint**   **What is the meaning of the term "half-life"?**

FIGURE 11
The half-life of a radioactive element is the amount of time it takes for half of the radioactive atoms to decay.
Calculating *After three half-lives, how much of the radioactive element remains?*

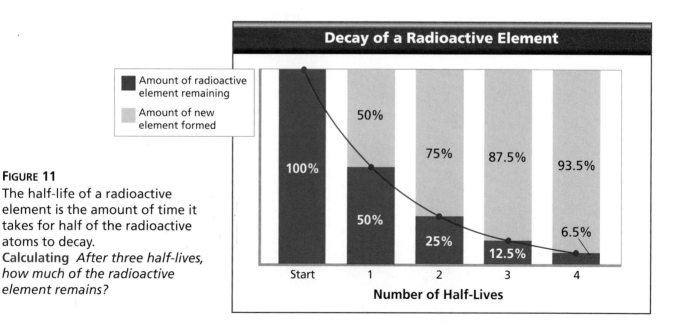

Decay of a Radioactive Element

- Amount of radioactive element remaining
- Amount of new element formed

50%
75%
87.5%
93.5%

100%
50%
25%
12.5%
6.5%

Start   1   2   3   4
Number of Half-Lives

Elements Used in Radioactive Dating		
Radioactive Element	Half-life (years)	Dating Range (years)
Carbon-14	5,730	500–50,000
Potassium-40	1.3 billion	50,000–4.6 billion
Rubidium-87	47 billion	10 million–4.6 billion
Thorium-232	14.1 billion	10 million–4.6 billion
Uranium-235	713 million	10 million–4.6 billion
Uranium-238	4.5 billion	10 million–4.6 billion

FIGURE 12
The half-lives of different radioactive elements vary greatly.

Determining Absolute Ages

Geologists use radioactive dating to determine the absolute ages of rocks. In radioactive dating, scientists first determine the amount of a radioactive element in a rock. Then they compare that amount with the amount of the stable element into which the radioactive element decays. Figure 12 lists several common radioactive elements and their half-lives.

Potassium–Argon Dating Scientists often date rocks using potassium-40. This form of potassium decays to stable argon-40 and has a half-life of 1.3 billion years. Potassium-40 is useful in dating the most ancient rocks because of its long half-life.

Carbon-14 Dating A radioactive form of carbon is carbon-14. All plants and animals contain carbon, including some carbon-14. As plants and animals grow, carbon atoms are added to their tissues. After an organism dies, no more carbon is added. But the carbon-14 in the organism's body decays. It changes to stable nitrogen-14. To determine the age of a sample, scientists measure the amount of carbon-14 that is left in the organism's remains. From this amount, they can determine its absolute age. Carbon-14 has been used to date fossils such as frozen mammoths, as well as pieces of wood and bone. Carbon-14 even has been used to date the skeletons of prehistoric humans.

Carbon-14 is very useful in dating materials from plants and animals that lived up to about 50,000 years ago. Carbon-14 has a half-life of only 5,730 years. For this reason, it can't be used to date very ancient fossils or rocks. The amount of carbon-14 left would be too small to measure accurately.

Math Skills

Percentage What percentage of a radioactive element will be left after 3 half-lives? First, multiply $\frac{1}{2}$ three times to determine what fraction of the element will remain.

$$\frac{1}{2} \times \frac{1}{2} \times \frac{1}{2} = \frac{1}{8}$$

You can convert this fraction to a percentage by setting up a proportion:

$$\frac{1}{8} = \frac{d\%}{100\%}$$

To find the value of d, begin by cross multiplying, as for any proportion:

$1 \times 100 = 8 \times d$

$d = \frac{100}{8}$

$d = 12.5\%$

Practice Problems What percentage of a radioactive element will remain after 5 half-lives?

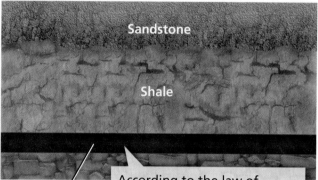
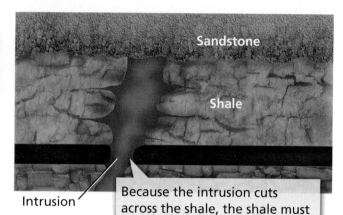

Sandstone

Shale

Extrusion

According to the law of superposition, the extrusion is older than the shale above it.

Sandstone

Shale

Intrusion

Because the intrusion cuts across the shale, the shale must be older than the intrusion.

FIGURE 13
Inferring the Age of Rocks
A layer of shale forms above an extrusion (left). Later (right), an intrusion crosses the shale. **Inferring** *What can you infer about the age of the shale?*

Go Online
PHSchool.com

For: More on radioactive dating
Visit: www.SciLinks.org
Web Code: cfd-2043

Radioactive Dating of Rock Layers Radioactive dating works well for igneous rocks, but not for sedimentary rocks. The rock particles in sedimentary rocks are from other rocks, all of different ages. Radioactive dating would provide the age of the particles. It would not provide the age of the sedimentary rock.

How, then, do scientists date sedimentary rock layers? They date the igneous intrusions and extrusions near the sedimentary rock layers. Look at Figure 13. As you can see, sedimentary rock above an igneous intrusion must be younger than that intrusion.

Reading Checkpoint **What are two types of radioactive dating?**

Section 3 Assessment

Target Reading Skill **Identifying Main Ideas** Use your graphic organizer to help you answer Question 2 below.

Reviewing Key Concepts

1. a. **Defining** In your own words, define the term *radioactive decay.*
   b. **Describing** How does the composition of a rock containing a radioactive element change over time?
   c. **Applying Concepts** How is a radioactive element's rate of decay like the ticking of a clock? Explain.

2. a. **Identifying** What method do geologists use to determine the absolute age of a rock?
   b. **Explaining** Why is it difficult to determine the absolute age of a sedimentary rock?

c. **Problem Solving** A geologist finds a fossil in a layer of sedimentary rock that lies in between two igneous extrusions. How could the geologist determine the age of the fossil?

Math **Practice**

3. **Percentage** What percentage of a radioactive element will remain after 7 half-lives?

The Geologic Time Scale

Reading Preview

Key Concepts
- Why is the geologic time scale used to show Earth's history?
- What are the different units of the geologic time scale?

Key Terms
- geologic time scale
- era
- period

Target Reading Skill

Sequencing As you read, make a flowchart like the one below that shows the eras and periods of geologic time. Write the name of each era and period in the flowchart in the order in which it occurs.

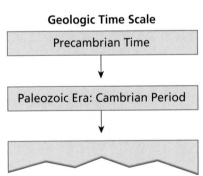

Geologic Time Scale

Precambrian Time

↓

Paleozoic Era: Cambrian Period

↓

Discover **Activity**

This Is Your Life!
1. Make a list of about 10 to 15 important events that you remember in your life.
2. On a sheet of paper, draw a timeline to represent your life. Use a scale of 3.0 cm to 1 year.
3. Write each event in the correct year along the timeline.
4. Now divide the timeline into parts that describe major periods in your life, such as preschool years, elementary school years, and middle school years.

Think It Over
Making Models Along which part of your timeline are most of the events located? Which period of your life does this part of the timeline represent? Why do you think this is so?

Imagine squeezing Earth's 4.6-billion-year history into a 24-hour day. Earth forms at midnight. About seven hours later, the earliest one-celled organisms appear. Over the next 14 hours, simple, soft-bodied organisms such as jellyfish and worms develop. A little after 9:00 P.M.—21 hours later—larger, more complex organisms evolve in the oceans. Reptiles and insects first appear about an hour after that. Dinosaurs arrive just before 11:00 P.M., but are extinct by 11:30 P.M. Modern humans don't appear until less than a second before midnight!

The Geologic Time Scale

Months, years, or even centuries aren't very helpful for thinking about Earth's long history. **Because the time span of Earth's past is so great, geologists use the geologic time scale to show Earth's history.** The **geologic time scale** is a record of the life forms and geologic events in Earth's history. You can see this time scale in Figure 14.

Scientists first developed the geologic time scale by studying rock layers and index fossils worldwide. With this information, scientists placed Earth's rocks in order by relative age. Later, radioactive dating helped determine the absolute age of the divisions in the geologic time scale.

FIGURE 14
The Geologic Time Scale

The eras and periods of the geologic time scale are used to date the events in Earth's long history.
Interpreting Diagrams *How long ago did the Paleozoic Era end?*

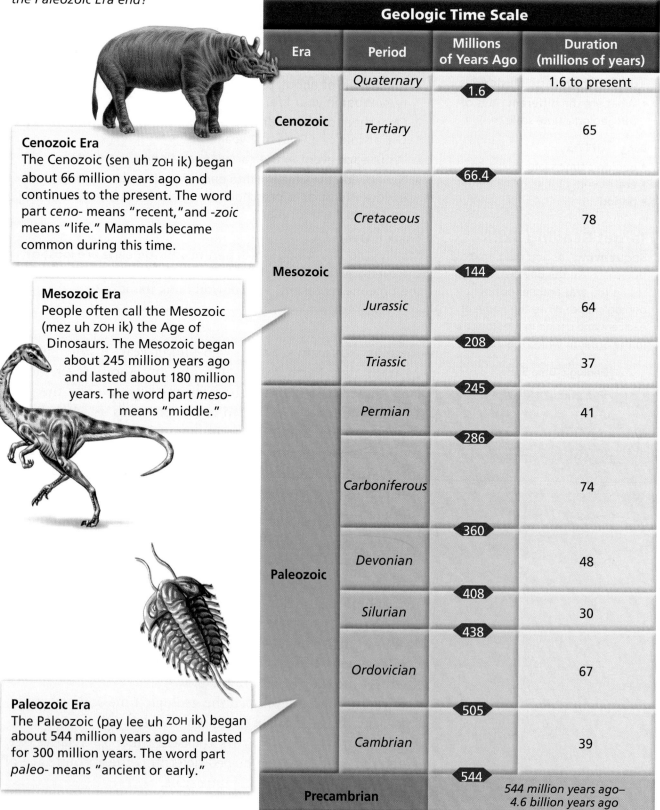

Geologic Time Scale			
Era	**Period**	**Millions of Years Ago**	**Duration (millions of years)**
Cenozoic	Quaternary	1.6	1.6 to present
	Tertiary		65
		66.4	
Mesozoic	Cretaceous		78
		144	
	Jurassic		64
		208	
	Triassic		37
		245	
Paleozoic	Permian		41
		286	
	Carboniferous		74
		360	
	Devonian		48
		408	
	Silurian		30
		438	
	Ordovician		67
		505	
	Cambrian		39
		544	
Precambrian			544 million years ago– 4.6 billion years ago

Cenozoic Era
The Cenozoic (sen uh ZOH ik) began about 66 million years ago and continues to the present. The word part *ceno-* means "recent," and *-zoic* means "life." Mammals became common during this time.

Mesozoic Era
People often call the Mesozoic (mez uh ZOH ik) the Age of Dinosaurs. The Mesozoic began about 245 million years ago and lasted about 180 million years. The word part *meso-* means "middle."

Paleozoic Era
The Paleozoic (pay lee uh ZOH ik) began about 544 million years ago and lasted for 300 million years. The word part *paleo-* means "ancient or early."

Divisions of Geologic Time

As geologists studied the fossil record, they found major changes in life forms at certain times. They used these changes to mark where one unit of geologic time ends and the next begins. Therefore the divisions of the geologic time scale depend on events in the history of life on Earth.

When speaking of the past, what names do you use for different spans of time? You probably use names such as century, decade, year, month, week, and day. Scientists use similar divisions for the geologic time scale.

Geologic time begins with a long span of time called Precambrian Time (pree KAM bree un). Precambrian Time, which covers about 88 percent of Earth's history, ended 544 million years ago. **After Precambrian Time, the basic units of the geologic time scale are eras and periods.** Geologists divide the time between Precambrian Time and the present into three long units of time called **eras.** They are the Paleozoic Era, the Mesozoic Era, and the Cenozoic Era.

Eras are subdivided into units of geologic time called **periods.** You can see in Figure 14 that the Mesozoic Era includes three periods: the Triassic Period, the Jurassic Period, and the Cretaceous Period.

The names of many of the geologic periods come from places around the world where geologists first described the rocks and fossils of that period. For example, the name Cambrian refers to Cambria, the old Roman name for Wales.

Reading Checkpoint To what era does the Jurassic Period belong?

FIGURE 15
Fossil of the Quaternary Period
This saber-toothed cat lived during the Quaternary Period.

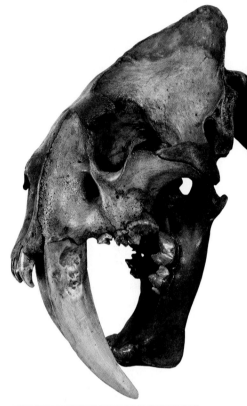

Go Online
PHSchool.com

For: More on the geologic time scale
Visit: PHSchool.com
Web Code: cfd-2044

Section 4 Assessment

Target Reading Skill Sequencing Refer to your flowchart about the geologic time scale as you answer Question 2.

Reviewing Key Concepts

1. a. **Defining** What is the geologic time scale?
   b. **Explaining** What information did geologists use in developing the geologic time scale?
2. a. **Listing** What are the basic units into which the geologic time scale is divided?
   b. **Interpreting Diagrams** Study Figure 14. Which major division of geologic time was the longest? When did it begin? When did it end?

c. **Sequencing** Place the following in the correct order from earliest to latest: Tertiary, Jurassic, Quaternary, Triassic, Cretaceous.

Writing in Science

An Address in Time Pick one of the periods in the geologic time scale. Write a paragraph that describes, as completely as you can, that period's place in geologic time relative to the other periods and eras.

Early Earth

Reading Preview

Key Concepts
- When did Earth form?
- How did Earth's physical features develop during Precambrian Time?
- What were early Precambrian organisms like?

Key Terms
- comet • continental drift

Target Reading Skill
Comparing and Contrasting As you read, compare and contrast early Earth with Earth later in Precambrian Time by completing a table like the one below.

Precambrian Earth

Feature	Early Earth	Later Precambrian Earth
Atmosphere		
Oceans		
Continents		

Discover **Activity**

How Could Planet Earth Form in Space?

1. Place a sheet of paper on top of a small magnet. The paper represents outer space and the magnet models gravity.
2. Sprinkle a half teaspoon of iron filings along one end of the paper to model the materials that formed Earth.
3. Gently blow through a straw for about 10 seconds from the end of the paper with the iron filings toward the magnet. **CAUTION:** *Be sure the straw is pointed away from other students.*
4. Observe what happens to the iron filings.

Think It Over
Making Models If you repeated Steps 2 and 3, what would happen to the size of your "planet"? How is this model like the early Earth? How is it different?

Your science class is going on a field trip, but this trip is a little out of the ordinary. You're going to travel back billions of years to the earliest days on Earth. Then you will move forward through time to the present. Enter the time machine and strap yourself in. Take a deep breath—you're off!

A dial on the dashboard shows the number of years before the present. You stare at the dial—it reads 4.6 billion years. You peer out the window as the time machine flies above the planet. Earth looks a little strange. Where are the oceans? Where are the continents? How will Earth change over the next billions of years? You'll answer these and other questions about Earth's history as you take this extraordinary trip.

The Planet Forms

Your journey starts at the beginning of Precambrian Time with the formation of planet Earth. **Scientists hypothesize that Earth formed at the same time as the other planets and the sun, roughly 4.6 billion years ago.**

The Age of Earth How do scientists know the age of Earth? Using radioactive dating, scientists have determined that the oldest rocks ever found on Earth are about 4 billion years old. But scientists think Earth formed even earlier than that.

FIGURE 16
Early Earth
This artist's illustration shows Earth shortly after the moon formed. Notice the rocky objects from space striking Earth, and the molten rock flowing over the surface.

According to this hypothesis, Earth and the moon are about the same age. When Earth was very young, it collided with a large object. The collision threw a large amount of material from both bodies into orbit around Earth. This material combined to form the moon. Scientists have dated moon rocks that were brought to Earth by astronauts during the 1970s. Radioactive dating shows that the oldest moon rocks are about 4.6 billion years old. Scientists infer that Earth is also roughly 4.6 billion years old—only a little older than those moon rocks.

Earth Takes Shape Scientists think that Earth began as a ball of dust, rock, and ice in space. Gravity pulled this mass together. As Earth grew larger, its gravity increased, pulling in dust, rock, and ice nearby. As objects made of these materials struck Earth at high speed, their kinetic energy was changed into thermal energy.

The energy from these collisions caused Earth's temperature to rise until the planet was very hot. Scientists think that Earth may have become so hot that it melted. Denser materials sank toward the center, forming Earth's dense, iron core. At the same time, Earth continuously lost heat to the cold of space. Less dense, molten material hardened to form Earth's outer layers—the solid crust and mantle.

As the growing Earth traveled around the sun, its gravity also captured gases such as hydrogen and helium. However, this first atmosphere was lost when the sun underwent a violent explosion.

✓ **Reading Checkpoint** What force caused the materials that formed Earth to come together?

Go Online
SCi LINKS NSTA

For: Links on Precambrian Earth
Visit: www.SciLinks.org
Web Code: scn-0745

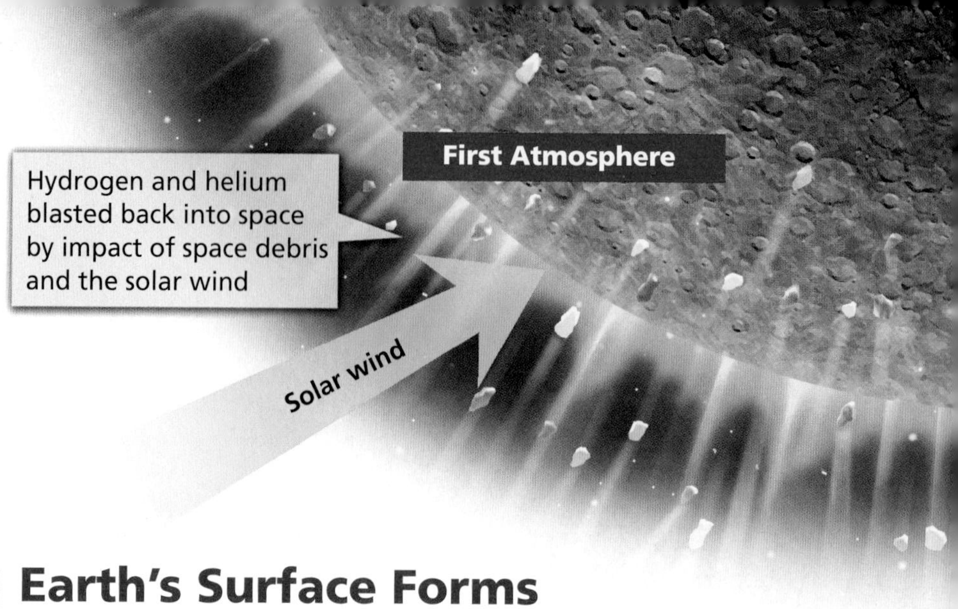

First Atmosphere

Hydrogen and helium blasted back into space by impact of space debris and the solar wind

Solar wind

FIGURE 17

Development of the Atmosphere
Earth soon lost its first atmosphere (left) of hydrogen and helium. Earth's second atmosphere (right) slowly developed the mixture of gases—nitrogen, oxygen, carbon dioxide, water vapor, and argon—of the atmosphere today. As oxygen levels increased, the ozone layer also developed.
Comparing and Contrasting *Compare and contrast Earth's first and second atmospheres.*

Lab zone Skills **Activity**

Calculating

Precambrian Time lasted about 4 billion years. What percentage is this of Earth's entire history of 4.6 billion years? If the first continents formed about 500 million years after Earth itself formed, what percentage of Precambrian Time had elapsed? (*Hint:* To review percentages, see the Math Review section in the Skills Handbook.)

Earth's Surface Forms

Watching early Earth from your time machine, you can see the planet change as the years speed by. **During the first several hundred million years of Precambrian Time, an atmosphere, oceans, and continents began to form.**

The Atmosphere After Earth lost its first atmosphere, a second atmosphere formed. This new atmosphere was made up mostly of carbon dioxide and water vapor. Volcanic eruptions released carbon dioxide, water vapor, and other gases from Earth's interior. Collisions with comets added other gases to the atmosphere. A **comet** is a ball of dust and ice that orbits the sun. The ice in a comet consists of water and frozen gases, including carbon dioxide.

The Oceans At first, Earth's surface was too hot for water to remain as a liquid. All water evaporated into water vapor. However, as Earth's surface cooled, the water vapor began to condense to form rain. Gradually, rainwater began to accumulate to form an ocean. Rain also began to erode Earth's rocky surface. Over time, the oceans affected the composition of the atmosphere by absorbing much of the carbon dioxide.

The Continents During early Precambrian Time, more and more of Earth's rock cooled and hardened. Less than 500 million years after Earth's formation, the less dense rock at the surface formed large landmasses called continents.

Scientists have found that the continents move very slowly over Earth's surface because of forces inside Earth. This process is called **continental drift.** The movement is very slow—only a few centimeters per year. Over billions of years, Earth's landmasses have repeatedly formed, broken apart, and then crashed together again, forming new continents.

Reading Checkpoint What is continental drift?

Second Atmosphere

Carbon dioxide, water vapor, and nitrogen from volcanic eruptions and comet impacts

Oxygen from bacteria in the oceans

Ozone layer gradually forms as amount of oxygen increases

Ozone layer

Ultraviolet light

Life Develops

Scientists cannot pinpoint when or where life began on Earth. **But scientists have found fossils of single-celled organisms in rocks that formed about 3.5 billion years ago. These earliest lifeforms were probably similar to present-day bacteria.** Scientists hypothesize that all other forms of life on Earth arose from these simple organisms.

About 2.5 billion years ago, organisms first began using energy from the sun to make their own food. This process is called photosynthesis. One waste product of photosynthesis is oxygen. As organisms released oxygen into the air, the amount of oxygen in the atmosphere slowly increased. Processes in the atmosphere changed some of this oxygen into a form called ozone. The atmosphere developed a layer rich in ozone that blocked out the deadly ultraviolet rays of the sun. Shielded from the sun's ultraviolet rays, organisms could live on land.

Section 5 Assessment

⟳ **Target Reading Skill** **Comparing and Contrasting** Use the information in your table about early Earth to answer the questions below.

Reviewing Key Concepts

1. a. Reviewing How long ago did Earth form?
   b. Summarizing Summarize the process by which scientists determined the age of Earth.
2. a. Listing What physical features formed during Earth's first several hundred million years?
   b. Explaining How did volcanic eruptions and comets change early Earth?
   c. Relating Cause and Effect What caused water erosion to begin on Earth's surface?

3. a. Identifying What do scientists think were the first organisms to evolve on Earth?
   b. Predicting How would Earth's atmosphere be different if organisms capable of photosynthesis had not evolved? Explain.

Writing in Science

Web Site Plan a Web site for early Earth. To plan your Web site, make a list of the topics you will include. Make sketches of the screens that visitors to the Web site will see. Then write short descriptions for each topic.

Eras of Earth's History

Reading Preview

Key Concepts
- What were the major events in the Paleozoic Era?
- What were the major events in the Mesozoic Era?
- What were the major events in the Cenozoic Era?

Key Terms
- invertebrate • vertebrate
- amphibian • reptile
- mass extinction • mammal

Target Reading Skill
Previewing Visuals Before you read, preview Figure 22. Then write three questions that you have about Earth's history in a graphic organizer like the one below. As you read, answer your questions.

Earth's History

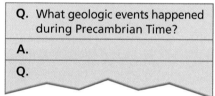

Q.	What geologic events happened during Precambrian Time?
A.	
Q.	

Lab zone Discover **Activity**

What Do Fossils Reveal About Earth's History?

1. Compare the two fossils in photos A and B. How did these organisms become fossils?
2. Work with one or two other students to study the organisms in the two photos. Think about how these organisms may have lived. Then make sketches showing what each of these organisms may have looked like.

Think It Over
Posing Questions If you were a paleontologist, what questions would you want to ask about these organisms?

As your time machine nears the end of Precambrian Time, you notice that Earth's organisms have begun to change. Along with organisms made up of single cells, living things resembling jellyfish now float in Earth's oceans. You also notice the fronds of feathery, plantlike organisms anchored to the seafloor. Scientists have found fossils of such organisms in Australia, Russia, and southern Africa. Fossils like the one in Figure 18 are more than 600 million years old! But a much greater variety of living things evolved during the next phase of geologic time—the Paleozoic Era.

FIGURE 18
Paleontologist at Work
This paleontologist in Australia is uncovering fossil animals from late Precambrian Time.

FIGURE 19
The Cambrian Explosion
During the early Cambrian period, Earth's oceans were home to many strange organisms unlike any animals that are alive today. The fossil above is an organism of the middle Cambrian called *Anomalocaris*.

The Paleozoic Era

Your time machine slows. You observe the "explosion" of life that began the Paleozoic Era.

The Cambrian Explosion During the Cambrian Period life took a big leap forward. **At the beginning of the Paleozoic Era, a great number of different kinds of organisms evolved.** Paleontologists call this event the Cambrian Explosion because so many new life forms appeared within a relatively short time. For the first time, many organisms had hard parts, including shells and outer skeletons.

At this time, all animals lived in the sea. Many were animals without backbones, or **invertebrates.** Invertebrates such as jellyfish, worms, and sponges drifted through the water, crawled along the sandy bottom, or attached themselves to the ocean floors.

Brachiopods and trilobites were common in the Cambrian seas. Brachiopods were small ocean animals with two shells. They resembled modern clams, but are only distantly related.

Vertebrates Arise During the Ordovician (awr duh VISH ee un) and Silurian (sih LOOR ee un) periods, the ancestors of the modern octopus and squid appeared. But these invertebrates soon shared the seas with a new type of organism. **During this time, jawless fishes evolved. Jawless fishes were the first vertebrates.** A **vertebrate** is an animal with a backbone. These fishes had suckerlike mouths, and they soon became common.

FIGURE 20
Devonian Armored Fish
Paleontologists have found fossils of huge armored fish, like this *Dunkleosteus,* that lived during the Devonian Period.

Life Reaches Land Until the Silurian Period, only one-celled organisms lived on the land. But during the Silurian Period, plants began to grow on land. These first, simple plants grew low to the ground in damp areas. By the Devonian Period (dih VOH nee un), plants that could grow in drier areas had evolved. Among these plants were the earliest ferns. The first insects also appeared during the Silurian Period.

Both invertebrates and vertebrates lived in the Devonian seas. Even though the invertebrates were more numerous, the Devonian Period is often called the Age of Fishes. Every main group of fishes was present in the oceans at this time. Most fishes now had jaws, bony skeletons, and scales on their bodies. Some fishes, like the one in Figure 20, were huge. Sharks appeared in the late Devonian Period.

During the Devonian Period, animals began to invade the land. The first vertebrates to crawl onto land were lungfish with strong, muscular fins. The first amphibians evolved from these lung fish. An **amphibian** (am FIB ee un) is an animal that lives part of its life on land and part of its life in water.

FIGURE 21
The Coal Forest
Forests of the Carboniferous Period later formed coal deposits. **Predicting** *What types of fossils would you expect to find from the Carboniferous Period?*

The Carboniferous Period Throughout the rest of the Paleozoic, life expanded over Earth's continents. Other vertebrates evolved from the amphibians. For example, small reptiles developed during the Carboniferous Period. **Reptiles** have scaly skin and lay eggs with tough, leathery shells. Some types of reptiles became very large during the later Paleozoic.

Math Analyzing Data

Mass Extinctions Since the Cambrian Period

Mass Extinctions

The graph shows how the number of families of animals in Earth's oceans has changed.

1. **Reading Graphs** What variable is shown on the *x*-axis? On the *y*-axis of the graph?

2. **Interpreting Data** How long ago did the most recent mass extinction occur?

3. **Interpreting Data** Which mass extinction produced the greatest drop in the number of families of ocean animals?

4. **Relating Cause and Effect** How did the number of families change after each mass extinction?

During the Carboniferous Period, winged insects evolved into many forms, including huge dragonflies and cockroaches. Giant ferns and cone-bearing plants and trees formed vast swampy forests called "coal forests." The remains of the coal forest plants formed thick deposits of sediment that changed into coal over millions of years.

Mass Extinction Ends the Paleozoic At the end of the Paleozoic Era, many kinds of organisms died out. This was a **mass extinction,** in which many types of living things became extinct at the same time. **The mass extinction at the end of the Paleozoic affected both plants and animals, on land and in the seas.** Scientists do not know what caused the mass extinction, but many kinds of organisms, such as trilobites, suddenly became extinct.

The Supercontinent Pangaea Scientists hypothesize that climate change resulting from continental drift may have caused the mass extinction at the end of the Paleozoic. **During the Permian Period, about 260 million years ago, Earth's continents moved together to form a great landmass, or supercontinent, called Pangaea** (pan JEE uh). The formation of Pangaea caused deserts to expand in the tropics. At the same time, sheets of ice covered land closer to the South Pole. Many organisms could not survive the new climate. After Pangaea formed, it broke apart again, as shown in Figure 22.

Reading Checkpoint What was Pangaea?

Go Online
active art

For: Continental Drift activity
Visit: PHSchool.com
Web Code: cfp-1015

Figure 22 Geologic History

Precambrian Time 4.6 billion–544 million years ago	Paleozoic Era 544–245 million years ago		
Period	**Cambrian**	**Ordovician**	**Silurian**
	544–505 million years ago	505–438 million years ago	438–408 million years ago

Geologic Events

- Earth forms about 4.6 billion years ago.
- Oceans form and cover Earth about 4 billion years ago.
- First sedimentary rocks form about 3.5 billion years ago.

- Shallow seas cover much of the land.
- Ancient continents lie near or south of the equator.

- Warm, shallow seas cover much of Earth.
- Ice cap covers what is now North Africa.

- Coral reefs develop.
- Early continents collide with what is now North America, forming mountains.

Development of Life

- Bacteria appear about 3.5 billion years ago.
- Soft-bodied, multi-cellular organisms develop late in the Precambrian.
- First mass extinction probably occurs near the end of the Precambrian.

Sea pen

Early bacteria

Jellyfish-like animal

Clam

- Great "explosion" of invertebrate life occurs in seas.
- Invertebrates with shells appear, including trilobites and mollusks.

Pikaia

Trilobite

Sponges

Cephalopod

- Invertebrates dominate the oceans.
- Early vertebrates—jawless fish—become common.

Crinoid

Jawless fish

Brachiopod

Eurypterid

- Fish with jaws develop.
- Land plants appear.
- Insects and spiders appear.

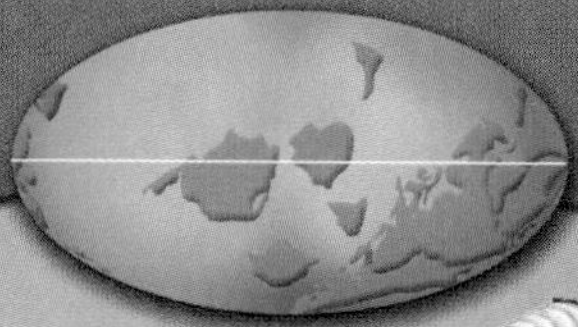

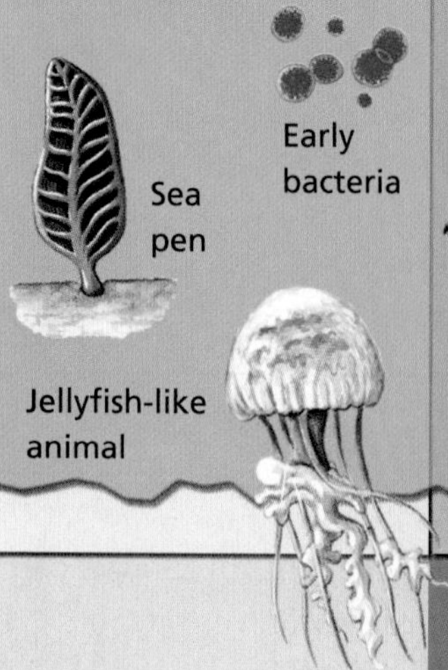

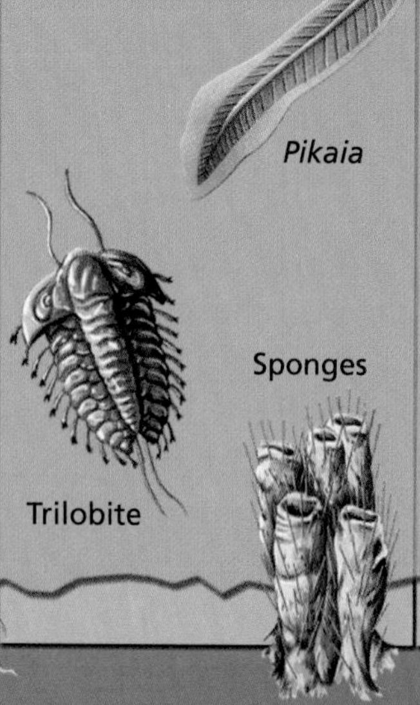

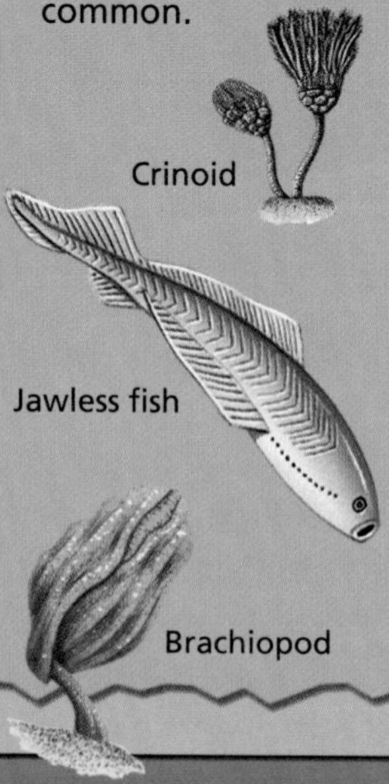

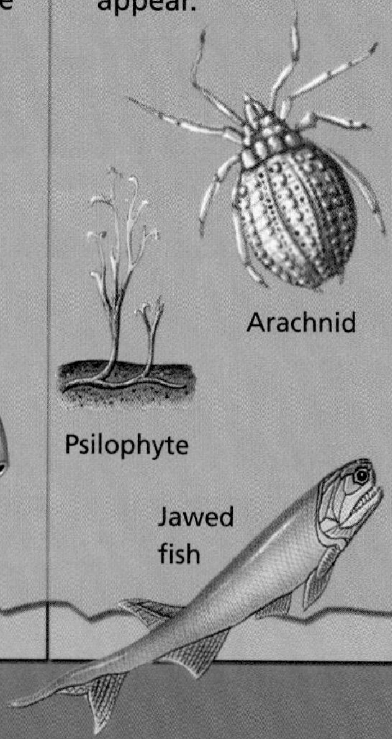

Arachnid

Psilophyte

Jawed fish

Paleozoic Era
544–245 million years ago

Devonian	Carboniferous 360–286 million years ago		Permian
408–360 million years ago	**Mississippian** 360–320 million years ago	**Pennsylvanian** 320–286 million years ago	286–245 million years ago

Geologic Events

Devonian
- Seas rise and fall over what is now North America.

Carboniferous
- Appalachian Mountains begin to form.
- North America and Northern Europe lie in warm, tropical region.

Permian
- Deserts become larger in tropical regions.
- The supercontinent Pangaea forms as all continents join together.

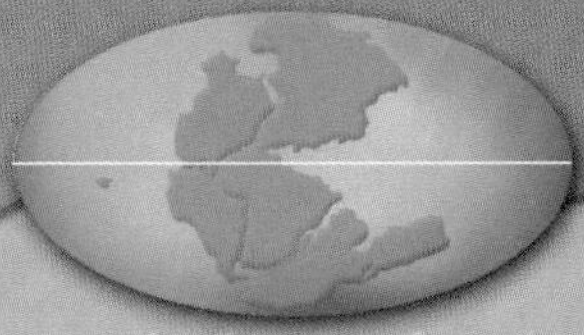

Development of Life

Devonian
- Age of Fishes begins as sharks and fish with scales and bony skeletons become common.
- Trilobites and corals flourish in the oceans.
- Lungfish develop.
- First amphibians reach land.

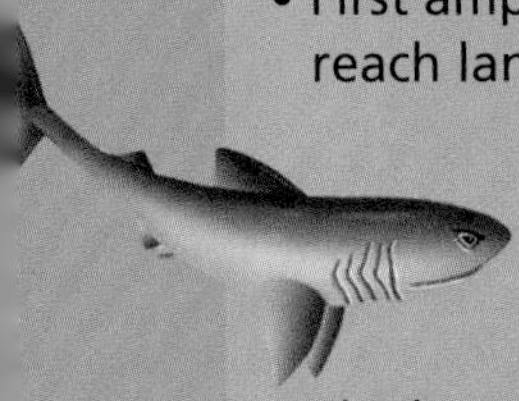

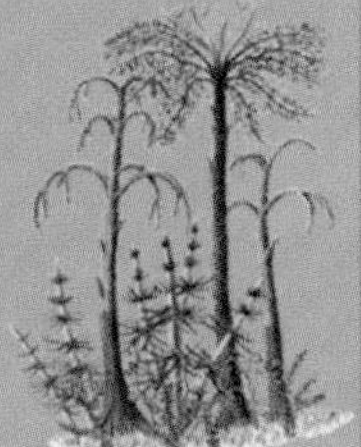

Carboniferous
- Great swamp forests of huge, woody trees cover eastern North America and parts of Europe.
- First true reptiles appear.
- Winged insects appear.

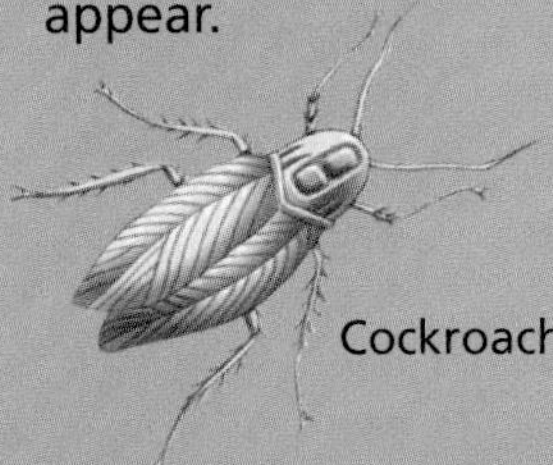

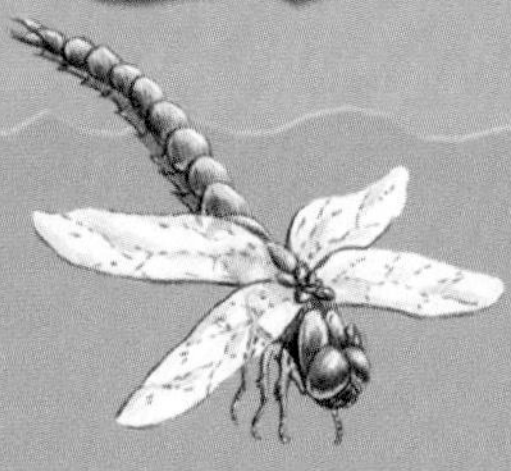

Dragonfly

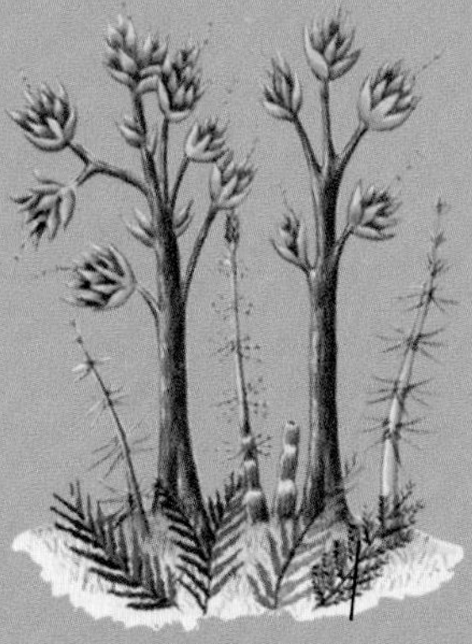

Permian
- Reptiles become dominant on land.
- Warm-blooded reptiles appear.
- Mass extinction of many marine invertebrates, including trilobites.

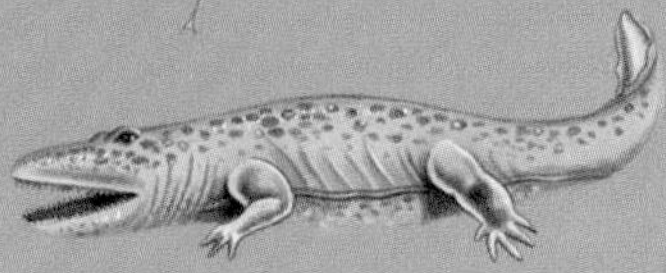

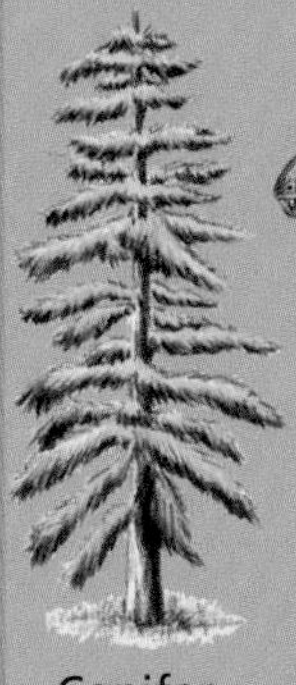

Shark

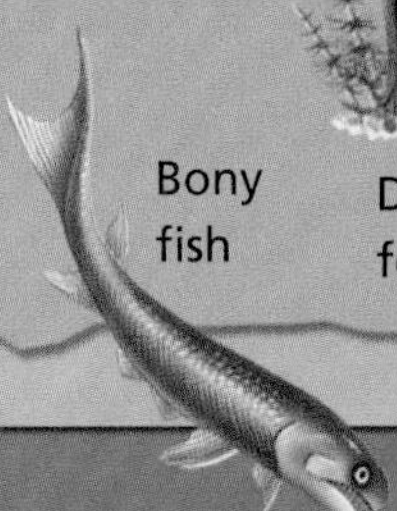

Bony fish

Devonian forest

Cockroach

Amphibian

Coal forest

Conifer

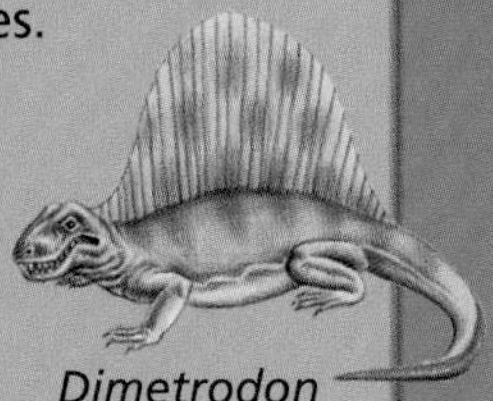

Dimetrodon

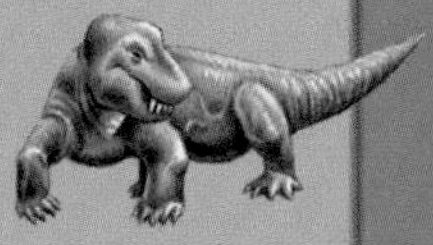

Dicynodon

Mesozoic Era

245–65 million years ago

Triassic	Jurassic
245–208 million years ago	208–144 million years ago

Geologic Events

- Pangaea holds together for much of the Triassic.
- Hot, dry conditions dominate the center of Pangaea.

- Pangaea breaks apart as North America separates from Africa and South America.

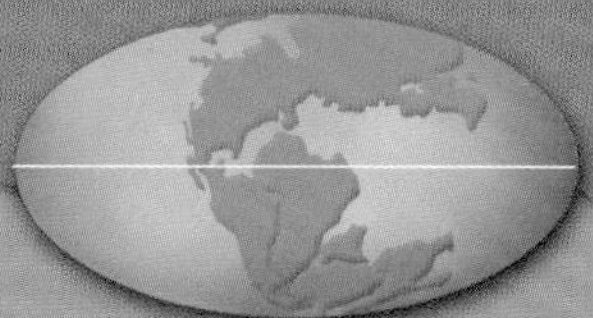

Archaeopteryx

Development of Life

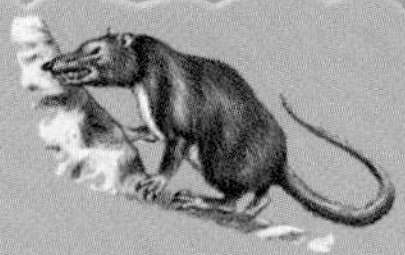

- Age of Reptiles begins.
- First dinosaurs appear.
- First mammals, which evolve from warm-blooded reptiles, appear.
- First turtles and crocodiles appear.
- Conifers, palmlike trees, and ginkgo trees dominate forests.

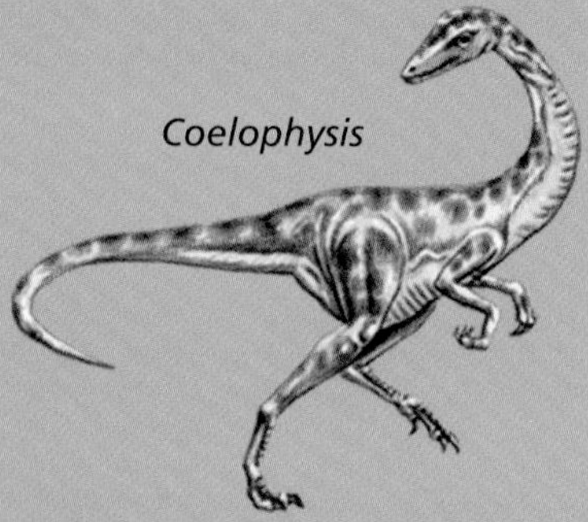

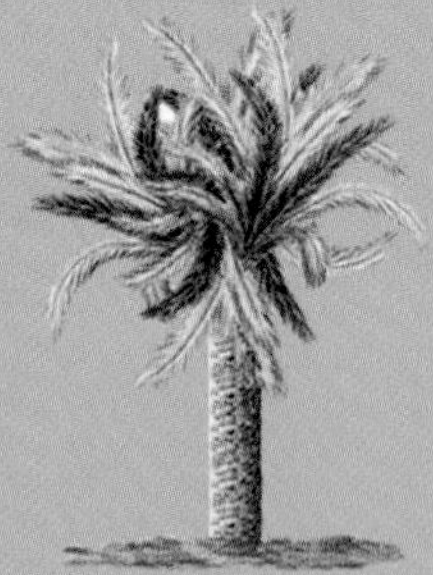

Morganucodon

- Largest dinosaurs thrive, including *Stegosaurus*, *Diplodocus*, and *Apatosaurus*.
- First birds appear.
- First flying reptiles, pterosaurs, appear.

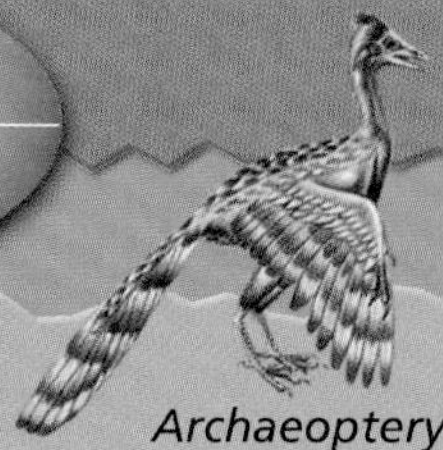

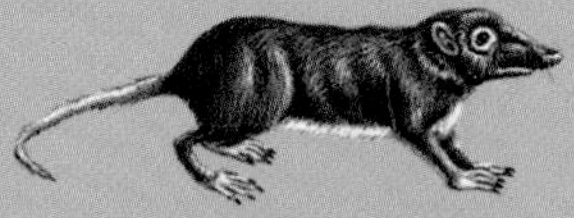

Megazostrodon

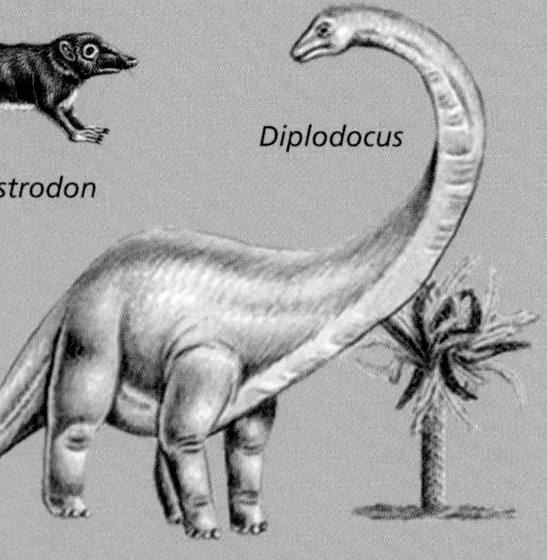

Diplodocus

Coelophysis

Cycad

Mesozoic Era
245–65 million years ago

Cenozoic Era
65 million years ago to present

Cretaceous	Tertiary	Quaternary
144–65 million years ago	65–1.6 million years ago	1.6 million years ago to the present

Geologic Events

- Continents move toward their present-day positions, as South America splits from Africa.
- Widespread volcanic activity occurs.

- The Rocky Mountains and Himalayas form.
- Continents continue to move into present-day positions.
- Continental glacier covers Antartica.

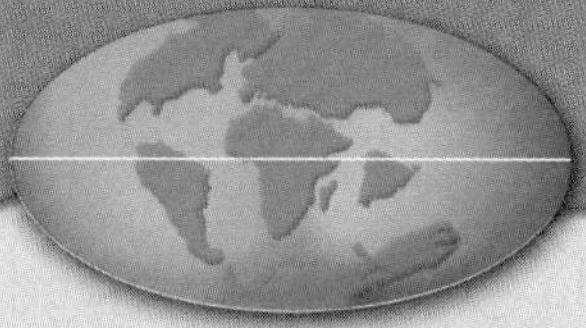

- Thick glaciers advance and retreat over much of North America and Europe, parts of South America and Asia, and all of Antarctica.

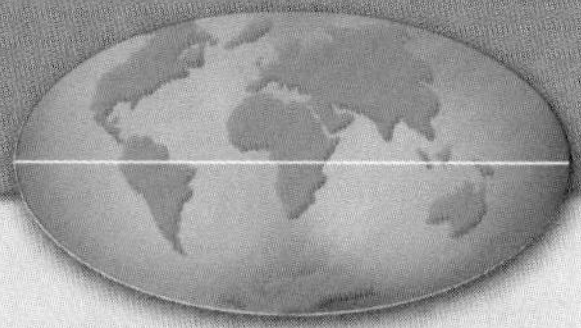

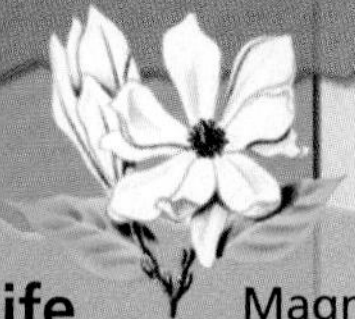

Development of Life

Magnolia

- First flowering plants appear.
- Dinosaurs, including *Tyrannosaurus rex,* dominate.
- First snakes appear.
- Mass extinction at end of period causes disappearance of many land and marine life forms, including dinosaurs.

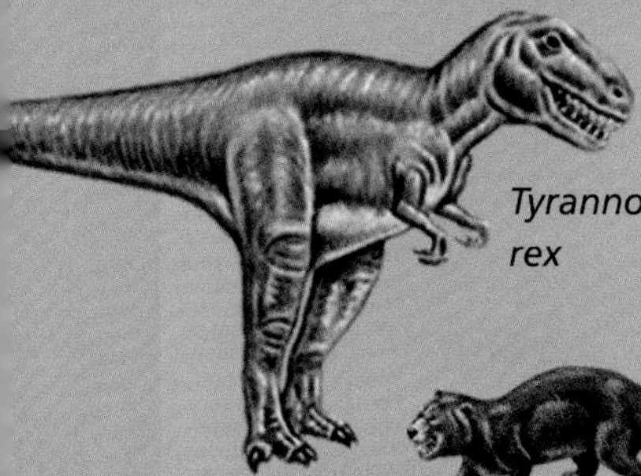

- Flowering plants thrive.
- First grasses appear.
- Age of Mammals begins.
- Modern groups such as horses, elephants, bears, rodents, and primates appear.
- Ancestors of humans evolve.

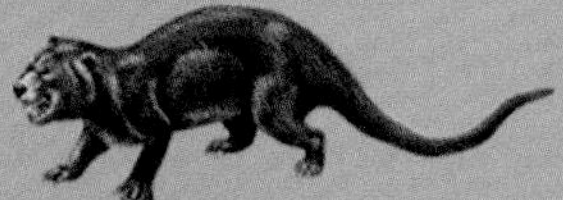

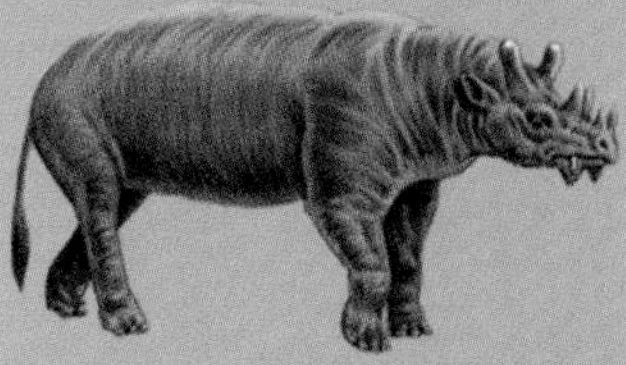

- Mammals, flowering plants, and insects dominate land.
- Modern humans evolve in Africa about 100,000 years ago.
- Giant mammals of North America and Eurasia become extinct when the Ice Age ends about 10,000 years ago.

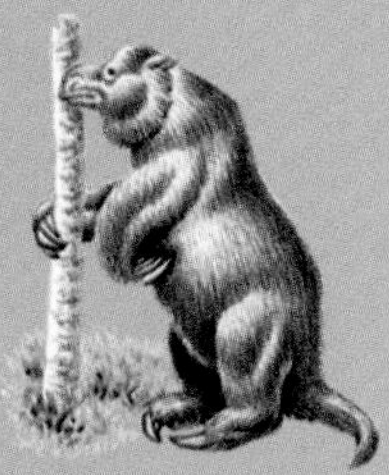

Tyrannosaurus rex

Creodonts

Uintatherium

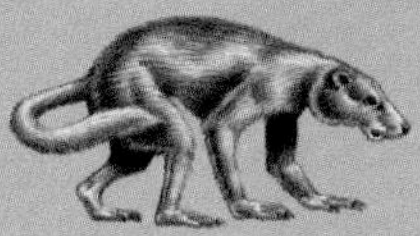

Plesiadapis

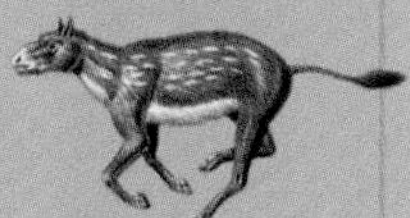

Hyracotherium

Megatherium

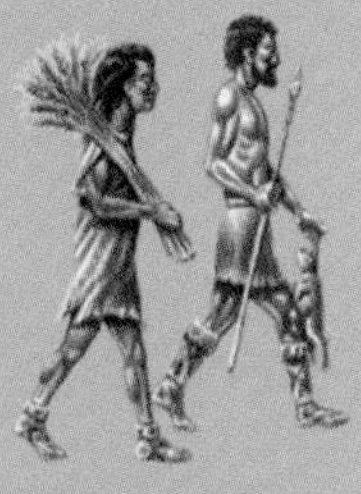

Homo sapiens

FIGURE 23
Flying Reptile
Dimorphodon was a flying reptile that lived during the Jurassic Period. Like dinosaurs, flying reptiles became extinct at the end of the Cretaceous period.
Comparing and Contrasting *How is Dimorphodon similar to the bird in Figure 24?*

The Mesozoic Era

Millions of years flash by as your time machine travels. Watch out—there's a dinosaur! You're observing an era that you've read about in books and seen in movies.

The Triassic Period Some living things survived the Permian mass extinction. These organisms became the main forms of life early in the Triassic Period (try AS ik). Plants and animals that survived included fish, insects, reptiles, and cone-bearing plants called conifers. **Reptiles were so successful during the Mesozoic Era that this time is often called the Age of Reptiles.** About 225 million years ago, the first dinosaurs appeared. Mammals also first appeared during the Triassic Period. A **mammal** is a warm-blooded vertebrate that feeds its young milk. Mammals probably evolved from warm-blooded reptiles. The mammals of the Triassic Period were very small, about the size of a mouse or shrew. From these first small mammals, all mammals that live today evolved.

The Jurassic Period During the Jurassic Period (joo RAS ik), dinosaurs became the dominant animals on land. Scientists have identified several hundred different kinds of dinosaurs. Some were plant eaters, while others were meat eaters. Dinosaurs "ruled" Earth for about 150 million years, but different types lived at different times.

One of the first birds, called *Archaeopteryx*, appeared during the Jurassic Period. The name *Archaeopteryx* means "ancient wing thing." Many paleontologists now think that birds evolved from dinosaurs.

FIGURE 24
Early Bird
The artist of the illustration (left) has given *Archaeopteryx* colorful feathers. From a fossil (right), paleontologists can tell that *Archaeopteryx* was about 30 centimeters long, had feathers and teeth, and also had claws on its wings.

The Cretaceous Period Reptiles, including dinosaurs, were still the dominant vertebrates throughout the Cretaceous Period (krih TAY shus). Flying reptiles and birds competed for places in the sky. The hollow bones and feathers of birds made them better adapted to their environment than the flying reptiles, which became extinct during the Cretaceous Period. The Cretaceous Period also brought new forms of life. Flowering plants like the ones you see today evolved. Unlike the conifers, flowering plants produce seeds that are inside a fruit. The fruit helps the seeds survive.

Another Mass Extinction **At the close of the Cretaceous Period, about 65 million years ago, another mass extinction occurred. Scientists hypothesize that this mass extinction occurred when an object from space struck Earth.** This object was probably an asteroid. Asteroids are rocky masses that orbit the sun between Mars and Jupiter. Once in many millions of years, an asteroid may collide with Earth.

When the asteroid hit Earth, the impact threw huge amounts of dust and water vapor into the atmosphere. Many organisms on land and in the oceans died immediately. Dust and heavy clouds blocked sunlight around the world for years. Without sunlight, plants died, and plant-eating animals starved. This mass extinction wiped out over half of all plant and animal groups. No dinosaurs survived.

Not all scientists agree that an asteroid impact caused the mass extinction. Some scientists think that climate changes caused by increased volcanic activity were responsible.

 Reading Checkpoint What major groups of organisms developed during the Mesozoic Era?

FIGURE 25
The End of the Dinosaurs
Many scientists hypothesize that during the Cretaceous an asteroid hit Earth near the present-day Yucatán Peninsula, in southeastern Mexico.

Life and Times

1. Place these events in their correct order: continental glaciers retreat; first fish appear; oldest fossils form; human ancestors appear; "explosion" of invertebrates occurs; dinosaurs become extinct; Pangaea forms.

2. Draw a timeline and graph these dates:

    3.5 billion years ago
    544 million years ago
    400 million years ago
    260 million years ago
    65 million years ago
    3.5 million years ago
    20,000 years ago

    Choose a scale so the oldest date fits on the paper.

Interpreting Data Match each event with the correct date on your timeline. How does the time since the dinosaurs became extinct compare with the time since the oldest fossil formed?

The Cenozoic Era

Your voyage through time continues on through the Cenozoic Era—often called the Age of Mammals. During the Mesozoic Era, mammals had a hard time competing with dinosaurs for food and places to live. **The extinction of dinosaurs created an opportunity for mammals. During the Cenozoic Era, mammals evolved to live in many different environments—on land, in water, and even in the air.**

The Tertiary Period During the Tertiary Period, Earth's climates were generally warm and mild. In the oceans, marine mammals such as whales and dolphins evolved. On land, flowering plants, insects, and mammals flourished. When grasses evolved, they provided a food source for grazing mammals. These were the ancestors of today's cattle, deer, sheep, and other grass-eating mammals. Some mammals became very large, as did some birds.

The Quaternary Period The mammals that had evolved during the Tertiary Period eventually faced a changing environment. **Earth's climate cooled, causing a series of ice ages during the Quaternary Period.** Thick continental glaciers advanced and retreated over parts of Europe and North America. Then, about 20,000 years ago, Earth's climate began to warm. Over thousands of years, the continental glaciers melted.

FIGURE 26
Ice-Age Environment
Large mammals roamed the ice-free parts of North America and Eurasia during the Ice Ages of the Quaternary Period.

In the oceans, algae, coral, mollusks, fish, and mammals thrived. Insects and birds shared the skies. On land, flowering plants and mammals such as bats, cats, dogs, cattle, and humans—just to name a few—became common.

The fossil record suggests that modern humans, or *Homo sapiens,* may have evolved as early as 100,000 years ago. By about 12,000 to 15,000 years ago, humans had migrated around the world to every continent except Antarctica.

Your time machine has now arrived back in the present. You and all organisms on Earth are living in the Quaternary Period of the Cenozoic Era. Is this the end of evolution and the changing of Earth's surface? No, these processes will continue as long as Earth exists. But you'll have to take your time machine into the future to see just what happens!

FIGURE 27
Ice Age Art
An early ancestor of modern humans painted these beautiful images of animals in a cave in France more than 20,000 years ago.

 Reading Checkpoint   **How did Earth's climate change during the Quaternary Period?**

Section 6 Assessment

Target Reading Skill Previewing Visuals Compare your questions and answers about Figure 22 with those of a partner.

Reviewing Key Concepts

1. a. **Listing** What are the periods of the Paleozoic Era?
   b. **Describing** How did Earth's organisms change during the first period of the Paleozoic?
   c. **Relating Cause and Effect** What event do scientists think may have caused the mass extinction at the end of the Paleozoic?
2. a. **Reviewing** Which group of animals was dominant during the Mesozoic Era?
   b. **Inferring** How was their small size helpful to the mammals of the Mesozoic?
   c. **Developing Hypotheses** Many scientists think that the asteroid impact at the end of the Cretaceous prevented plant growth for many years. Although many dinosaurs were plant eaters, some were meat eaters. Develop a hypothesis to explain why no dinosaurs survived.

3. a. **Identifying** What term do scientists apply to the Cenozoic Era?
   b. **Inferring** What conditions allowed so many different kinds of mammals to evolve during the Cenozoic Era?

Writing in Science

Description Suppose that you are going on a tour of Earth during one era of geologic time. Write a paragraph describing the organisms and environments that you see on the tour. Your tour should include at least one stop in each geologic period of the era you chose.

As Time Goes By

Problem

How can you make a model of geologic time?

Skills

measuring, calculating, making models

Materials

- worksheet with 2,000 asterisks
- one ream of paper

Procedure

PART 1 Table A

1. Copy Table A into your lab notebook. Figure how long ago these historic events happened and write the answers on your chart.

2. Obtain a worksheet with 2,000 asterisks printed on it. Each asterisk represents one year. The first asterisk at the top represents one year ago.

3. Starting from this asterisk, circle the asterisk that represents how many years ago each event in Table A occurred.

4. Label each circled asterisk to indicate the event.

5. Obtain a ream of copy paper. There are 500 sheets in a ream. If each sheet had 2,000 asterisks on it, there would be a total of 1 million asterisks. Therefore, each ream would represent 1 million years.

Table A: Historic Events		
Event	**Date**	**Number of Years Ago**
You are born.		
One of your parents is born.		
First space shuttle sent into space.	1981	
Neil Armstrong first walks on the moon.	1969	
World War I ends.	1918	
Civil War ends.	1865	
Declaration of Independence is signed.	1776	
Columbus crosses Atlantic Ocean.	1492	
Leif Ericson visits North America.	1000	

Table B: Geologic Events			
Event	Number of Years Ago	Reams or Sheets of Paper	Thickness of Paper
Last ice age ends.	10,000		
Whales evolve.	50 million		
Pangaea begins to break up.	225 million		
First vertebrates develop.	530 million		
Multicellular organisms (algae) develop.	1 billion		
Single-celled organisms develop.	3.5 billion		
Oldest known rocks form.	4.0 billion		
Earth forms.	4.6 billion		

PART 2 Table B

6. Copy Table B into your lab notebook. Determine how much paper in reams or sheets would be needed to represent the events in geologic time found in Table B. (*Hint:* Recall that each ream represents 1 million years.)

7. Measure the thickness of a ream of paper. Use this thickness to calculate how thick a stack of paper would need to be to represent how long ago each geologic event occurred. (*Hint:* Use a calculator to multiply the thickness of the ream of paper by the number of reams.) Enter your results in Table B.

Analyze and Conclude

1. **Measuring** Measure the height of your classroom. How many reams of paper would you need to reach the ceiling? How many years would the height of the ceiling represent? Which geologic events listed in Table B would fall on a ream of paper inside your classroom?

2. **Calculating** At this scale, how many classrooms would have to be stacked on top of each other to represent the age of Earth? The time when vertebrates appeared?

3. **Calculating** How many times higher would the thickness of the stack be for the age of Earth than for the breakup of Pangaea?

4. **Making Models** On your model, how could you distinguish one era or period from another? How could you show when particular organisms evolved and when they became extinct?

5. **Communicating** Is the scale of your model practical? What would be the advantages and disadvantages of a model that fit geologic time on a timeline 1 meter long?

More to Explore

This model represents geologic time as a straight line. Can you think of other ways of representing geologic time graphically? Using colored pencils, draw your own version of the geologic time scale so that it fits on a single sheet of typing paper. (*Hint:* You could represent geologic time as a wheel, a ribbon, or a spiral.)

① Fossils

Key Concepts

- Most fossils form when living things die and are buried by sediments. The sediments slowly harden into rock and preserve the shapes of the organisms.

- Fossils found in rock include petrified fossils, molds and casts, carbon films, and trace fossils. Other fossils form when the remains of organisms are preserved in substances such as tar, amber, or ice.

- The fossil record provides evidence about the history of life and past environments on Earth. The fossil record also shows that different groups of organisms have changed over time.

Key Terms

fossil	trace fossil
sedimentary rock	paleontologist
mold	scientific theory
cast	evolution
petrified fossil	extinct
carbon film	

② The Relative Age of Rocks

Key Concepts

- According to the law of superposition, in horizontal sedimentary rock layers the oldest layer is at the bottom. Each higher layer is younger than the layers below it.

- To determine relative age, geologists also study extrusions and intrusions of igneous rock, faults, and gaps in the geologic record.

- Index fossils are useful because they tell the relative ages of the rock layers in which they occur.

Key Terms

relative age	intrusion
absolute age	fault
law of superposition	unconformity
extrusion	index fossil

③ Radioactive Dating

Key Concepts

- During radioactive decay, the atoms of one element break down to form atoms of another.

- Geologists use radioactive dating to determine the absolute ages of rocks.

Key Terms

atom	radioactive decay
element	half-life

④ The Geologic Time Scale

Key Concepts

- Geologists use the geologic time scale to show the time span of Earth's history.

- After Precambrian Time, the basic units of the geologic time scale are eras and periods.

Key Terms

geologic time scale	era	period

⑤ Early Earth

Key Concepts

- Scientists hypothesize that Earth formed at the same time as the other planets and the sun, roughly 4.6 billion years ago.

- During early Precambrian Time, an atmosphere, oceans, and continents formed.

- Scientists have found fossils of single-celled organisms in rocks that formed about 3.5 billion years ago.

Key Terms

comet	continental drift

⑥ Eras of Earth's History

Key Concepts

- At the beginning of the Paleozoic Era, many different kinds of organisms evolved.

- During the Permian Period, about 260 million years ago, the supercontinent Pangaea formed.

Key Terms

invertebrate	amphibian	mass extinction
vertebrate	reptile	mammal

Review and Assessment

Organizing Information

Concept Mapping Copy the concept map about fossils onto a piece of paper. Then complete it and add a title. (For more on concept maps, see the Skills Handbook.)

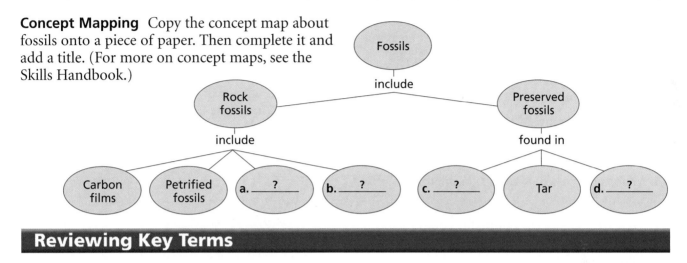

Reviewing Key Terms

Choose the letter of the best answer.

1. A hollow area in sediment in the shape of all or part of an organism is called a
   a. mold.
   b. cast.
   c. trace fossil.
   d. carbon film.

2. A gap in the geologic record formed when sedimentary rocks cover an eroded surface is called a(n)
   a. intrusion.
   b. unconformity.
   c. fault.
   d. extrusion.

3. The time it takes for half of a radioactive element's atoms to decay is a(n)
   a. era.
   b. half-life.
   c. relative age.
   d. absolute age.

4. The geologic time scale is subdivided into
   a. relative ages.
   b. absolute ages.
   c. unconformities.
   d. eras and periods.

5. An animal that doesn't have a backbone is called a(n)
   a. vertebrate.
   b. mammal.
   c. invertebrate.
   d. amphibian.

If the statement is true, write *true*. If it is false, change the underlined word or words to make the statement true.

6. A dinosaur footprint in rock is an example of a <u>trace fossil</u>.

7. A <u>carbon film</u> is a fossil in which minerals have replaced all or part of an organism.

8. The <u>relative age</u> of something is the exact number of years since an event has occurred.

9. Earth's landmasses move slowly in a process called <u>continental drift</u>.

10. Scientists think dinosaurs became extinct as part of a(n) <u>intrusion</u> at the end of the Cretaceous Period.

Writing in Science

Field Guide Write a field guide for visitors to the Grand Canyon. In your guide, explain how geologists have learned about Earth's past by studying the canyon walls and the fossils they contain.

A Trip Through Geologic Time
Video Preview
Video Field Trip
▶ Video Assessment

Review and Assessment

Checking Concepts

11. How does a petrified fossil form?

12. Which organism has a better chance of leaving a fossil: a jellyfish or a bony fish? Explain.

13. Describe a process that could cause an unconformity.

14. What evidence would a scientist use to determine the absolute age of a fossil found in a sedimentary rock?

15. When and how do scientists think that Earth's oceans formed?

16. How did Earth's environments change from the Tertiary Period to the Quarternary Period? Explain.

Thinking Critically

17. **Applying Concepts** Paleontologists find a trilobite fossil in a rock layer at the top of a hill in South America. Then they find the same kind of fossil in a rock layer at the bottom of a cliff in Africa. What could the paleontologists conclude about the two rock layers?

18. **Problem Solving** Which of the elements in the table below would be better to use in dating a fossil from Precambrian time? Explain.

Radioactive Elements	
Element	**Half-life (years)**
Carbon-14	5,730
Uranium-235	713 million

19. **Relating Cause and Effect** When Pangaea formed, the climate changed and the land on Earth became drier. How was this climate change more favorable to reptiles than amphibians?

20. **Making Judgments** If you see a movie in which early humans fight giant dinosaurs, how would you judge the scientific accuracy of that movie? Give reasons for your judgment.

Math Practice

21. **Percentage** What percentage of a radioactive element will remain after 9 half-lives?

Applying Skills

Use the diagram of rock layers below to answer Questions 22–25.

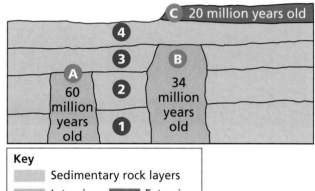

Key
Sedimentary rock layers
Intrusion   Extrusion

22. **Inferring** Which is the oldest layer of sedimentary rock? Which is the youngest? How do you know?

23. **Measuring** What method did a scientist use to determine the age of the intrusion and extrusion?

24. **Interpreting Data** What is the relative age of layer 3? (*Hint:* With what absolute ages can you compare it?)

25. **Interpreting Data** What is the relative age of layer 4?

 Chapter **Project**

Performance Assessment You have completed your illustrations for the timeline and travel brochure. Now you are ready to present the story of the geologic time period you researched. Be sure to include the awesome sights people will see when they travel to this time period. Don't forget to warn them of any dangers that await them. In your journal, reflect on what you have learned about Earth's history. If you could travel back in time, how far back would you go?

Standardized Test Prep

Choose the letter of the best answer.

1. A geologist finds identical trilobite fossils in a rock layer in the Grand Canyon in Arizona and in a rock layer in northern Utah, over 675 kilometers away. What inference can she make about the ages of the two rock layers?
   A the rock layer in the Grand Canyon is older
   B the rock layer in Utah is older
   C the two rock layers are about the same age
   D no inferences

2. What should you use so that the geologic time scale covering Earth's 4.6 billion year history can be drawn as a straight line on a poster board one meter high?
   F 1 cm = 1 million years
   G 1 cm = 10,000 years
   H 1 cm = 100,000 years
   J 1 cm = 50,000,000 years

Use the diagram below and your knowledge of science to answer Question 3.

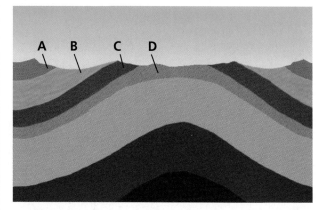

3. According to the law of superposition, the youngest layer of rock in this diagram is
   A Layer A
   B Layer B
   C Layer C
   D Layer D

4. What was used by geologists to define the beginnings and ends of the divisions of the geologic time scale?
   F radioactive dating
   G major changes in life forms
   H types of rocks present
   J volcanic events

5. A leaf falls into a shallow lake and is rapidly buried in the sediment that changes to rock over millions of years. Which type of fossil would be formed?
   A mold and cast
   B carbon film
   C trace fossil
   D amber

Constructed Response

6. Describe two methods geologists use to determine the age of a rock. In your answer, be sure to mention igneous rock, sedimentary rock, the law of superposition, index fossils, radioactive decay, and half-life.

Nile River
The Nile River gives life
to the Egyptian desert.

The Gift of the Nile

What water . . .

- flows from south to north?
- travels through a scorching desert for much of its length?
- nourished a remarkable ancient culture?
- is the longest river in the world?

Water Lily
Blue water lilies
grow in the Nile.

It's the Nile River. More than 5,000 years ago, people first began planting seeds and harvesting crops in the valley of the Nile. The great civilization of Egypt rose in these fertile lands. The Nile supplied water for drinking, growing crops, raising animals, and fishing. When the river flooded every year, it brought a new layer of rich soil to the flood plain.

This productive strip of land was the envy of many nations. Fortunately, the deserts west and east of the Nile helped protect ancient Egypt from invaders. The river provided a trade route from central Africa downstream to the Mediterranean Sea. Around 600 B.C., Egypt expanded its trade by digging a canal to the Red Sea.

During the months when the Nile flooded, peasants worked as builders for the Pharaoh, or king. They constructed magnificent pyramids and temples, some of which still stand today.

Lifeline of Egypt

The wealth of ancient Egypt and the lives of its people depended on the fertile flood plains that bordered the Nile River. Egyptian society was organized in classes to support agriculture. The Pharaoh was the supreme ruler to whom all Egyptians paid taxes. Below the Pharaoh was a small upper class of priests, scribes, and nobles. Traders and skilled workers, who made tools, pottery, and clothing, formed a small middle class. But the largest group in Egyptian society consisted of the peasants. Peasants used the Nile waters to raise crops that fed all of Egypt.

Priests and nobles recorded the history and literature of ancient Egypt on the walls of monuments and temples. They also wrote on papyrus, a paper made from reeds that grew in marshes along the Nile. Many writings were about the Nile.

When scholars finally found the key to hieroglyphics (hy ur oh GLIF iks), Egyptian writing, they discovered hymns, poems, legends, adventure stories, and lessons for young people. The poem at the right is from a hymn to Hapy, the god of the Nile. "Darkness by day" is the Nile filled with silt.

▼ Egyptian Hieroglyphics

Adoration of Hapy

Hail to you, Hapy,
Sprung from earth,
Come to nourish Egypt!
Of secret ways,
A darkness by day,
To whom his followers sing!
Who floods the fields that Re* has made,
To nourish all who thirst;
Lets drink the waterless desert,
His dew descending from the sky.

Food provider, bounty maker,
Who creates all that is good!
Lord of awe, sweetly fragrant,
Gracious when he comes.
Who makes herbage for the herds,
Gives sacrifice for every god.
He fills the stores,
Makes bulge the barns,
Gives bounty to the poor.

Oh joy when you come!
O joy when you come, O Hapy,
Oh joy when you come!

*Amon-Re, god of the sun

Language Arts Activity

In this poem, Hapy is a personification of the Nile River. When writers and poets use personification, they give an object or animal human qualities. Write your own story or poem using personification. Choose a subject found in nature, such as a mountain, stream, river, or glacier. Jot down human behaviors and actions for your subject—"the stream gurgles, murmurs, and sighs." Before writing, think about the time, place, characters, and sequence of events in your story.

Egyptian Jar
The god Hapy is represented here on a wooden jar from 700 B.C.

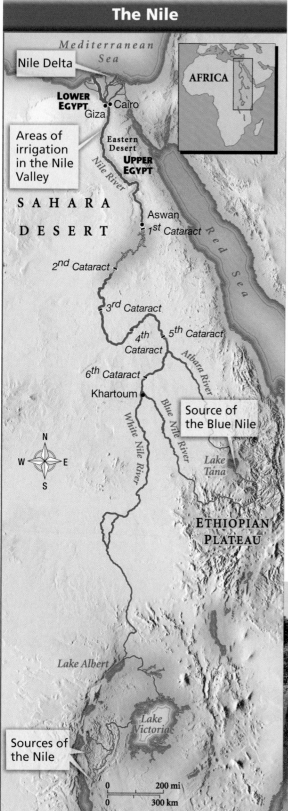

The Nile

Mediterranean Sea

Nile Delta

AFRICA

LOWER EGYPT
Giza · Cairo

Areas of irrigation in the Nile Valley

Eastern Desert

UPPER EGYPT

Nile River

S A H A R A
D E S E R T

Aswan
1st Cataract

Red Sea

2nd Cataract

3rd Cataract

4th Cataract   5th Cataract

Atbara River

6th Cataract

Khartoum

Source of the Blue Nile

White Nile River

Blue Nile River

Lake Tana

ETHIOPIAN PLATEAU

N
W · E
S

Lake Albert

Lake Victoria

Sources of the Nile

0 ——— 200 mi
0 ——— 300 km

Fertilizing the Fields

In some parts of Egypt, it hasn't rained in years. Only about 3 percent of Egypt can be farmed. The rest is sunbaked desert. But hot weather and the silt and water brought by the Nile River make the Nile Valley highly productive.

The Nile River is the longest river on Earth, stretching 6,650 kilometers. Its drainage basin is about 3.3 million square kilometers, larger than that of the Mississippi River. Three major rivers form the Nile—the White Nile, the Blue Nile, and the Atbara.

The source of the White Nile is just south of the equator, near Lake Victoria (about 1,135 meters above sea level). A fairly constant volume of water flows north over rapids and through swamplands to Khartoum. Here the Blue Nile and the White Nile meet to form the great Nile River.

The Blue Nile starts in the eastern plateau of Ethiopia near Lake Tana (about 1,800 meters above sea level). The Atbara River, the last major tributary of the Nile, also flows in from Ethiopia. Between Khartoum and Aswan, the Nile flows north over six cataracts—huge waterfalls. From Aswan to Cairo, the flood plain stretches out on both sides of the river. It gradually widens to about 19 kilometers. Then in Lower Egypt, the river branches out to form the Nile Delta.

The Blue Nile
The rushing waters of the Blue Nile carry silt from the Ethiopian highlands to the Nile.

Between May and August, heavy rains soak the eastern plateau of Ethiopia and wash rock and silt from the highlands into the Blue Nile. The dark water rushes over rapids and through deep gorges into the Nile River. For thousands of years, this rush of water from the Blue Nile and the Atbara caused the seasonal flooding on the Nile. In mid July, the Nile would begin to rise north of Aswan. When the flood waters went down, the silt remained on the land.

Then in the 1800s and 1900s, the government of Egypt built dams on the Nile to try to control the flood waters. The Aswan High Dam, the largest of these dams, was completed in 1970. The dam enabled Egyptians to gain control over annual flooding. The Aswan High Dam holds back water for use during dry periods.

In recent years, the population of Egypt and other nations in the Nile basin has grown rapidly. Feeding more people means increasing the area of irrigated cropland. To avoid conflicts, nations must agree to share water. Most of the water in the Blue Nile, for example, comes from Ethiopia. Yet Egypt and Sudan, the nations farther downstream, use about 90 percent of that water. Today, Ethiopia's growing population needs more Nile water. Using water efficiently and sharing it fairly are essential in the Nile basin.

Aswan High Dam
Today, the Aswan High Dam provides irrigation and electricity throughout Egypt.

Science Activity

Use the stream table (pages 82–83) to observe how the Nile builds its delta and how the Aswan High Dam affects the river. Pour water into the lower end of the stream table to model the sea.

- Make a dam. Cut off the top 2 centimeters from a plastic foam cup. Cut the cup into a semicircle to make your dam. Cut a small notch in the top of the dam for a spillway.

- Start the dripper to create the Nile. Allow it to flow for 5 minutes. What do you observe where the river flows into the sea?

- Now place the dam halfway down the river. Scoop out a small, shallow reservoir behind the dam. Start the dripper. Observe for 5 minutes.

What effect would you say the Aswan High Dam has on the movement of sediment down the Nile?

Farming Around 1200 B.C.
This painting from the Tomb of Sennedjem
in Thebes shows Sennedjem and his wife
farming in the afterworld. They plant and
harvest grain and cultivate fruit-bearing
trees, such as the date palm.

Basin Irrigation

The ancient Egyptians may have been the first
people to irrigate their lands. The slope of the
flood plain in Egypt is good for irrigation. From
south to north, the land slopes down slightly. The
land also slopes slightly down to the desert from
the river banks on either side of the Nile.

Egyptians used basin irrigation. They divided
the flood plain into a series of basins by building
low banks of dirt. When the Nile flooded from
July to October, it filled the basins. Then, the
water level in the Nile and in the basins gradually
dropped. This left a rich sediment layer ready for
planting.

In November, peasants plowed the fields and
scattered seeds. To push the seeds into the
ground, they drove sheep over the fields.

Egyptians grew crops of wheat, barley, lentils,
onions, beans, garlic, vegetables, and fruits in the
Nile Valley. The crops usually could feed all of
Egypt. The Egyptians traded any surplus crops for
lumber, copper, and beautiful minerals that they
used for decorations.

When the fields became dry, peasants brought
water from irrigation channels, or deep ditches.
They also used a tool called a shaduf to take water
directly from the Nile. A shaduf works like a
plank on a seesaw: A wooden beam balances on a
pivot. Hanging from one end of the beam is a
bucket. Weighing down the other end is a large
stone. A farmer tips the beam to scoop water from
the Nile, swivels the beam, and empties the
bucket into an irrigation channel.

▲ **Modern market in Cairo, Egypt**

Shaduf
Egyptians still use the shaduf today. It dates back to about 2200 B.C.

After the harvest in April, farm animals grazed on the lands until the Nile rose again in mid July. Then a new cycle began.

The flooding of the Nile determined the lives of early Egyptians. Their year began on the day the Nile began to rise, about July 19 on our calendar. The Egyptians were the first people to have a calendar of 365 days. Their year was divided into three seasons based on the Nile's flood cycle. Each season had four months of 30 days. At the end of the 12 months, the Egyptians had five festival days to complete the year.

Social Studies Activity

Divide into groups of three to make a timeline of an Egyptian calendar year. Each member of the group should choose a four-month season—flooding, planting, or harvesting—to label and illustrate.

- Draw the timeline to begin on July 19 and end on July 18.

- Divide the timeline into 12 months and 5 days.

- Label the months and seasons.

- Illustrate the seasonal work of the farmers.

Mathematics

Pyramids at Giza
These pyramids were built around 2500 B.C.
Egyptians used geometry to measure triangles,
squares, and circles as they built pyramids.

Measuring the Land

Have you ever measured the length of a room using your feet as the unit of measurement? Around 3000 B.C., ancient Egyptians developed the cubit system of measurement. It was based on the lengths of parts of the arm and hand, rather than the foot. The Egyptian cubit was the length of a forearm from the tip of the elbow to the end of the middle finger. The cubit was subdivided into smaller units of spans, palms, digits, and parts of digits.

Of course, the length of a cubit varied from person to person. So Egypt established a standard cubit, called the Royal Cubit. It was based on the length of the Pharaoh's forearm. The Royal Cubit was a piece of black granite about 52.3 centimeters long. Although the royal architect kept the Royal Cubit, wooden copies were distributed throughout the land.

Measurement was important to Egyptian life. Every year when the Nile flooded, it wiped out the boundaries for the fields. So after the annual floods, farmers had to measure off new areas. Drawings on the walls of early tombs show that the Egyptians probably had a system for measuring distances and angles on land.

Standard measurement was also necessary for building the massive temples and pyramids that lined the Nile Valley. The cubit sticks must have been very accurate, because the lengths of the sides of the Great Pyramid at Giza vary by only a few centimeters.

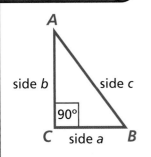

A

side *b*   side *c*

90°

C   side *a*   B

To measure fields and build pyramids, the Egyptians needed to understand geometry. They laid out their fields in squares by first making a right triangle. Look at the diagram. The two shorter sides are the legs of the triangle. The side opposite the right angle is the hypotenuse. The Egyptians might have known that the sum of the squares of the lengths of the legs is equal to the square of the hypotenuse. The equation is $a^2 + b^2 = c^2$. So if side *a* is 3, side *b* is 4, and side *c* is 5, then $3^2 + 4^2 = 5^2$, or $9 + 16 = 25$. Now work in groups of three to make your own right triangle.

- Measure one student's arm to make a cubit stick.
- Use the cubit stick to cut one rope 12 cubits long; mark off each of the 12 cubits.
- Have three students hold the rope at points *A, B,* and *C* so that side *a* is 3 cubits, side *b* is 4 cubits, and side *c* is 5 cubits.

Have you made a right triangle? How do you know? How could you make a square?

Egyptian Exhibition

Plan a brochure to promote a special exhibition on Egypt at a museum. Half the class can focus on ancient Egypt. The other half can find out about the changes that have occurred on the Nile in the last 100 years. Work in small groups to research and assemble the information and illustrations. You might want to include the following:

- the Rosetta Stone and hieroglyphics
- directions for making a mummy
- the Great Pyramid at Giza
- history and treasures of King Tutankhamen

King Tutankhamen
This is a section of the King's gold mummy case.

- religion in ancient Egypt
- model of an irrigation system for fields on the Nile
- maps of ancient and modern Egypt
- construction of the Aswan Dam, 1959–1970
- water control on the Nile in Egypt today
- Nile Delta today

Think Like a Scientist

Although you may not know it, you think like a scientist every day. Whenever you ask a question and explore possible answers, you use many of the same skills that scientists do. Some of these skills are described on this page.

Observing

When you use one or more of your five senses to gather information about the world, you are **observing.** Hearing a dog bark, counting twelve green seeds, and smelling smoke are all observations. To increase the power of their senses, scientists sometimes use microscopes, telescopes, or other instruments that help them make more detailed observations.

An observation must be an accurate report of what your senses detect. It is important to keep careful records of your observations in science class by writing or drawing in a notebook. The information collected through observations is called evidence, or data.

Inferring

When you interpret an observation, you are **inferring,** or making an inference. For example, if you hear your dog barking, you may infer that someone is at your front door. To make this inference, you combine the evidence— the barking dog—and your experience or knowledge—you know that your dog barks when strangers approach—to reach a logical conclusion.

Notice that an inference is not a fact; it is only one of many possible interpretations for an observation. For example, your dog may be barking because it wants to go for a walk. An inference may turn out to be incorrect even if it is based on accurate observations and logical reasoning. The only way to find out if an inference is correct is to investigate further.

Predicting

When you listen to the weather forecast, you hear many predictions about the next day's weather—what the temperature will be, whether it will rain, and how windy it will be. Weather forecasters use observations and knowledge of weather patterns to predict the weather. The skill of **predicting** involves making an inference about a future event based on current evidence or past experience.

Because a prediction is an inference, it may prove to be false. In science class, you can test some of your predictions by doing experiments. For example, suppose you predict that larger paper airplanes can fly farther than smaller airplanes. How could you test your prediction?

Activity

Use the photograph to answer the questions below.

Observing Look closely at the photograph. List at least three observations.

Inferring Use your observations to make an inference about what has happened. What experience or knowledge did you use to make the inference?

Predicting Predict what will happen next. On what evidence or experience do you base your prediction?

Classifying

Could you imagine searching for a book in the library if the books were shelved in no particular order? Your trip to the library would be an all-day event! Luckily, librarians group together books on similar topics or by the same author. Grouping together items that are alike in some way is called **classifying.** You can classify items in many ways: by size, by shape, by use, and by other important characteristics.

Like librarians, scientists use the skill of classifying to organize information and objects. When things are sorted into groups, the relationships among them become easier to understand.

Activity

Classify the objects in the photograph into two groups based on any characteristic you choose. Then use another characteristic to classify the objects into three groups.

Activity

This student is using a model to demonstrate what causes day and night on Earth. What do the flashlight and the tennis ball in the model represent?

Making Models

Have you ever drawn a picture to help someone understand what you were saying? Such a drawing is one type of model. A model is a picture, diagram, computer image, or other representation of a complex object or process. **Making models** helps people understand things that they cannot observe directly.

Scientists often use models to represent things that are either very large or very small, such as the planets in the solar system, or the parts of a cell. Such models are physical models—drawings or three-dimensional structures that look like the real thing. Other models are mental models—mathematical equations or words that describe how something works.

Communicating

Whenever you talk on the phone, write a letter, or listen to your teacher at school, you are communicating. **Communicating** is the process of sharing ideas and information with other people. Communicating effectively requires many skills, including writing, reading, speaking, listening, and making models.

Scientists communicate to share results, information, and opinions. Scientists often communicate about their work in journals, over the telephone, in letters, and on the Internet.

They also attend scientific meetings where they share their ideas with one another in person.

Activity

On a sheet of paper, write out clear, detailed directions for tying your shoe. Then exchange directions with a partner. Follow your partner's directions exactly. How successful were you at tying your shoe? How could your partner have communicated more clearly?

Making Measurements

When scientists make observations, it is not sufficient to say that something is "big" or "heavy." Instead, scientists use instruments to measure just how big or heavy an object is. By measuring, scientists can express their observations more precisely and communicate more information about what they observe.

Measuring in SI

The standard system of measurement used by scientists around the world is known as the International System of Units, which is abbreviated as SI (in French, **Système International d'Unités**). SI units are easy to use because they are based on multiples of 10. Each unit is ten times larger than the next smallest unit and one tenth the size of the next largest unit. The table lists the prefixes used to name the most common SI units.

Common SI Prefixes		
Prefix	**Symbol**	**Meaning**
kilo-	k	1,000
hecto-	h	100
deka-	da	10
deci-	d	0.1 (one tenth)
centi-	c	0.01 (one hundredth)
milli-	m	0.001 (one thousandth)

Length To measure length, or the distance between two points, the unit of measure is the **meter (m).** The distance from the floor to a doorknob is approximately one meter. Long distances, such as the distance between two cities, are measured in kilometers (km). Small lengths are measured in centimeters (cm) or millimeters (mm). Scientists use metric rulers and meter sticks to measure length.

Common Conversions	
1 km	= 1,000 m
1 m	= 100 cm
1 m	= 1,000 mm
1 cm	= 10 mm

Activity

The larger lines on the metric ruler in the picture show centimeter divisions, while the smaller, unnumbered lines show millimeter divisions. How many centimeters long is the shell? How many millimeters long is it?

Liquid Volume To measure the volume of a liquid, or the amount of space it takes up, you will use a unit of measure known as the **liter (L).** One liter is the approximate volume of a medium-size carton of milk. Smaller volumes are measured in milliliters (mL). Scientists use graduated cylinders to measure liquid volume.

Activity

The graduated cylinder in the picture is marked in milliliter divisions. Notice that the water in the cylinder has a curved surface. This curved surface is called the *meniscus*. To measure the volume, you must read the level at the lowest point of the meniscus. What is the volume of water in this graduated cylinder?

Common Conversion	
1 L	= 1,000 mL

Mass To measure mass, or the amount of matter in an object, you will use a unit of measure known as the **gram (g).** One gram is approximately the mass of a paper clip. Larger masses are measured in kilograms (kg). Scientists use a balance to find the mass of an object.

Common Conversion

1 kg = 1,000 g

Activity

The mass of the potato in the picture is measured in kilograms. What is the mass of the potato? Suppose a recipe for potato salad called for one kilogram of potatoes. About how many potatoes would you need?

0.25 KG

Temperature To measure the temperature of a substance, you will use the **Celsius scale.** Temperature is measured in degrees Celsius (°C) using a Celsius thermometer. Water freezes at 0°C and boils at 100°C.

Time The unit scientists use to measure time is the **second (s).**

Activity

What is the temperature of the liquid in degrees Celsius?

Converting SI Units

To use the SI system, you must know how to convert between units. Converting from one unit to another involves the skill of **calculating,** or using mathematical operations. Converting between SI units is similar to converting between dollars and dimes because both systems are based on multiples of ten.

Suppose you want to convert a length of 80 centimeters to meters. Follow these steps to convert between units.

1. Begin by writing down the measurement you want to convert—in this example, 80 centimeters.

2. Write a conversion factor that represents the relationship between the two units you are converting. In this example, the relationship is 1 meter = 100 centimeters. Write this conversion factor as a fraction, making sure to place the units you are converting from (centimeters, in this example) in the denominator.

3. Multiply the measurement you want to convert by the fraction. When you do this, the units in the first measurement will cancel out with the units in the denominator. Your answer will be in the units you are converting to (meters, in this example).

Example

80 centimeters = ■ meters

$$80 \text{ centimeters} \times \frac{1 \text{ meter}}{100 \text{ centimeters}} = \frac{80 \text{ meters}}{100}$$

$$= 0.8 \text{ meters}$$

Activity

Convert between the following units.

1. 600 millimeters = ■ meters
2. 0.35 liters = ■ milliliters
3. 1,050 grams = ■ kilograms

Conducting a Scientific Investigation

In some ways, scientists are like detectives, piecing together clues to learn about a process or event. One way that scientists gather clues is by carrying out experiments. An experiment tests an idea in a careful, orderly manner. Although experiments do not all follow the same steps in the same order, many follow a pattern similar to the one described here.

Posing Questions

Experiments begin by asking a scientific question. A scientific question is one that can be answered by gathering evidence. For example, the question "Which freezes faster—fresh water or salt water?" is a scientific question because you can carry out an investigation and gather information to answer the question.

Developing a Hypothesis

The next step is to form a hypothesis. A **hypothesis** is a possible explanation for a set of observations or answer to a scientific question. In science, a hypothesis must be something that can be tested. A hypothesis can be worded as an *If . . . then . . .* statement. For example, a hypothesis might be *"If I add salt to fresh water, then the water will take longer to freeze."* A hypothesis worded this way serves as a rough outline of the experiment you should perform.

Designing an Experiment

Next you need to plan a way to test your hypothesis. Your plan should be written out as a step-by-step procedure and should describe the observations or measurements you will make.

Two important steps involved in designing an experiment are controlling variables and forming operational definitions.

Controlling Variables In a well-designed experiment, you need to keep all variables the same except for one. A **variable** is any factor that can change in an experiment. The factor that you change is called the manipulated variable. In this experiment, the **manipulated variable** is the amount of salt added to the water. Other factors, such as the amount of water or the starting temperature, are kept constant.

The factor that changes as a result of the manipulated variable is called the **responding variable.** The responding variable is what you measure or observe to obtain your results. In this experiment, the responding variable is how long the water takes to freeze.

An experiment in which all factors except one are kept constant is called a **controlled experiment.** Most controlled experiments include a test called the control. In this experiment, Container 3 is the control. Because no salt is added to Container 3, you can compare the results from the other containers to it. Any difference in results must be due to the addition of salt alone.

Forming Operational Definitions Another important aspect of a well-designed experiment is having clear operational definitions. An **operational definition** is a statement that describes how a particular variable is to be measured or how a term is to be defined. For example, in this experiment, how will you determine if the water has frozen? You might decide to insert a stick in each container at the start of the experiment. Your operational definition of "frozen" would be the time at which the stick can no longer move.

Experimental Procedure
1. Fill 3 containers with 300 milliliters of cold tap water.
2. Add 10 grams of salt to Container 1; stir. Add 20 grams of salt to Container 2; stir. Add no salt to Container 3.
3. Place the 3 containers in a freezer.
4. Check the containers every 15 minutes. Record your observations.

Interpreting Data

The observations and measurements you make in an experiment are called **data.** At the end of an experiment, you need to analyze the data to look for any patterns or trends. Patterns often become clear if you organize your data in a data table or graph. Then think through what the data reveal. Do they support your hypothesis? Do they point out a flaw in your experiment? Do you need to collect more data?

Drawing Conclusions

A **conclusion** is a statement that sums up what you have learned from an experiment. When you draw a conclusion, you need to decide whether the data you collected support your hypothesis or not. You may need to repeat an experiment several times before you can draw any conclusions from it. Conclusions often lead you to pose new questions and plan new experiments to answer them.

Activity

Is a ball's bounce affected by the height from which it is dropped? Using the steps just described, plan a controlled experiment to investigate this problem.

Technology Design Skills

Engineers are people who use scientific and technological knowledge to solve practical problems and design new technologies. To design new products, engineers usually follow the process described here, even though they may not follow these steps in the exact order. As you read the steps, think about how you might apply them in technology labs.

Identify a Need

Before engineers begin designing a new product, they must first identify the need they are trying to meet. For example, suppose you are a member of a design team in a company that manufactures toys. Your team has identified a need: a toy boat that is powered by wind. The new toy needs to be inexpensive and easy to assemble.

Research the Problem

Engineers need to research the problem to gather information that will help them with their new design. This research may include finding articles in books, magazines, or on the Internet. It may also include talking to other designers who have developed similar technologies or solved similar problems. Engineers almost always perform experiments related to the product they want to design.

For your wind-powered toy boat, you could look at toys that are similar to the one you want to design. You might also do research on the Internet. You will probably want to test some materials to see how well they float and other materials to see whether they can function as sails.

Design a Solution

Research gives engineers information that lets them begin designing the product. When engineers design new products, they usually work in groups.

Generating Ideas Often design groups hold brainstorming meetings in which any group member can contribute ideas. Brainstorming is a creative process in which one group member's suggestions often spark ideas in other group members. Together, the creativity of different group members leads to proposed solutions.

Evaluating Constraints Chances are good that during brainstorming, a design group will come up with several possible designs. The group must then evaluate each proposal.

As part of their evaluation, engineers consider constraints, which are factors that place limitations or restrictions on a product design. Physical characteristics, such as the properties of the materials used to make products, are typical constraints. The materials in your proposed toy boat, for example, can't be too heavy, or the boat won't float. The sails need to be made of materials that are lightweight enough not to weigh down the boat. But they also need to be sturdy enough that the sails won't collapse in breezes.

Money and time are other typical constraints. If the materials in a product cost a lot, or if the product takes a long time to manufacture, the design may be impractical.

Making Trade-offs Design teams usually need to make trade-offs, in which they give up one benefit of a proposed design in order to obtain another. In designing your toy boat, you may have to make trade-offs when choosing materials. For example, suppose one material is lightweight but not fully waterproof. An alternative material is sturdy and more waterproof, but also heavier. You may decide to give up the benefit of low weight in order to obtain the benefits of sturdiness and waterproofing.

Build and Evaluate a Prototype

Once the team has chosen a design plan, the engineers build a prototype of the product. A prototype is a working version of the chosen design, made of the materials that have been proposed for the product. Engineers construct a prototype so that it can be tested and evaluated. They evaluate the product to see whether it works well, is easy to operate, is safe to use, and holds up to repeated use.

Think of your wind-powered boat. What would the prototype be like? Of what materials would it be made? How would you test it?

Troubleshoot and Redesign

Few prototypes work perfectly, which is why they need to be tested. Once a design team has tested a prototype, the members analyze the results and identify any problems. The team then tries to troubleshoot, or correct the problems. The design of the prototype is changed or adjusted to address any problems. For example, if your prototype toy boat leaks or wobbles, the boat should be redesigned to eliminate those problems.

Communicate the Solution

Once a team has decided on a final design, the team needs to communicate the design to people who will manufacture and use the product. Teams often use a variety of methods, including sketches and word descriptions, to communicate the design of their product.

Activity

Now it's your turn. Design and build a toy boat that is powered by wind. Follow the steps in the technology design process.

Your boat must

- be made of materials approved by your teacher
- be no longer than 10 cm
- float the length of a rectangular dishpan in 10 seconds or less, powered by a breeze from an electric fan
- be built following the safety guidelines in Appendix A

Creating Data Tables and Graphs

How can you make sense of the data in a science experiment?
The first step is to organize the data to help you understand them.
Data tables and graphs are helpful tools for organizing data.

Data Tables

You have gathered your materials and set up your experiment. But before you start, you need to plan a way to record what happens during the experiment. By creating a data table, you can record your observations and measurements in an orderly way.

Suppose, for example, that a scientist conducted an experiment to find out how many Calories people of different body masses burn while doing various activities. The data table shows the results.

Notice in this data table that the manipulated variable (body mass) is the heading of one column. The responding variable (for

Calories Burned in 30 Minutes			
Body Mass	Experiment 1: Bicycling	Experiment 2: Playing Basketball	Experiment 3: Watching Television
30 kg	60 Calories	120 Calories	21 Calories
40 kg	77 Calories	164 Calories	27 Calories
50 kg	95 Calories	206 Calories	33 Calories
60 kg	114 Calories	248 Calories	38 Calories

Experiment 1, the number of Calories burned while bicycling) is the heading of the next column. Additional columns were added for related experiments.

Bar Graphs

To compare how many Calories a person burns doing various activities, you could create a bar graph. A bar graph is used to display data in a number of separate, or distinct, categories. In this example, bicycling, playing basketball, and watching television are the three categories.

To create a bar graph, follow these steps.

1. On graph paper, draw a horizontal, or *x*-, axis and a vertical, or *y*-, axis.

2. Write the names of the categories to be graphed along the horizontal axis. Include an overall label for the axis as well.

3. Label the vertical axis with the name of the responding variable. Include units of measurement. Then create a scale along the axis by marking off equally spaced numbers that cover the range of the data collected.

4. For each category, draw a solid bar using the scale on the vertical axis to determine the height. Make all the bars the same width.

5. Add a title that describes the graph.

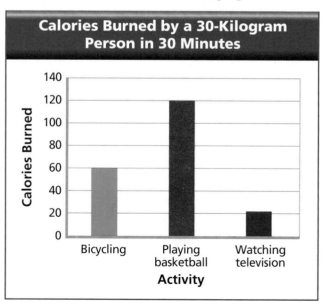

Line Graphs

To see whether a relationship exists between body mass and the number of Calories burned while bicycling, you could create a line graph. A line graph is used to display data that show how one variable (the responding variable) changes in response to another variable (the manipulated variable). You can use a line graph when your manipulated variable is **continuous,** that is, when there are other points between the ones that you tested. In this example, body mass is a continuous variable because there are other body masses between 30 and 40 kilograms (for example, 31 kilograms). Time is another example of a continuous variable.

Line graphs are powerful tools because they allow you to estimate values for conditions that you did not test in the experiment. For example, you can use the line graph to estimate that a 35-kilogram person would burn 68 Calories while bicycling.

To create a line graph, follow these steps.

1. On graph paper, draw a horizontal, or *x*-, axis and a vertical, or *y*-, axis.

2. Label the horizontal axis with the name of the manipulated variable. Label the vertical axis with the name of the responding variable. Include units of measurement.

3. Create a scale on each axis by marking off equally spaced numbers that cover the range of the data collected.

4. Plot a point on the graph for each piece of data. In the line graph above, the dotted lines show how to plot the first data point (30 kilograms and 60 Calories). Follow an imaginary vertical line extending up from the horizontal axis at the 30-kilogram mark. Then follow an imaginary horizontal line extending across from the vertical axis at the 60-Calorie mark. Plot the point where the two lines intersect.

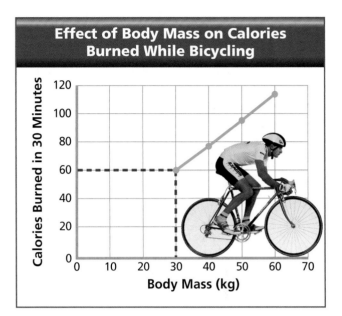

Effect of Body Mass on Calories Burned While Bicycling

5. Connect the plotted points with a solid line. (In some cases, it may be more appropriate to draw a line that shows the general trend of the plotted points. In those cases, some of the points may fall above or below the line. Also, not all graphs are linear. It may be more appropriate to draw a curve to connect the points.)

6. Add a title that identifies the variables or relationship in the graph.

Activity

Create line graphs to display the data from Experiment 2 and Experiment 3 in the data table.

Activity

You read in the newspaper that a total of 4 centimeters of rain fell in your area in June, 2.5 centimeters fell in July, and 1.5 centimeters fell in August. What type of graph would you use to display these data? Use graph paper to create the graph.

Circle Graphs

Like bar graphs, circle graphs can be used to display data in a number of separate categories. Unlike bar graphs, however, circle graphs can only be used when you have data for *all* the categories that make up a given topic. A circle graph is sometimes called a pie chart. The pie represents the entire topic, while the slices represent the individual categories. The size of a slice indicates what percentage of the whole a particular category makes up.

The data table below shows the results of a survey in which 24 teenagers were asked to identify their favorite sport. The data were then used to create the circle graph at the right.

Favorite Sports	
Sport	Students
Soccer	8
Basketball	6
Bicycling	6
Swimming	4

To create a circle graph, follow these steps.

1. Use a compass to draw a circle. Mark the center with a point. Then draw a line from the center point to the top of the circle.

2. Determine the size of each "slice" by setting up a proportion where *x* equals the number of degrees in a slice. (*Note:* A circle contains 360 degrees.) For example, to find the number of degrees in the "soccer" slice, set up the following proportion:

$$\frac{\text{Students who prefer soccer}}{\text{Total number of students}} = \frac{x}{\text{Total number of degrees in a circle}}$$

$$\frac{8}{24} = \frac{x}{360}$$

Cross-multiply and solve for *x*.

$$24x = 8 \times 360$$
$$x = 120$$

The "soccer" slice should contain 120 degrees.

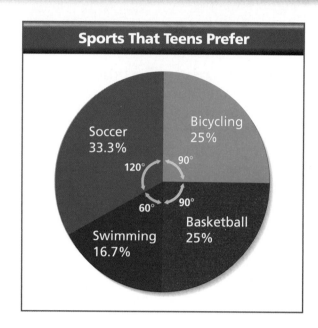

Sports That Teens Prefer

Soccer 33.3%
Bicycling 25%
120°
90°
60°
90°
Swimming 16.7%
Basketball 25%

3. Use a protractor to measure the angle of the first slice, using the line you drew to the top of the circle as the 0° line. Draw a line from the center of the circle to the edge for the angle you measured.

4. Continue around the circle by measuring the size of each slice with the protractor. Start measuring from the edge of the previous slice so the wedges do not overlap. When you are done, the entire circle should be filled in.

5. Determine the percentage of the whole circle that each slice represents. To do this, divide the number of degrees in a slice by the total number of degrees in a circle (360), and multiply by 100%. For the "soccer" slice, you can find the percentage as follows:

$$\frac{120}{360} \times 100\% = 33.3\%$$

6. Use a different color for each slice. Label each slice with the category and with the percentage of the whole it represents.

7. Add a title to the circle graph.

Activity

In a class of 28 students, 12 students take the bus to school, 10 students walk, and 6 students ride their bicycles. Create a circle graph to display these data.

Math Review

Math is a key tool in the study of science. Scientists use math to organize, analyze, and present data. This appendix will help you review some basic math skills.

Mean, Median, and Mode

When scientists analyze data, they may use the terms *mean*, *median*, and *mode*. The **mean** is the average, or the sum of the data divided by the number of data items. The **median** is the middle number in a set of ordered data. The **mode** is the number that appears most often in a set of data.

Example

A scientist counted the number of distinct songs sung by seven different male birds and collected the data shown below.

Male Bird Songs							
Bird	A	B	C	D	E	F	G
Number of Songs	36	29	40	35	28	36	27

To determine the mean number of songs, add the total number of songs and divide by the number of data items—in this case, the number of male birds.

$$\text{Mean} = \frac{231}{7} = 33 \text{ songs}$$

To find the median number of songs, arrange the data in numerical order and find the number in the middle of the series.

27 28 29 35 36 36 40

The number in the middle is 35, so the median number of songs is 35.

The mode is the value that appears most frequently. In the data, 36 appears twice, while each other item appears only once. Therefore, 36 songs is the mode.

Practice

Find out how many minutes it takes each student in your class to get to school. Then find the mean, median, and mode for the data.

Area

The **area** of a surface is the number of square units that cover it. The front cover of your textbook has an area of about 600 cm^2.

Area of a Rectangle and a Square To find the area of a rectangle, multiply its length times its width. The formula for the area of a rectangle is

$$A = \ell \times w, \text{ or } A = \ell w$$

Since all four sides of a square have the same length, the area of a square is the length of one side multiplied by itself, or squared.

$$A = s \times s, \text{ or } A = s^2$$

Example

A scientist is studying the plants in a field that measures 75 m × 45 m. What is the area of the field?

$$A = \ell \times w$$
$$A = 75 \text{ m} \times 45 \text{ m}$$
$$A = 3,375 \text{ m}^2$$

Area of a Circle The formula for the area of a circle is

$$A = \pi \times r \times r, \text{ or } A = \pi r^2$$

The length of the radius is represented by r, and the value of π is approximately $\frac{22}{7}$.

Example

Find the area of a circle with a radius of 14 cm.

$$A = \pi r^2$$
$$A = 14 \times 14 \times \frac{22}{7}$$
$$A = 616 \text{ cm}^2$$

Practice

Find the area of a circle that has a radius of 21 m.

Circumference

The distance around a circle is called the circumference. The formula for finding the circumference of a circle is

$$C = 2 \times \pi \times r, \text{ or } C = 2\pi r$$

Example

The radius of a circle is 35 cm. What is its circumference?

$$C = 2\pi r$$
$$C = 2 \times 35 \times \frac{22}{7}$$
$$C = 220 \text{ cm}$$

Practice

What is the circumference of a circle with a radius of 28 m?

Volume

The volume of an object is the number of cubic units it contains. The volume of a wastebasket, for example, might be about 26,000 cm^3.

Volume of a Rectangular Object To find the volume of a rectangular object, multiply the object's length times its width times its height.

$$V = \ell \times w \times h, \text{ or } V = \ell wh$$

Example

Find the volume of a box with length 24 cm, width 12 cm, and height 9 cm.

$$V = \ell wh$$
$$V = 24 \text{ cm} \times 12 \text{ cm} \times 9 \text{ cm}$$
$$V = 2,592 \text{ cm}^3$$

Volume of a Cylinder To find the volume of a cylinder, multiply the area of its base times its height. Since the base of a cylinder is a circle, the formula for its area is $A = \pi r^2$. Therefore, the formula for the volume of a cylinder is

$$V = (\pi r^2)h$$

Example

Find the volume of a coffee can with radius 5 cm and height 14 cm.

$$V = (\pi r^2)h$$
$$V = \frac{22}{7} \times 5 \text{ cm} \times 5 \text{ cm} \times 14 \text{ cm}$$
$$V = 1,100 \text{ cm}^3$$

Practice

What is the volume of a cylinder with height 5 m and base radius of 7 m?

Fractions

A **fraction** is a way to express a part of a whole. For example, a baseball team has nine players. The three outfielders make up three parts of the nine-part team. This can be expressed as $\frac{3}{9}$ of the team. In the fraction $\frac{3}{9}$, 3 is the numerator and 9 is the denominator.

Adding and Subtracting Fractions To add or subtract two or more fractions that have a common denominator, first add or subtract the numerators. Then write the sum or difference over the common denominator.

Example

$$\frac{2}{7} + \frac{3}{7} = \frac{2+3}{7} = \frac{5}{7}$$

To find the sum or difference of fractions with different denominators, first find the least common multiple of the denominators. This is known as the least common denominator. Then convert each fraction to equivalent fractions with the least common denominator. Add or subtract the numerators. Then write the sum or difference over the common denominator.

Example

$$\frac{5}{6} - \frac{3}{4} = \frac{10}{12} - \frac{9}{12} = \frac{10 - 9}{12} = \frac{1}{12}$$

Multiplying Fractions To multiply two fractions, first multiply the two numerators to find the product's numerator. Then multiply the two denominators to find the product's denominator.

Example

$$\frac{5}{6} \times \frac{2}{3} = \frac{5 \times 2}{6 \times 3} = \frac{10}{18} = \frac{5}{9}$$

Dividing Fractions Dividing by a fraction is the same as multiplying by its reciprocal. Reciprocals are numbers whose numerators and denominators have been switched. To divide one fraction by another, first invert the fraction you are dividing by—in other words, turn it upside down. Then multiply the two fractions.

Example

$$\frac{2}{5} \div \frac{7}{8} = \frac{2}{5} \times \frac{8}{7} = \frac{2 \times 8}{5 \times 7} = \frac{16}{35}$$

Practice

Solve the following: $\frac{3}{7} \div \frac{4}{5}$.

Decimals

Fractions whose denominators are 10, 100, or some other power of 10 are often expressed as decimals. For example, the fraction $\frac{9}{10}$ can be expressed as the decimal 0.9, and the fraction $\frac{7}{100}$ can be written as 0.07.

Adding and Subtracting With Decimals
To add or subtract decimals, line up the decimal points before you carry out the operation.

Example

27.4	278.635
+ 6.19	− 191.4
33.59	87.235

Multiplying With Decimals When you multiply two numbers with decimals, the number of decimal places in the product is equal to the total number of decimal places in each number being multiplied.

Example

46.2 (one decimal place)
× 2.37 (two decimal places)
109.494 (three decimal places)

Dividing With Decimals To divide a decimal by a whole number, put the decimal point in the quotient above the decimal point in the dividend.

Example

15.5 ÷ 5

$$\begin{array}{r} 3.1 \\ 5\overline{)15.5} \end{array}$$

To divide a decimal by a decimal, you need to rewrite the divisor as a whole number. Do this by multiplying both the divisor and dividend by the same multiple of 10.

Example

1.68 ÷ 4.2 = 16.8 ÷ 42

$$\begin{array}{r} 0.4 \\ 42\overline{)16.8} \end{array}$$

Practice

Multiply 6.21 by 8.5.

Converting Fractions to Decimals To convert a fraction to a decimal, divide the numerator by the denominator.

Example

$$\frac{5}{8} = \begin{array}{r} 0.625 \\ 8\overline{)5} \end{array}$$

Ratio and Proportion

A **ratio** compares two numbers by division. For example, suppose a scientist counts 800 wolves and 1,200 moose on an island. The ratio of wolves to moose can be written as a fraction, $\frac{800}{1,200}$, which can be reduced to $\frac{2}{3}$. The same ratio can also be expressed as 2 to 3 or 2 : 3.

A **proportion** is a mathematical sentence saying that two ratios are equivalent. For example, a proportion could state that $\frac{800 \text{ wolves}}{1,200 \text{ moose}} = \frac{2 \text{ wolves}}{3 \text{ moose}}$. You can sometimes set up a proportion to determine or estimate an unknown quantity. For example, suppose a scientist counts 25 beetles in an area of 10 square meters. The scientist wants to estimate the number of beetles in 100 square meters.

Example

1. Express the relationship between beetles and area as a ratio: $\frac{25}{10}$, simplified to $\frac{5}{2}$.
2. Set up a proportion, with x representing the number of beetles. The proportion can be stated as $\frac{5}{2} = \frac{x}{100}$.
3. Begin by cross-multiplying. In other words, multiply each fraction's numerator by the other fraction's denominator.

   $$5 \times 100 = 2 \times x, \text{ or } 500 = 2x$$

4. To find the value of x, divide both sides by 2. The result is 250, or 250 beetles in 100 square meters.

Practice

Find the value of x in the following proportion: $\frac{6}{7} = \frac{x}{49}$.

Percentage

A **percentage** is a ratio that compares a number to 100. For example, there are 37 granite rocks in a collection that consists of 100 rocks. The ratio $\frac{37}{100}$ can be written as 37%. Granite rocks make up 37% of the rock collection.

You can calculate percentages of numbers other than 100 by setting up a proportion.

Example

Rain falls on 9 days out of 30 in June. What percentage of the days in June were rainy?

$$\frac{9 \text{ days}}{30 \text{ days}} = \frac{d\%}{100\%}$$

To find the value of d, begin by cross-multiplying, as for any proportion:

$$9 \times 100 = 30 \times d \qquad d = \frac{900}{30} \qquad d = 30$$

Practice

There are 80 beans in a jar, and 24 of those beans are red. What percentage of the beans are red?

Precision and Significant Figures

The **precision** of a measurement depends on the instrument you use to take the measurement. For example, suppose you measure a box with a ruler. If the smallest unit on the ruler is millimeters, then the most precise measurement you can make will be in millimeters.

The sum or difference of measurements can only be as precise as the least precise measurement being added or subtracted. Round your answer so that it has the same number of digits after the decimal as the least precise measurement. Round up if the last digit is 5 or more, and round down if the last digit is 4 or less.

Example

Subtract a temperature of 5.2°C from the temperature 75.47°C.

$$75.46 - 5.2 = 70.26$$

5.2 has the fewest digits after the decimal, so it is the least precise measurement. Since the last digit of the answer is 6, round up to 3. The most precise difference between the measurements is 70.3°C.

Practice

Add 26.4 m to 8.37 m. Round your answer according to the precision of the measurements.

Significant figures are the number of nonzero digits in a measurement. Zeroes between nonzero digits are also significant. For example, the measurements 12,500 L, 0.125 cm, and 2.05 kg all have three significant figures. When you multiply and divide measurements, the one with the fewest significant figures determines the number of significant figures in your answer.

Example

Multiply 110 g by 5.75 g.

110 × 5.75 = 632.5

Because 110 has only two significant figures, round the answer to 630 g.

Practice

Divide 306 L by 2.5 L.

Scientific Notation

A **factor** is a number that divides into another number with no remainder. In the example, the number 3 is used as a factor four times.

Example

3 × 3 × 3 × 3 = 81

An **exponent** tells how many times a number is used as a factor. For example, $3 \times 3 \times 3 \times 3$ can be written as 3^4. The exponent ^{4} indicates that the number 3 is used as a factor four times. Another way of expressing this is to say that 81 is equal to 3 to the fourth power.

Scientific notation uses exponents and powers of ten to write very large or very small numbers in shorter form. When you write a number in scientific notation, you write the number as two factors. The first factor is any number between 1 and 10. The second factor is a power of 10, such as 10^3 or 10^6.

Example

The average distance between the planet Mercury and the sun is 58,000,000 km. To write the first factor in scientific notation, insert a decimal point in the original number so that you have a number between 1 and 10. In the case of 58,000,000, the number is 5.8.

To determine the power of 10, count the number of places that the decimal point moved. In this case, it moved 7 places.

58,000,000 km = 5.8×10^7 km

Practice

Express 6,590,000 in scientific notation.

Probability

Probability is the chance that an event will occur. Probability can be expressed as a ratio, a fraction, or a percentage. For example, when you flip a coin, the probability that the coin will land heads up is 1 in 2, or $\frac{1}{2}$, or 50 percent.

The probability that an event will happen can be expressed in the following formula.

$$P(\text{event}) = \frac{\text{Number of times the event can occur}}{\text{Total number of possible events}}$$

Example

A paper bag contains 25 blue marbles, 5 green marbles, 5 orange marbles, and 15 yellow marbles. If you close your eyes and pick a marble from the bag, what is the probability that it will be yellow?

$$P(\text{yellow marbles}) = \frac{15 \text{ yellow marbles}}{50 \text{ marbles total}}$$

$$P = \frac{15}{50}, \text{ or } \frac{3}{10}, \text{ or } 30\%$$

Practice

Each side of a cube has a letter on it. Two sides have *A*, three sides have *B*, and one side has *C*. If you roll the cube, what is the probability that *A* will land on top?

Target Reading Skills

Your textbook is an important source of science information. As you read your science textbook, you will find that the book has been written to assist you in understanding the science concepts.

Introduction: Learning From Science Textbooks

As you study science in school, you will learn science concepts in a variety of ways. Sometimes you will do interesting activities and experiments to explore science ideas. To fully understand what you observe in experiments and activities, you will need to read your science textbook. To help you read, some of the important ideas are highlighted so that you can easily recognize what they are. In addition, a target reading skill in each section will help you understand what you read.

By using the target reading skills, you will become a strategic reader—that is, one who can easily apply the appropriate reading skills. As you learn science, you will build knowledge that will help you understand even more of what you read. This knowledge will help you learn about all the topics presented in this textbook.

And—guess what?—these reading skills can be useful whenever you are reading. Reading to learn is important for your entire life. You have an opportunity to begin that process now.

The target reading skills that will make you a strategic reader are described below.

Building Vocabulary

To understand the science concepts taught in this textbook, you need to remember the meanings of the Key Terms. One strategy consists of writing the definitions of these terms in your own words. You can also practice using the terms in sentences and make lists of words or phrases you associate with each term.

Using Prior Knowledge

Your prior knowledge is what you already know before you begin to read about a topic. Building on what you already know gives you a head start on learning new information. Before you begin a new assignment, think about what you know. You might page through your reading assignment, looking at the headings and the visuals to spark your memory. You can list what you know in the graphic organizer provided in the section opener. Then, as you read, consider questions like the ones below to connect what you learn to what you already know.

- How does what you learn relate to what you know?
- How did something you already know help you learn something new?
- Did your original ideas agree with what you have just learned? If not, how would you revise your original ideas?

Asking Questions

Asking yourself questions is an excellent way to focus on and remember new information in your textbook. You can learn how to ask good questions.

One way is to turn the text headings into questions. Then your questions can guide you to identify and remember the important information as you read. Look at these examples:

Heading: Using Seismographic Data
Question: How are seismographic data used?
Heading: Kinds of Faults
Question: What are the kinds of faults?

You do not have to limit your questions to the text headings. Ask questions about anything that you need to clarify or that will help you understand the content. *What* and *how* are probably the most common question words, but you may also ask *why*, *who*, *when*, or *where* questions. Here is an example:

Properties of Waves

Question	Answer
What is amplitude?	Amplitude is . . .

Previewing Visuals

Visuals are photographs, graphs, tables, diagrams, and illustrations. Visuals, such as this diagram of a normal fault, contain important information. Look at visuals and their captions before you read. This will help you prepare for what you will be reading about.

Often you will be asked what you want to learn about a visual. For example, after you look at the normal fault diagram, you might ask: What is the movement along a normal fault? Questions about visuals give you a purpose for reading—to answer your questions. Previewing visuals also helps you see what you already know.

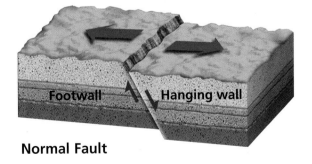

Footwall **Hanging wall**

Normal Fault

Outlining

An outline shows the relationship between main ideas and supporting ideas. An outline has a formal structure. You write the main ideas, called topics, next to Roman numerals. The supporting ideas, sometimes called subtopics, are written under the main ideas and labeled A, B, C, and so on. An outline looks like this:

Technology and Society

I. Technology through history

II. The impact of technology on society

  A.

  B.

When you have completed an outline like this, you can see at a glance the structure of the section. You can use this outline as a study tool.

Identifying Main Ideas

When you are reading, it is important to try to understand the ideas and concepts that are in a passage. As you read science material, you will recognize that each paragraph has a lot of information and detail. Good readers try to identify the most important—or biggest—idea in every paragraph or section. That's the main idea. The other information in the paragraph supports or further explains the main idea.

Sometimes main ideas are stated directly. In this book, some main ideas are identified for you as key concepts. These are printed in boldface type. However, you must identify other main ideas yourself. In order to do this, you must identify all the ideas within a paragraph or section. Then ask yourself which idea is big enough to include all the other ideas.

Comparing and Contrasting

When you compare and contrast, you examine the similarities and differences between things. You can compare and contrast in a Venn diagram or in a table. Your completed diagram or table shows you how the items are alike and how they are different.

Venn Diagram A Venn diagram consists of two overlapping circles. In the space where the circles overlap, you write the characteristics that the two items have in common. In one of the circles outside the area of overlap, you write the differing features or characteristics of one of the items. In the other circle outside the area of overlap, you write the differing characteristics of the other item.

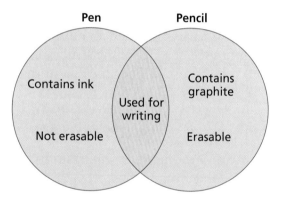

Table In a compare/contrast table, you list the items to be compared across the top of the table. Then list the characteristics or features to be compared in the left column. Complete the table by filling in information about each characteristic or feature.

	Loop One	Loop Two
Side of heart		
Blood flows to		
Blood returns from		

Sequencing

A sequence is the order in which a series of events occurs. Recognizing and remembering the sequence of events is important to understanding many processes in science. Sometimes the text uses words like *first, next, during,* and *after* to signal a sequence. A flowchart or a cycle diagram can help you visualize a sequence.

Flowchart To make a flowchart, write a brief description of each step or event in a box. Place the boxes in order, with the first event at the top of the page. Then draw an arrow to connect each step or event to the next.

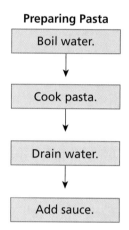

Cycle Diagram A cycle diagram shows a sequence that is continuous, or cyclical. A continuous sequence does not have an end because when the final event is over, the first event begins again. To create a cycle diagram, write the starting event in a box placed at the top of a page in the center. Then, moving in a clockwise direction around an imaginary circle, write each event in a box in its proper sequence. Draw arrows that connect each event to the one that occurs next, forming a continuous circle.

Identifying Supporting Evidence

A hypothesis is a possible explanation for observations made by scientists or an answer to a scientific question. A hypothesis is tested over and over again. The tests may produce evidence that supports the hypothesis. When enough supporting evidence is collected, a hypothesis may become a theory.

Identifying the supporting evidence for a hypothesis or theory can help you understand the hypothesis or theory. Evidence consists of facts—information whose accuracy can be confirmed by testing or observation.

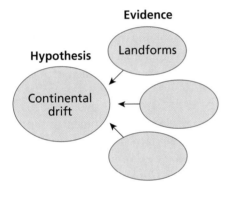

Relating Cause and Effect

Identifying causes and effects helps you understand relationships among events. A cause makes something happen. An effect is what happens. When you recognize that one event causes another, you are relating cause and effect. Words like *cause, because, effect, affect,* and *result* often signal a cause or an effect.

Sometimes an effect can have more than one cause, or a cause can produce several effects. For example, car exhaust and smoke from industrial plants are two causes of air pollution. Some effects of air pollution include breathing difficulties for some people, death of plants along some highways, and damage to some building surfaces.

Science involves many cause-and-effect relationships. Seeing and understanding these relationships helps you understand science processes.

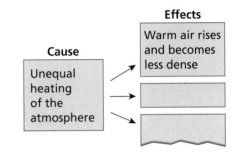

Concept Mapping

Concept maps are useful tools for organizing information on any topic. A concept map begins with a main idea or core concept and shows how the idea can be subdivided into related subconcepts or smaller ideas. In this way, relationships between concepts become clearer and easier to understand.

You construct a concept map by placing concepts (usually nouns) in ovals and connecting them with linking words. The biggest concept or idea is placed in an oval at the top of the map. Related concepts are arranged in ovals below the big idea. The linking words are often verbs and verb phrases and are written on the lines that connect the ovals.

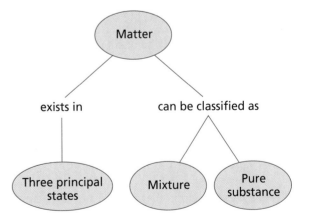

Safety Symbols

These symbols warn of possible dangers in the laboratory and remind you to work carefully.

 Safety Goggles Wear safety goggles to protect your eyes in any activity involving chemicals, flames or heating, or glassware.

 Lab Apron Wear a laboratory apron to protect your skin and clothing from damage.

 Breakage Handle breakable materials, such as glassware, with care. Do not touch broken glassware.

 Heat-Resistant Gloves Use an oven mitt or other hand protection when handling hot materials such as hot plates or hot glassware.

 Plastic Gloves Wear disposable plastic gloves when working with harmful chemicals and organisms. Keep your hands away from your face, and dispose of the gloves according to your teacher's instructions.

 Heating Use a clamp or tongs to pick up hot glassware. Do not touch hot objects with your bare hands.

 Flames Before you work with flames, tie back loose hair and clothing. Follow instructions from your teacher about lighting and extinguishing flames.

 No Flames When using flammable materials, make sure there are no flames, sparks, or other exposed heat sources present.

 Corrosive Chemical Avoid getting acid or other corrosive chemicals on your skin or clothing or in your eyes. Do not inhale the vapors. Wash your hands after the activity.

 Poison Do not let any poisonous chemical come into contact with your skin, and do not inhale its vapors. Wash your hands when you are finished with the activity.

 Fumes Work in a ventilated area when harmful vapors may be involved. Avoid inhaling vapors directly. Only test an odor when directed to do so by your teacher, and use a wafting motion to direct the vapor toward your nose.

 Sharp Object Scissors, scalpels, knives, needles, pins, and tacks can cut your skin. Always direct a sharp edge or point away from yourself and others.

 Animal Safety Treat live or preserved animals or animal parts with care to avoid harming the animals or yourself. Wash your hands when you are finished with the activity.

 Plant Safety Handle plants only as directed by your teacher. If you are allergic to certain plants, tell your teacher; do not do an activity involving those plants. Avoid touching harmful plants such as poison ivy. Wash your hands when you are finished with the activity.

 Electric Shock To avoid electric shock, never use electrical equipment around water, or when the equipment is wet or your hands are wet. Be sure cords are untangled and cannot trip anyone. Unplug equipment not in use.

 Physical Safety When an experiment involves physical activity, avoid injuring yourself or others. Alert your teacher if there is any reason you should not participate.

 Disposal Dispose of chemicals and other laboratory materials safely. Follow the instructions from your teacher.

 Hand Washing Wash your hands thoroughly when finished with the activity. Use antibacterial soap and warm water. Rinse well.

 General Safety Awareness When this symbol appears, follow the instructions provided. When you are asked to develop your own procedure in a lab, have your teacher approve your plan before you go further.

Science Safety Rules

General Precautions

Follow all instructions. Never perform activities without the approval and supervision of your teacher. Do not engage in horseplay. Never eat or drink in the laboratory. Keep work areas clean and uncluttered.

Dress Code

Wear safety goggles whenever you work with chemicals, glassware, heat sources such as burners, or any substance that might get into your eyes. If you wear contact lenses, notify your teacher.

Wear a lab apron or coat whenever you work with corrosive chemicals or substances that can stain. Tie back long hair. Remove or tie back any article of clothing or jewelry that can hang down and touch chemicals, flames, or equipment. Roll up long sleeves. Never wear open shoes or sandals.

First Aid

Report all accidents, injuries, or fires to your teacher, no matter how minor. Be aware of the location of the first-aid kit, emergency equipment such as the fire extinguisher and fire blanket, and the nearest telephone. Know whom to contact in an emergency.

Heating and Fire Safety

Keep all combustible materials away from flames. When heating a substance in a test tube, make sure that the mouth of the tube is not pointed at you or anyone else. Never heat a liquid in a closed container. Use an oven mitt to pick up a container that has been heated.

Using Chemicals Safely

Never put your face near the mouth of a container that holds chemicals. Never touch, taste, or smell a chemical unless your teacher tells you to.

Use only those chemicals needed in the activity. Keep all containers closed when chemicals are not being used. Pour all chemicals over the sink or a container, not over your work surface. Dispose of excess chemicals as instructed by your teacher.

Be extra careful when working with acids or bases. When mixing an acid and water, always pour the water into the container first and then add the acid to the water. Never pour water into an acid. Wash chemical spills and splashes immediately with plenty of water.

Using Glassware Safely

If glassware is broken or chipped, notify your teacher immediately. Never handle broken or chipped glass with your bare hands.

Never force glass tubing or thermometers into a rubber stopper or rubber tubing. Have your teacher insert the glass tubing or thermometer if required for an activity.

Using Sharp Instruments

Handle sharp instruments with extreme care. Never cut material toward you; cut away from you.

Animal and Plant Safety

Never perform experiments that cause pain, discomfort, or harm to animals. Only handle animals if absolutely necessary. If you know that you are allergic to certain plants, molds, or animals, tell your teacher before doing an activity in which these are used. Wash your hands thoroughly after any activity involving animals, animal parts, plants, plant parts, or soil.

During field work, wear long pants, long sleeves, socks, and closed shoes. Avoid poisonous plants and fungi as well as plants with thorns.

End-of-Experiment Rules

Unplug all electrical equipment. Clean up your work area. Dispose of waste materials as instructed by your teacher. Wash your hands after every experiment.

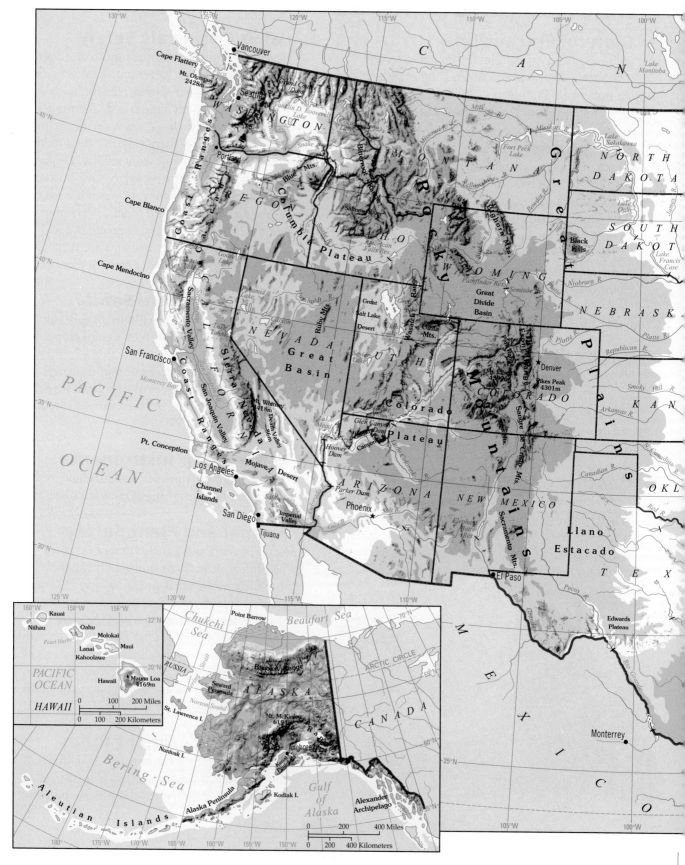

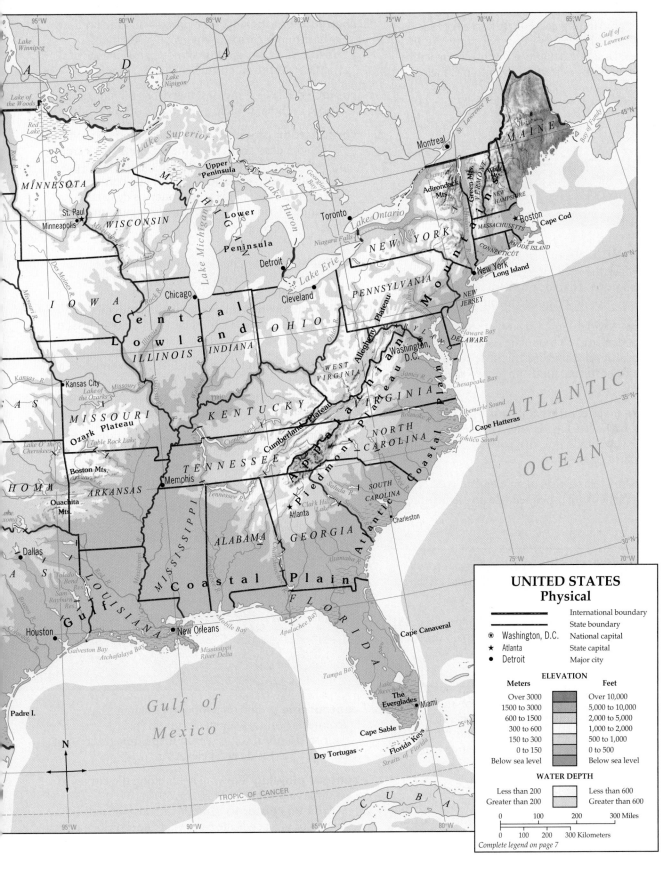

UNITED STATES
Physical

	International boundary
	State boundary
⊛ Washington, D.C.	National capital
★ Atlanta	State capital
● Detroit	Major city

ELEVATION

Meters		Feet
Over 3000		Over 10,000
1500 to 3000		5,000 to 10,000
600 to 1500		2,000 to 5,000
300 to 600		1,000 to 2,000
150 to 300		500 to 1,000
0 to 150		0 to 500
Below sea level		Below sea level

WATER DEPTH

Less than 200		Less than 600
Greater than 200		Greater than 600

0   100   200   300 Miles

0 100 200 300 Kilometers

Complete legend on page 7

English and Spanish Glossary

A

abrasion The grinding away of rock by other rock particles carried in water, ice, or wind. (pp. 41, 87)
abrasión Desgaste de la roca por otras partículas de roca llevadas por el agua, el viento o el hielo.

absolute age The age of a rock given as the number of years since the rock formed. (p. 117)
edad absoluta Edad de una roca basada en el número de años desde que se formó la roca.

alluvial fan A wide, sloping deposit of sediment formed where a stream leaves a mountain range. (p. 77)
abanico aluvial Depósito ancho de sedimento en declive, que se forma donde un arroyo sale de una cordillera.

amphibian A vertebrate that lives part of its life on land and part of its life in water. (p. 136)
anfibio Vertebrado que vive parte de su vida en la tierra y parte en el agua.

atom The smallest particle of an element. (p. 124)
átomo Partícula más pequeña de un elemento.

B

beach Wave-washed sediment along a coast. (p. 99)
playa Sedimento depositado por las olas a lo largo de una costa.

bedrock The solid layer of rock beneath the soil. (p. 48)
lecho rocoso Capa sólida de roca debajo del suelo.

C

carbon film A type of fossil consisting of an extremely thin coating of carbon on rock. (p. 112)
película de carbono Tipo de fósil que consiste en una capa de carbono extremadamente fina que recubre la roca.

cast A fossil that is a copy of an organism's shape, formed when minerals seep into a mold. (p. 111)
vaciado Fósil que es una copia de la forma de un organismo, formado cuando los minerales penetran en un molde.

chemical weathering The process that breaks down rock through chemical changes. (p. 42)
desgaste químico Proceso que erosiona la roca mediante cambios químicos.

comet A ball of ice and dust that orbits the sun. (p. 132)
cometa Bola de hielo y polvo que orbita el Sol.

conservation plowing Soil conservation method in which the dead stalks from the previous year's crop are left in the ground to hold the soil in place. (p. 59)
arada de conservación Método de conservación del suelo en el cual los tallos muertos de la cosecha del año anterior se dejan en la tierra para que sujeten el suelo en su lugar.

continental drift The slow movement of the continents over Earth's surface caused by forces inside Earth. (p. 132)
deriva continental Movimiento lento de los continentes sobre la superficie de la Tierra causado por las fuerzas dentro de la Tierra.

continental glacier A glacier that covers much of a continent or large island. (p. 92)
glaciar continental Glaciar que cubre gran parte de un continente o una isla grande.

contour interval The difference in elevation from one contour line to the next. (p. 27)
intervalo entre curvas de nivel Diferencia de elevación de una curva de nivel a otra.

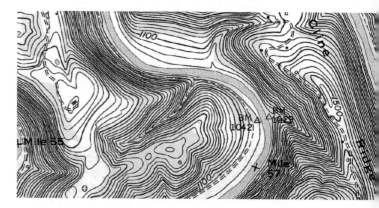

contour line A line on a topographic map that connects points of equal elevation. (p. 27)
curva de nivel Línea en un mapa topográfico que conecta puntos de igual elevación.

contour plowing Plowing fields along the curves of a slope to prevent soil loss. (p. 59)
arada en contarno Arar los campos siguiendo las curvas de una pendiente para evitar que el suelo se suelte.

crop rotation The planting of different crops in a field each year to maintain the soil's fertility. (p. 59)
rotación de las cosechas Plantación de cosechas diferentes en un campo cada año para mantener la fertilidad del suelo.

D

decomposer Soil organism that breaks down the remains of organisms and digests them. (p. 53)
descomponedor Organismo del suelo que desintegra los restos de organismos y los digiere.

deflation Wind erosion that removes surface materials. (p. 102)
deflación Erosión por viento que se lleva materiales superficiales.

degree A unit used to measure distances around a circle. One degree equals 1/360 of a full circle. (p. 13)
grado Unidad usada para medir distancias alrededor de un círculo. Un grado es igual a 1/360 de un círculo completo.

delta A landform made of sediment that is deposited where a river flows into an ocean or lake. (p. 77)
delta Accidente geográfico formado por sedimentos que se depositan en la desembocadura de un río en un océano o lago.

deposition Process in which sediment is laid down in new locations. (p. 67)
sedimentación Proceso por el cual se asientan sedimentos en sitios nuevos.

digitizing Converting information to numbers for use by a computer. (p. 21)
digitalizar Convertir información a números para que pueda ser usada por una computadora.

Dust Bowl The area of the Great Plains where wind erosion caused soil loss during the 1930s. (p. 58)
Cuenca del polvo Área de las Grandes Llanuras donde la erosión por el viento causó la pérdida de suelo durante la década de 1930.

E

element A type of matter in which all the atoms are the same. (p. 124)
elemento Tipo de materia en la cual todos los átomos son iguales.

elevation Height above sea level. (p. 7)
elevación Altura sobre el nivel del mar.

energy The ability to do work or cause change. (p. 86)
energía Capacidad para realizar un trabajo o producir cambios.

equator An imaginary line that circles Earth halfway between the North and South poles. (p. 14)
ecuador Línea imaginaria que rodea la Tierra por el centro, entre los polos Norte y Sur.

era One of the three long units of geologic time between the Precambrian and the present. (p. 129)
era Cada una de las tres unidades largas del tiempo geológico entre el Precámbrico y el presente.

erosion The process by which water, ice, wind, or gravity moves weathered rock and soil. (p. 39, 66)
erosión Proceso por el cual el agua, el hielo, el viento o la gravedad desplazan rocas meteorizadas y suelo.

evolution The process by which all the different kinds of living things have changed over time. (p. 116)
evolución Proceso por el cual los diferentes tipos de seres vivos han cambiado con el tiempo.

extinct Describes a type of organism that no longer exists anywhere on Earth. (p. 116)
extinto Describe un tipo de organismo que ya no existe en la Tierra.

extrusion An igneous rock layer formed when lava flows onto Earth's surface and hardens. (p. 119)
extrusión Capa de roca ígnea formada cuando la lava fluye hacia la superficie de la Tierra y se endurece.

F

fault A break or crack in Earth's lithosphere along which the rocks move. (p. 119)
falla Fisura o grieta en la litosfera de la Tierra a lo largo de la cual se mueven las rocas.

English and Spanish Glossary

fertility A measure of how well soil supports plant growth. (p. 49)
fertilidad Medida de lo apropiado de un suelo para mantener el crecimiento de las plantas.

flood plain Wide valley through which a river flows. (p. 75)
llanura de aluvión Valle ancho por el cual fluye un río.

fossil The preserved remains or traces of living things. (p. 110)
fósil Restos preservados o huellas de seres vivos.

friction The force that opposes the motion of one surface as it moves across another surface. (p. 89)
fricción La fuerza que se opone al movimiento de una superficie con la que está en contacto.

G

geologic time scale A record of the geologic events and life forms in Earth's history. (p. 127)
escala de tiempo geológico Registro de los sucesos geológicos y de las formas de vida en la historia de la Tierra.

glacier A large mass of moving ice and snow on land. (p. 92)
glaciar Gran masa de hielo y nieve que se mantiene en movimiento sobre la tierra.

Global Positioning System A method of finding latitude and longitude using a network of satellites. (p. 23)
Sistema de posicionamiento global Método para hallar la latitud y longitud usando una red de satélites.

globe A sphere that represents Earth's entire surface. (p. 12)
globo terráqueo Esfera que representa toda la superficie de la Tierra.

gravity A force that moves rocks and other materials downhill. (p. 67)
gravedad Fuerza que mueve rocas y otros materiales hacia abajo en una pendiente.

groundwater Water that fills the cracks and spaces in underground soil and rock layers. (p. 80)
aguas freáticas Agua que llena las grietas y huecos de las capas subterráneas de tierra y roca.

gully A large channel in soil formed by erosion. (p. 74)
barranco Canal grande en el suelo, formado por la erosión.

H

half-life The time it takes for half of the atoms of a radioactive element to decay. (p. 124)
vida media Tiempo que demoran en desintegrarse a la mitad de los átomos de un elemento radioactivo.

headland A part of the shore that sticks out into the ocean. (p. 97)
promontorio Parte de la costa que se interna en el mar.

hemisphere One half of the sphere that makes up Earth's surface. (p. 14)
hemisferio La mitad de la esfera que forma la superficie de la Tierra.

humus Dark-colored organic material in soil. (p. 49)
humus Material orgánico de color oscuro en el suelo.

I

ice age Times in the past when continental glaciers covered large parts of Earth's surface. (p. 92)
glaciación Épocas del pasado en las que glaciares continentales cubrieron grandes extensiones de la superficie terrestre.

ice wedging Process that splits rock when water seeps into cracks, then freezes and expands. (p. 41)
calza de hielo Proceso que parte la roca cuando el agua penetra en las grietas, y luego se congela y expande.

index contours On a topographic map, a heavier contour line that is labeled with elevation of that contour line in round units. (p. 27)
curva de nivel índice En un mapa topográfico, una curva de nivel más gruesa que lleva rotulada la elevación de esa curva de nivel en unidades redondeadas.

index fossil Fossils of widely distributed organisms that lived during only one short period. (p. 120)
fósil indicador Fósiles de organismos ampliamente dispersos que vivieron durante un período corto.

intrusion An igneous rock layer formed when magma hardens beneath Earth's surface. (p. 119)
intrusión Capa de roca ígnea formada cuando el magma se endurece bajo la superficie de la Tierra.

invertebrate An animal without a backbone. (p. 135)
invertebrado Animal sin columna vertebral.

karst topography A region in which a layer of limestone close to the surface creates deep valleys, caverns and sinkholes. (p. 80)
topografía kárstica Tipo de terreno de regiones lluviosas en las que hay piedra caliza cerca de la superficie; se caracteriza por tener grutas, pozas hundidas y valles.

kettle A small depression that forms when a chunk of ice is left in glacial till. (p. 94)
cazuela Pequeña depresión que se forma cuando queda un trozo de hielo en arcilla glaciárica.

key A list of the symbols used on a map. (p. 12)
clave Lista de símbolos usados en un mapa.

kinetic energy The energy an object has due to its motion. (p. 86)
energía cinética Energía que tiene un objeto por el hecho de estar en movimiento.

landform A feature of topography formed by the processes that shape Earth's surface. (p. 7)
accidente geográfico Característica de la topografía creada por los procesos de formación de la superficie terrestre.

landform region A large area of land where the topography is similar. (p. 10)
región con accidentes geográficos Gran extensión de tierra con topografía y estructura generales similares.

latitude The distance in degrees north or south of the equator. (p. 16)
latitud Distancia en grados al norte o al sur del ecuador.

law of superposition The geologic principle that states that in horizontal layers of sedimentary rock, each layer is older than the layer above it and younger than the layer below it. (p. 118)
ley de la superposición Principio geológico que enuncia que en las capas horizontales de la roca sedimentaria, cada capa es más vieja que la capa superior y más joven que la capa inferior.

litter The loose layer of dead plant leaves and stems on the surface of the soil. (p. 52)
hojarasca Capa suelta de hojas y tallos de plantas muertas en la superficie del suelo.

load The amount of sediment that a river or stream carries. (p. 87)
carga La cantidad de sedimento que lleva un río o arroyo.

loam Rich, fertile soil that is made up of about equal parts of clay, sand, and silt. (p. 49)
marga Suelo rico y fértil que está formado por partes casi iguales de arcilla, arena y cieno.

loess A wind-formed deposit made of fine particles of clay and silt. (p. 103)
loes Depósito de partículas finas de arcilla y limo arrastradas por el viento.

longitude The distance in degrees east or west of the prime meridian. (p. 16)
longitud Distancia en grados al este o al oeste del primer meridiano.

longshore drift The movement of water and sediment down a beach caused by waves coming in to shore at an angle. (p. 99)
deriva litoral Movimiento de agua y sedimentos paralelo a una playa debido a la llegada de olas inclinadas respecto a la costa.

English and Spanish Glossary

M

mammal A warm-blooded vertebrate that feeds its young milk. (p. 142)
mamífero Vertebrado de sangre caliente que alimenta con leche a su crías.

map A flat model of all or part of Earth's surface as seen from above. (p. 12)
mapa Modelo plano de toda la superficie de la Tierra o parte de ella tal y como se ve desde arriba.

map projection A framework of lines that helps to show landmasses on a flat surface. (p. 18)
proyección de mapa Sistema de líneas que ayuda a mostrar volúmenes de tierra en una superficie plana.

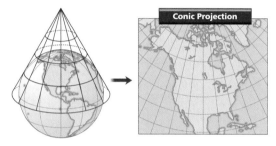

Conic Projection

mass extinction When many types of living things become extinct at the same time. (p. 137)
extinción en masa Cuando muchos tipos de seres vivos se extinguen al mismo tiempo.

mass movement Any one of several processes by which gravity moves sediment downhill. (p. 67)
movimiento masivo Cualquiera de varios procesos por los cuales la gravedad desplaza sedimentos cuesta abajo.

meander A looplike bend in the course of a river. (p. 76)
meandro Curva muy pronunciada en el curso de un río.

mechanical weathering The type of weathering in which rock is physically broken into smaller pieces. (p. 40)
desgaste mecánico Tipo de desgaste en el cual una roca se rompe físicamente en trozos más pequeños.

mold A fossil formed when an organism buried in sediment dissolves, leaving a hollow area. (p. 111)
molde Fósil que se forma cuando un organismo enterrado en sedimento se disuelve y deja un área hueca.

moraine A ridge formed by the till deposited at the edge of a glacier. (p. 94)
morrena Montículo formado por la arcilla glaciárica depositada en el borde de un glaciar.

mountain A landform with high elevation and high relief. (p. 9)
montaña Accidente geográfico con una elevación alta y un relieve alto.

mountain range A series of mountains that have the same general shape and structure. (p. 9)
cordillera Serie de montañas que tienen la misma forma y estructura general.

N

natural resource Anything in the environment that humans use. (p. 57)
recurso natural Cualquier cosa de la naturaleza que usan los humanos.

O

oxbow lake A meander cut off from a river. (p. 76)
lago de recodo Meandro que ha quedado aislado de un río.

oxidation A chemical change in which a substance combines with oxygen, as when iron oxidizes, forming rust. (p. 43)
oxidación Cambio químico en el cual una sustancia se combina con el oxígeno, como cuando el hierro se oxida y se forma herrumbre.

P

paleontologist A scientist who studies fossils to learn about organisms that lived long ago. (p. 114)
paleontólogo Científico que estudia fósiles para aprender acerca de los organismos que vivieron hace mucho tiempo.

period One of the units of geologic time into which geologists divide eras. (p. 129)
período Una de las unidades del tiempo geológico dentro de las cuales los geólogos dividen las eras.

permeable Characteristic of a material that is full of tiny, connected air spaces that water can seep through. (p. 44)
permeable Característica de un material que está lleno de diminutos espacios de aire conectados entre sí, por los que puede penetrar el agua.

petrified fossil A fossil in which minerals replace all or part of an organism. (p. 112)
fósil petrificado Fósil en el cual los minerales reemplazan todo el organismo o parte de él.

pixels The tiny dots in a satellite image. (p. 22)
pixels Puntos diminutos en una imagen de satélite.

plain A landform made up of flat or gently rolling land with low relief. (p. 8)
llanura Accidente geográfico que consiste en un terreno plano o ligeramente ondulado con un relieve bajo.

plateau A landform that has high elevation and a more or less level surface. (p. 9)
meseta Accidente geográfico que tiene una elevación alta y cuya superficie está más o menos nivelada.

plucking The process by which a glacier picks up rocks as it flows over the land. (p. 93)
extracción Proceso por el cual un glaciar arranca rocas al fluir sobre la tierra.

potential energy Energy that is stored and available to be used later. (p. 86)
energía potencial Energía que se encuentra almacenada y puede utilizarse posteriormente.

prime meridian The line that makes a half circle from the North Pole to the South Pole and that passes through Greenwich, England. (p. 15)
primer meridiano Línea que forma medio círculo desde el Polo Norte al Polo Sur y que pasa por Greenwich, Inglaterra.

 R

radioactive decay The breakdown of a radioactive element, releasing particles and energy. (p. 124)
desintegración radiactiva Descomposición de un elemento radioactivo que libera partículas y energía.

relative age The age of a rock compared to the ages of rock layers. (p. 117)
edad relativa Edad de una roca comparada con la edad de las capas de roca.

relief The difference in elevation between the highest and lowest parts of an area. (p. 7)
relieve Diferencia en la elevación entre las partes más altas y más bajas en un área.

reptile A vertebrate with scaly skin that lays eggs with tough, leathery shells. (p. 136)
reptil Vertebrado con piel de escamas que pone huevos de cascarón duro y correoso.

rill A tiny groove in soil made by flowing water. (p. 74)
arroyuelo Pequeño surco en el suelo que deja el agua al fluir.

runoff Water that flows over the ground surface rather than soaking into the ground. (p. 73)
escurrimiento Agua que fluye sobre la superficie del suelo en lugar de ser absorbida por éste.

S

sand dune A deposit of wind-blown sand. (p. 101)
duna de arena Depósito de arena arrastrada por el viento.

satellite images Pictures of the land surface based on computer data collected from satellites. (p. 22)
imágenes satelitales Fotografías de la superficie terrestre basadas en información computarizada reunida por satélites.

scale Used to compare distance on a map or globe to distance on Earth's surface. (p. 12)
escala Se usa para comparar la distancia en un mapa o globo terráqueo con la distancia en la superficie de la Tierra.

scientific theory A well-tested concept that explains a wide range of observations. (p. 116)
teoría científica Concepto bien comprobado que explica un amplia gama de observaciones.

sediment Earth materials deposited by erosion. (p. 67)
sedimento Materiales terrestres depositados por la erosión.

sedimentary rock The type of rock that is made of hardened sediment. (p. 110)
roca sedimentaria Tipo de roca formada de sedimento endurecido.

sod A thick mass of grass roots and soil. (p. 56)
tepe Masa gruesa de raíces de hierbas y suelo.

soil The loose, weathered material on Earth's surface in which plants can grow. (p. 48)
suelo Material suelto y desgastado sobre la superficie de la Tierra en donde crecen las plantas.

soil conservation The management of soil to prevent its destruction (p. 59)
conservación del suelo Cuidado del suelo para prevenir su destrucción.

soil horizon The layer of soil that differs in color and texture from the layers above or below it. (p. 50)
horizonte de suelo Capa de suelo que se diferencia en color y textura de las capas que tiene encima o debajo.

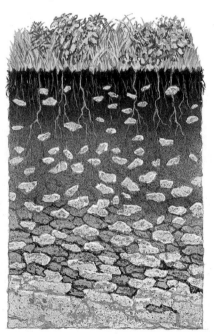

spit A beach formed by longshore drift that projects like a finger out into the water. (p. 100)
banco de arena Playa formada por la deriva litoral

stalactite A calcite deposit that hangs from the roof of a cave. (p. 80)
estalactita Depósito de calcita que cuelga del techo de una gruta.

stalagmite A cone-shaped calcite deposite that builds up from the floor of a cave. (p. 80)
estalagmita Depósito cónico de calcita que se forma en el piso de una gruta

stream A channel through which water is continually flowing downhill. (p. 74)
arroyo Canal por el cual fluye continuamente agua cuesta abajo.

subsoil The layer of soil beneath the topsoil that contains mostly clay and other minerals. (p. 50)
subsuelo Capa del suelo bajo el mantillo que contiene principalmente arcilla y otros minerales.

surveying The process of gathering data for a map by using instruments and the principles of geometry to determine distance and elevations. (p, 21)
agrimensura Proceso de reunir información para un mapa usando instrumentos y los principios de geometría para determinar distancias y elevaciones.

symbol On a map, pictures used by mapmakers to stand for features on Earth's surface. (p, 12)
símbolos En un mapa, los dibujos que usan los cartógrafos para representar características de la superficie de la Tierra.

T

till The sediments deposited directly by a glacier. (p. 94)
arcilla glaciárica Sedimentos depositados directamente por un glaciar.

topographic map A map that shows the surface features of an area. (p. 27)
mapa topográfico Mapa que muestra los accidentes geográficos de la superficie terrestre de un área.

topography The shape of the land determined by elevation, relief, and landforms. (p. 6)
topografía Forma del terreno determinada por la elevación, el relieve y los accidentes geográficos.

topsoil Mixture of humus, clay, and other minerals that forms the crumbly, topmost layer of soil. (p, 50)
mantillo Mezcla de humus, arcilla y otros minerales que forman la capa superior y suelta del suelo.

trace fossil A type of fossil that provides evidence of the activities of ancient organisms. (p. 112)
vestigios fósiles Tipo de fósil que da evidencia de las actividades de los organismos antiguos.

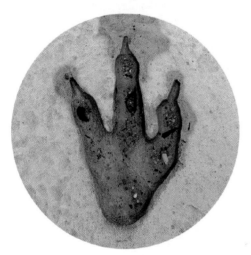

tributary A stream that flows into a larger stream. (p. 74)
afluente Arroyo que desemboca en una corriente de agua más grande.

turbulence A type of movement of water in which, rather than moving downstream, the water moves every which way. (p. 89)
turbulencia Tipo de movimiento del agua en el que, en vez de moverse corriente abajo, el agua se mueve en todas direcciones.

U

unconformity A place where an old, eroded rock surface is in contact with a newer rock layer. (p. 120)
discordancia Lugar donde una superficie rocosa erosionada y vieja está en contacto con una capa de rocas más nueva.

uniformitarianism The geologic principle that the same geologic processes that operate today operated in the past to change Earth's surface. (p. 39)
uniformitarianismo Principio geológico que enuncia que los mismos procesos geológicos que cambian la superficie de la Tierra en la actualidad, ocurrían en el pasado.

V

valley glacier A long, narrow glacier that forms when snow and ice build up in a mountain valley. (p. 92)
glaciar de valle Glaciar largo y angosto que se forma por acumulación de hielo y nieve en un valle de montaña.

vertebrate An animal with a backbone. (p. 135)
vertebrado Animal con columna vertebral.

W

weathering The chemical and physical processes that break down rock at Earth's surface. (p. 39)
desgaste Procesos químicos y físicos que rompen la roca de la superficie de la Tierra.

Index

Page numbers for key terms are printed in **boldface** type.
Page numbers for illustrations, maps, and charts are printed in *italics*.

Index

Page numbers for key terms are printed in **boldface** type.
Page numbers for illustrations, maps, and charts are printed in *italics*.

minerals
   chemical weathering producing new 42
   fossil formation and 111, 112
   in rock, rate of weathering and 44
minutes (division of degree) 13
Mississippi River 76
   delta of 77, *78*
   tributaries of 74
mites, as soil decomposers 53
mode 171
molds (fossils) 111, *113*
moon, formation of 131
moraine 94
mountain belt 9
mountain building, process of 39
mountain range 9
   age of 38
mountains 9
mountain system 9
mudflows (mass movement) 66, 68

N

Namib Desert 101
natural resource 57. *See also* **soil**
Nile 152–159
nitrogen-fixing bacteria 57
Northern Hemisphere 14
no-till plowing 59
nutrients in soil 49
   crop rotation and 59

O

observing, skill of 160
oceans
   development of 132
   life in Quaternary Period in 145
Ocean waves. *See* **waves**
operational definition 165
Ordovician Period 135
organisms
   chemical weathering caused by 43
   classification of 114
   development of living 133
   in soil 52–54
orienteering 26
oxbow lake *76*
oxidation 43
oxygen
   in aerated soil 54

in atmosphere, photosynthesis and 133
   chemical weathering caused by 43
ozone 133

P

paleontologists 114, *134*
Paleozoic Era 135–137
   Cambrian Explosion 135
   Carboniferous Period 136–137
   life on land 136
   mass extinction at end of 137, 142
   Pangaea, formation of 137
   Permian Period 137, 142
   vertebrates, evolution of **135**
Pangaea 137
percentage 125, **174**
periods, geologic *128*, *129*
   organisms of *138–141*
permeable material 44
Permian Period 137
   mass extinction at end of 137, 142
petrified fossils 112, *113*
photosynthesis 133
pixels 22
plains 8. *See also* **Great Plains**
plants
   chemical weathering caused by 43
   coal forests *136*, 137
   first growth on land 136
   flowering 143
   humus formed from 52–53
   nutrients in soil and 49
   soil texture and 49
   soil types classified by 51
plateaus 9
plowing, soil conservation and 59
plucking *93*
potassium-argon dating 125
potential energy 86
prairies 56, 57
Precambrian Time 129, 130, 132, 134
precision 174
predicting, skill of 160
preserved remains, fossils as 113
prime meridian 14, 15
   longitude of 16
probability 175

proportion 174
pyramids 158–159

Q

Quaternary Period 144–145
   fossil of *129*

R

radioactive dating 123–126, 127
   age of Earth using 130
   to determine absolute ages 125–126
   of moon rocks 131
radioactive decay *124*
rain
   acid 43
   runoff and amount of 73
Rancho La Brea tar pits 113
rapids 75
ratio 12, **174**
relative age 117–121
   determining 119–120
relief 7
replacement, petrified fossils formed by 112
reptiles 136
   flying *142*, 143
   during Mesozoic Era 142
responding variable 165
rills *74*
rivers 74
   course of *79*
   deposits by 76–77
   erosion by 75–76
   factors affecting erosion and deposition 90
   power to erode 88–90
   sediment load in 87
   slope of 88
   stream bed shape 89
   tributaries of **74**
   volume of flow 88
rocks 38–45. *See also* **sedimentary rock**
   igneous 119, 124, 126
   position of rock layers 118
   relative age of **117**–121
   soil and weathering of **48**, 50
   using fossils to date 120–*121*
   weathering of **39**–45
Rocky Mountains 9, 10

Index

Page numbers for key terms are printed in **boldface** type.
Page numbers for illustrations, maps, and charts are printed in *italics*.

Acknowledgments

Acknowledgment for page 153: Excerpt from "The Hymn to Hapy" from volume 1 of *Ancient Egyptian Literature*, by Miriam Lichtheim. Copyright ©1973–1980 Regents of the University of California. Reprinted by permission of the University of California Press.

Staff Credits

Diane Alimena, Michele Angelucci, Scott Andrews, Jennifer Angel, Carolyn Belanger, Barbara A. Bertell, Suzanne Biron, Peggy Bliss, Stephanie Bradley, James Brady, Anne M. Bray, Sarah M. Carroll, Kerry Cashman, Jonathan Cheney, Joshua D. Clapper, Lisa J. Clark, Bob Craton, Patricia Cully, Patricia M. Dambry, Kathy Dempsey, Leanne Esterly, Emily Ellen, Thomas Ferreira, Jonathan Fisher, Patricia Fromkin, Paul Gagnon, Kathy Gavilanes, Joel Gendler, Holly Gordon, Robert Graham, Ellen Granter, Diane Grossman, Barbara Hollingdale, Linda Johnson, Anne Jones, John Judge, Kevin Keane, Kelly Kelliher, Toby Klang, Sue Langan, Russ Lappa, Carolyn Lock, Rebecca Loveys, Constance J. McCarty, Carolyn B. McGuire, Ranida Touranont McKneally, Anne McLaughlin, Eve Melnechuk, Natania Mlawer, Janet Morris, Karyl Murray, Francine Neumann, Baljit Nijjar, Marie Opera, Jill Ort, Kim Ortell, Joan Paley, Dorothy Preston, Maureen Raymond, Laura Ross, Rashid Ross, Siri Schwartzman, Melissa Shustyk, Laurel Smith, Emily Soltanoff, Jennifer A. Teece, Elizabeth Torjussen, Amanda M. Watters, Merce Wilczek, Amy Winchester, Char Lyn Yeakley. **Additional Credits** Allen Gold, Andrea Golden, Etta Jacobs, Meg Montgomery, Kim Schmidt, Adam Teller, Joan Tobin.

Illustration

Morgan Cain & Associates: 49, 52, 53, 68, 69, 90, 102, 107, 124, 126; **Kerry Cashman:** 35, 44; **John Edwards and Associates:** 14t, 16, 17t, 27, 44, 87, 88, 93r, 95, 111, 132, 133; **GeoSystems Global Corporation:** 7b, 10, 55, 58, 77, 92; **Kevin Jones Associates:** 8, 9, 40, 41, 67, 74, 93b, 98, 99, 103, 106, 114, 115; **Martucci Design:** 28; **Richard McMahon, with J/B Woolsey Associates:** 128, 138, 139, 140, 141; **Karen Minot:** 73; **Matthew Pippin:** 51, 78, 79, 94, 95; **J/B Woolsey Associates:** 62, 116, 118, 121, 122; **XNR Productions:** 12, 13, 17b, 18, 19, 29, 80. **All charts and graphs by Matt Mayerchak.**

Photography

Photo Research Paula Wehde

Cover Image top, Jeff Drewitz/DRK Photo; **bottom,** Gavriel Jecan/Corbis. **Page vi t,** Howard Grey/Getty Images, Inc.; **vi b,** Tom Bean; **vii,** Richard Haynes; **viii,** Richard Haynes; **x t,** Dave King/Dorling Kindersley; **x b,** Courtesy of Karen Chin; **1all,** Courtesy of Karen Chin; **2tl,** Douglas Henderson; **2tr,** Courtesy of Karen Chin; **2b,** Courtesy of Karen Chin; **3,** Courtesy of Karen Chin.

Chapter 1
Pages 4–5, Image courtesy of NASA Landsat Project Science Office and USGS EROS Data Center; **6,** National Museum of American History/Smithsonian Institution; **8,** Tom Bean; **9l,** David Muench; **9r,** Tom Bean; **11,** Russ Lappa; **13,** Jim Wark/Airphoto; **14l,** The Granger Collection; **14m,** Bodleian Library, Oxford, U.K.; **14r,** Royal Geographical Society, London, UK/Bridgeman Art Library; **15l,** British Library, London/Bridgeman Art Library, London/Superstock, Inc.; **15m,** The Granger Collection; **15r,** The Granger Collection; **19,** Richard Haynes; **21t,** Russ Lappa; **21b,** Geographix; **22l,** Library of Congress; **22r,** U.S. Geological Survey; **24t,** © Boeing, all rights reserved; **24b,** Forest Johnson/Masterfile Corporation; **24–25,** Index Stock Imagery; **25,** Richard Haynes; **26t,** Richard Haynes; **26b,** Mitch Wojnarowicz/The Image Works; **27l,** Elliot Cohen/Janelco; **28,** U.S. Geological Survey; **30,** Robert Rathe/Stock Boston; **31,** Richard Haynes; **32,** British Library, London/Bridgeman Art Library, London/Superstock, Inc.; **34,** U.S. Geological Survey.

Chapter 2
Pages 36–37, Frozen Images/The Image Works; **37r,** Richard Haynes; **38,** Richard Haynes; **39t,** Jerry D. Greer; **39b,** Ron Watts/Corbis; **40t,** Susan Rayfield/Photo Researchers, Inc.; **40m,** Breck P. Kent/Animals Animals/Earth Scenes; **40b,** E.R. Degginger/Photo Researchers, Inc.; **41l,** John Sohlden/Visuals Unlimited; **41r,** Jim Steinberg/Animals Animals/Earth Scenes; **43,** Mike Mazzaschi/Stock Boston; **45all,** T.C. Meierding; **47,** Richard Haynes; **48t,** Richard Haynes; **48–49b,** Tom Bean; **54,** J.M. Labat/Jacana/Photo Researchers, Inc.; **55,** Richard Haynes; **56t,** Richard Haynes; **56b,** Tom Bean; **57t,** Corbis; **57b,** Grant Heilman Photography, Inc.; **58,** AP/Wide World Photos; **59,** Larry Lefever/Grant Heilman Photography, Inc.

Chapter 3
Pages 64–65, Ron Watts/Corbis; **65r,** Richard Haynes; **66,** AP/Wide World Photos; **68l,** Martin Miller/Visuals Unlimited; **68r,** Thomas G. Rampton/Grant Heilman Photography, Inc.; **69,** Steven Holt/Stockpix.com; **70,** Richard Haynes; **71,** Richard Haynes; **72–73,** Walter Bibikow/The Viesti Collection; **74,** Jim Wark/Airphoto; **75,** Dorling Kindersley; **76,** Tom Bean; **77t,** Martin Miller; **77b,** NASA/SADO/Tom Stack & Associates, Inc.; **81,** Dorling Kindersley; **81inset,** Laurence Parent; **82,** Russ Lappa; **83,** Richard Haynes; **84–85b,** David Sailors/Corbis; **85t,** Alex Wong/Getty Images, Inc.; **86t,** Richard Haynes; **86b,** Eliot Cohen; **87,** Michael Quinton/Minden Pictures; **89,** Corbis; **91t,** Richard Haynes; **91b,** Marc Muench/Muench Photography, Inc.; **92,** Dorling Kindersley; **96t,** Richard Haynes; **96b,** Corbis; **97,** Dick Roberts/Visuals Unlimited; **100,** F. Stuart Westmoreland/Photo Researchers, Inc.; **101t,** Richard Haynes; **101b,** Jess Stock/Getty Images, Inc.; **102,** Tom Bean.

Chapter 4
Pages 108–109, Dave G. Houser/Corbis; **109r,** Richard Haynes; **110,** Sinclair Stammers/Photo Researchers, Inc.; **111,** Dorling Kindersley; **112l,** Francois Gohier/Photo Researchers, Inc.; **112m,** Runk/Schoenberger/Grant Heilman Photography, Inc.; **112r,** Breck P. Kent; **113l,** Park Street/PhotoEdit; **113m,** Michelle Bridwell/PhotoEdit; **113r,** Howard Grey/Stone/Getty Images, Inc.; **114t,** Peabody Museum of Natural History; **114b,** Ken Lucas/Visuals Unlimited; **115,** T. Wiewandt/DRK Photo; **116,** Frans Lanting/Minden Pictures; **117t,** Richard Haynes; **117b,** Zephyr Picture/Index Stock Imagery/PictureQuest; **118,** Jeff Greenberg/Photo Researchers, Inc.; **119all,** PH Photo; **121,** Photo Researchers, Inc.; **123t,** Richard Haynes; **123bl,** Dr. Dennis Kunkel/Visuals Unlimited; **123br,** Michael Fogden/DRK Photo; **129,** The Natural History Museum, London; **131,** Mark Garlick/Science Photo Library/Photo Researchers, Inc.; **134t,** Breck P. Kent; **134m,** Runk/Schoenberger/Grant Heilman Photography, Inc.; **134b,** Auscape International; **135l,** John Sibbick; **135r,** The Natural History Museum, London; **136t,** Chip Clark/Smithsonian Institution; **136b,** © The Field Museum, Neg.#CSGEO 75400c.; **142,** Dorling Kindersley; **143tl,** Jane Burton/Bruce Coleman, Inc.; **143tr,** David M. Dennis/Tom Stack & Associates, Inc.; **143b,** D. Van Ravenswaay/Photo Researchers, Inc.; **144,** © 2002 Mark Hallett, all rights reserved; **145,** Photo Researchers, Inc.; **146,** Richard Haynes. **152t,** Robert Caputo/Stock Boston; **152b,** David Sanger Photography; **153t,** Brian Braker/Photo Researchers, Inc.; **153b,** British Museum/The Image Works; **154,** Groenendyk/Photo Researchers, Inc.; **155,** Corbis; **156,** Robert Caputo/Stock Boston; **157t,** Charlie Waite/Getty Images Inc.; **157b,** Robert Caputo/Stock Boston; **158,** David Ball/The Picture Cube/Index Stock Imagery, Inc.; **159t,** Richard Haynes; **159b,** Erich Lessing/Art Resource; **160,** Tony Freeman/PhotoEdit; **161t,** Russ Lappa; **161m,** Richard Haynes; **161b,** Russ Lappa; **162,** Richard Haynes; **164,** Richard Haynes; **166,** Morton Beebe/Corbis; **167,** Catherine Karnow/Corbis; **169t,** Dorling Kinderlsey; **169b,** Richard Haynes; **181,** Richard Haynes; **184,** U.S. Geological Survey; **185,** NASA/SADO/Tom Stack & Associates, Inc.; **190,** Laurence Parent; **191,** Park Street/PhotoEdit.